Aligning for Advantage

Aligning for Advantage

Competitive Strategies for the Political and Social Arenas

Thomas C. Lawton, Jonathan P. Doh, and
Tazeeb Rajwani

OXFORD
UNIVERSITY PRESS

OXFORD
UNIVERSITY PRESS

Great Clarendon Street, Oxford, OX2 6DP,
United Kingdom

Oxford University Press is a department of the University of Oxford.
It furthers the University's objective of excellence in research, scholarship,
and education by publishing worldwide. Oxford is a registered trade mark of
Oxford University Press in the UK and in certain other countries

© Thomas C. Lawton, Jonathan P. Doh, and Tazeeb Rajwani 2014

The moral rights of the authors have been asserted

First Edition published in 2014
Impression: 1

Published in the United States of America by Oxford University Press
198 Madison Avenue, New York, NY 10016, United States of America

British Library Cataloguing in Publication Data
Data available

Library of Congress Control Number: 2013954175

ISBN 978–0–19–960474–6 (hbk.)
ISBN 978–0–19–960475–3 (pbk.)

Printed and bound in Great Britain by
CPI Group (UK) Ltd, Croydon, CR0 4YY

Links to third party websites are provided by Oxford in good faith and
for information only. Oxford disclaims any responsibility for the materials
contained in any third party website referenced in this work.

To Katalin, Robin, and Carly

Preface

Samuel Johnson once noted that, "knowledge is of two kinds: we know a subject ourselves, or we know where we can find information upon it."[1] Accumulating and utilizing information—facts, figures, and ideas—are essential to any strategic management process, allowing business leaders to answer such questions as "What do our customers need?" and "What markets should we be in?" Possessing the most robust, legitimate, and original information— and doing so ahead of others—is key to gaining competitive advantage.

The same holds true in nonmarket settings, where social, political, regulatory, and cultural considerations constrain or facilitate business endeavors.[2] In these contexts, the range and diversity of stakeholders and issues can be daunting, even for the most seasoned managers. Despite this, businesspeople routinely tackle challenges and opportunities that emanate from the political and social environments in which they operate.[3] Managers and entrepreneurs often view these interfaces as obstacles to be overcome rather than as opportunities to leverage information, knowledge, and relationships to gain competitive advantage.[4] If managers do not fully understand the implications of these contextual forces or appreciate how best to deal with their influence and outcomes, they may respond with practices that are obsolete or ineffective. The result can be a corporate strategy that is no longer effectual in a complex business environment in which subnational, national, supranational, and nongovernmental actors and issues are increasingly important and even vie with each other for authority and influence. For example, a U.S. company doing business in Germany might have to understand and respond to regulatory demands from the European Union in Brussels, the federal government in Berlin, and the provincial government in Munich. The company might also need to consider the views and positions of nongovernmental organizations (NGOs) at all three levels and reconcile any variances in approach and attitude. Local community groups and other stakeholders, such as employee unions and trade councils, might also have to be considered. Therefore, as Bach and Allen noted, if money is the currency of markets, information is the currency of the nonmarket environment.[5]

In *Aligning for Advantage*, we advance a framework for aligning a company's business objectives and market positions with its political requirements and social obligations. Alignment is key, because companies are not separate from, but embedded within, the political, social, and economic environments in which they operate.[6] As such, political and social strategies must be aligned with overall corporate strategy to have an impact and be successful.[7] Our premise is that most companies should strive for a balanced and mutually reinforcing approach to corporate strategy, political activity, and social responsibility. In some cases, alignment may mean deep, strategically embedded partnerships with governments, NGOs, or other stakeholders. In others, alignment may take the form of looser, more ad hoc collaborations with outside organizations and institutions. No matter what the approach, however, the relationship between nonmarket and market strategies should be conscious and deliberate, not accidental nor artificially constructed. Truly aligned strategies seek to reconcile and modulate the sometimes conflicting external demands that a company encounters in a way that is appropriate for the firm's geographic and market positions, while at the same time leveraging the overall nonmarket strategy (NMS) as a source of competitive advantage.

Consider these examples from three multinational enterprises (MNEs) illustrating the variety and complexity of interactions between firms and nonmarket actors, and the various ways—defensive, proactive, and collaborative—that firms respond to social and political pressures. After being accused by authorities of allowing tainted products to be sold and receiving criticism for its water resource practices generally, Coca-Cola developed an affirmative strategy to encourage water conservation and efficiency practices in China and globally. Organized partly through a partnership with the World Wildlife Fund (WWF), Coca-Cola's approach resulted in environmental sustainability benefits. But it is equally valuable to the company's market growth strategy in China, which depends on a consistent, sanitary water supply. Similarly, DuPont turned its environmental conservation and sustainability practices into market opportunities by developing products that conserve resources, save money, and protect against environmental threats. Also, Microsoft, after facing widespread and rampant piracy of its products, partnered with the Chinese government to promote licensed adoption of its products instead of pirated copies.

Aligning for Advantage starts from the premise that corporate political and social activity needs to be synchronized with the business strategy process if it is to add real value for companies. Furthermore, we argue that strategy for industry and market competition and strategy for political and social contexts must be equally in tune with corporate vision, values, and objectives. Research shows that the policy environment is a dynamic and self-renewing system, populated by large and small companies, interest groups, and individuals striving to get their voices heard.[8] In this world, companies—not government agencies, political parties, or social actors—are often center stage.

However, as events such as the 2008–2012 global financial and economic crises illustrate, governments are resurgent and social actors within civil society are also on the rise. In a world in which change is endemic, companies must align strategies to take account of, and be ready for, any and all forces and agents of change. Building on the view of companies as important political actors,[9] our central notion is that of strategic alignment: the organizational process by which enterprises balance their political and social resources and responsibilities with their business objectives to achieve industry and market advantage.

Aligning for Advantage reveals that aligning market and nonmarket environments is a crucial determinant of corporate success.[10] Some newer companies such as Reddit, Sina Weibo, and Twitter have used their social influence to gain an advantage over competitors, while established companies such as Danone, Diageo, and PepsiCo have aligned their political and social resource portfolio with their business objectives to create or enter new markets at home and abroad, which has allowed them to sustain advantage. Of course, for every example of strategic success there are examples of companies that failed to adjust to political and social trends. The abortive GE-Honeywell merger bid—shot down by European competition authorities in 2001—illustrates the downside of failing to align the business objectives and political context of corporate strategy. In this case, the companies underestimated the influence exerted by European Commission decisions on the corporate objectives of U.S.-based companies.

When we refer to alignment, we have in mind two complementary ideas. First, we explicitly argue for closer coordination between market and nonmarket strategies. Secondly, we refer to alignment between those activities and actions within the company that support and underpin strategy, and the acknowledgement, assessment, and internalization of the external social and political environment alongside those strategic processes and actions. We believe that these two related forms of alignment constitute a form of strategic fit between commercial and political/social strategy and between internal and external factors and variables. The driving force that advances and facilitates this alignment, however, must always be the corporate-level vision and strategy of the firm itself, beginning with the senior executive team. In other words, only when the value and logic of strategic alignment between market and nonmarket—and internal and external environments— are obvious and clear to senior management and only when it emanates from the firm's core vision and values can such alignment be achieved. This process—together with the logic behind it—is the essence of this book.

Aligning for Advantage provides a strategic roadmap for enterprising leaders who want to raise a business from a subordinate to a dominant market position and for those who wish to retain a position of market prominence or preeminence. Although our language and examples are tilted towards large, international corporations, the ideas, approaches, and implications are applicable to all companies, regardless of size, sector, or location. For students, scholars, and consultants, the book offers a synthesis of recent thinking on corporate political and social strategy and our own concepts and recommendations for the interplay with business strategy. In writing this book, we drew on our experience as academic researchers, management consultants, and executive educators with governmental, business, and civil society organizations across Africa, Asia-Pacific, Europe, Latin America, the Middle East, and North America. The result is an integrative research approach to an international managerial challenge.

Notes

1. Samuel Johnson cited in Boswell, J. (1791). *The Life of Samuel Johnson*. Reprinted, 2008. London: Penguin.
2. Doh, J.P., Lawton, T.C., and Rajwani, T. (2012). Advancing nonmarket strategy research: institutional perspectives in a changing world. *Academy of Management Perspectives*, 26(3): 22–39.
3. Frynas, J.G., Mellahi, K., and Pigman, G.A. (2006). First-mover advantages in international business and firm-specific political resources. *Strategic Management Journal*, 27(4): 321–345.
4. Getz, K.A. (1997). Research in corporate political action: integration and assessment. *Business and Society*, 36(1): 32–72.
5. Bach, D. and Allen, D.B. (2010). What every CEO needs to know about nonmarket strategy. *MIT Sloan Management Review*, 51(3): 41–48 (43).
6. Hillman, A.J. and Hitt, M.A. (1999). Corporate political strategy formulation: a model of approach, participation, and strategy decisions. *Academy of Management Review*, 24(4): 825–842.
7. Baron, D.P. (1995a). The nonmarket strategy system. *Sloan Management Review*, 37(1): 73–85.
8. Coen, D. (1998). The European business interest and the nation state: large-firm lobbying in the European Union and member states. *Journal of Public Policy*, 18(1): 75–100.
9. Epstein, E. (1969). *The corporation in American politics*. Englewood Cliffs, NJ: Prentice-Hall.
10. Baron, D.P. (2001). Private politics, corporate social responsibility, and integrated strategy. *Journal of Economics & Management Strategy*, 10(1): 7–45.

Acknowledgements

As with all projects of this magnitude, we could not have reached completion without the help and support of others. At an institutional level, Thomas would like to thank the Open University Business School, EMLYON Business School, and the Tuck School of Business at Dartmouth. Jonathan wishes to express his gratitude to Villanova University School of Business and Tazeeb is grateful for the support of Cranfield University School of Management.

We owe a collective debt of gratitude to those in business, academia, government, and the nonprofit sector who have given their time and thought to facilitate and bolster our research. A special word of thanks to Antoine Boatwright and Michele Glaze of Dell, Jan Janssen at Bank of America Merrill Lynch, Sean Greenwood and Jostein Solheim of Ben & Jerry's, and Malcolm Lane of Tata Group. Our thanks also to Donald Siegel, co-editor of *Academy of Management Perspectives,* for supporting the publication of our symposium on nonmarket strategies in a multipolar world and to our co-contributors on that project and on related nonmarket strategy panels at the Strategic Management Society annual conference in Miami in 2011 and the Academy of International Business annual conference in Washington, DC in 2012.

There are others who deserve a special mention for assisting us at various stages along the journey to publication. In particular, Jason Guo, Kate Hudson, Timothy Haas, Charles Harvey, Charles Mbalyohere, Steve McGuire, Terry O'Sullivan, Sotirios Paroutis, Philippe Riot, Danielle Rousson, and Huyen Anh Tham.

A word of thanks to our editorial team, David Musson and Emma Booth, at Oxford University Press. We appreciate their patience and support throughout.

We would like to express our appreciation for permission to reproduce and adapt portions of previously published papers. Some parts of Chapter 1 were published in *International Journal of Management Reviews,* volume 15 (Lawton, McGuire, and Rajwani, 2013). Segments of Chapter 2 originally appeared in somewhat different form in *U.S. News & World Report,* Economic Intelligence blog (Lawton, May 4, 2012). An earlier version of Chapter 3 appeared in the *Oxford Handbook of Business and Government* (Story and Lawton, 2010). Chapter 4 was partly adapted from an article published in *Journal of Management Studies,* volume 41 (Doh and Pearce, 2004). An article published in *International Business Review,* volume 22 (Lawton, Rajwani, and Doh, 2013) provided the basis for Chapter 5 and Chapter 7. Fanny D'Onofrio also provided helpful research assistance for Chapter 5, including the production of Figure 5.1 and the preparation of article summaries from which a portion of the chapter is derived. In addition, Chapter 6 includes material previously published in *Journal of Management,* volume 36 (Doh, Howton, Howton, and Siegel, 2010). Portions of Chapter 6 and Chapter 7 have been adapted from the above-mentioned article published in *International Journal of Management Reviews,* volume 15 (Lawton, McGuire, and Rajwani, 2013). Finally, Chapter 9 draws on two previously published articles—the first in *California Management Review,* volume 42 (Cummings and Doh, 2000), and the second in *Journal of World Business,* volume 44 (Oetzel and Doh, 2009).

On a personal note, each of us could not have completed this work without the steadfast encouragement and affection of friends and family. In particular, for Thomas, his wife Katalin and daughter Méabh were a source of motivation, support, and endless smiles. For Jonathan, his wife Robin and daughters Alyssa and Lorelei provided great diversions, humor, and love throughout. For Tazeeb, his wife Carly provided inspiration, care, and sustenance during the development of the book.

Thomas Lawton, Jonathan Doh, and Tazeeb Rajwani
London, U.K. and Philadelphia, U.S.A.

Contents

List of Figures

List of Tables

Section I
Foundations of Alignment

1

Establishing Alignment*

> Those who do not know the lay of the land cannot maneuver their forces.[1]
>
> *Sun Tzu*

In August 2012, Johnson & Johnson (J&J) found itself in a sensitive public relations position. Having previously promised to eliminate one known and one potential carcinogen and several other chemicals from its baby products by 2013, the company announced its intention to do the same for its entire line of personal-care products by 2015. This included such flagship brands as Neutrogena, Aveeno, and Clean & Clear. On the one hand, J&J naturally wanted to promote its position as the first major consumer-products manufacturer to make these fundamental changes, but on the other hand, it had to reassure customers that the existing product formulations were still safe. The success of the initiative, which the company called "Moving Beyond Safety," was especially critical since, as *The New York Times* noted, the company had "experienced serious recalls and quality lapses in recent years."[2]

The J&J example, like countless others before and many since, illustrates the complex and challenging nature of the nonmarket environment and the range of actions—proactive and defensive, preemptive and responsive—that firms pursue to advance their positions within that environment. The challenges that firms like J&J encounter in their social and political interactions directly affect the bottom line of shareholders and customers. Given the increasing share of corporate balance sheets that encompass intangibles such as goodwill—highly volatile elements influenced by reputation and legitimacy—it is no surprise that the stakes for companies like J&J are high. Indeed, it may be that J&J's 2012 announcement and its strategy for phasing out potentially harmful chemicals were based in part on lessons learned from the infamous Tylenol scandal that rocked the company in 1982. At the time,

J&J, which had a strong reputation for ethical practices and social responsibility, was lauded for its decision to recall an estimated 31 million bottles of Tylenol after only two bottles were found to have been laced with cyanide. This decision resulted in $100 million in losses and a 30 percent drop in its market share for pain relievers. But J&J recovered, partly because it was viewed as having been highly responsible in its approach to this safety challenge. Since then, however, the company has endured subsequent scandals, including accusations of kickbacks, illegally promoting an epilepsy drug, and rampant quality-control problems at a J&J facility. These provided a clear incentive to regain public trust—something the decision to remove certain chemicals from its entire line was designed to do.

Even entire industries have had to respond to "Tylenol moments" and learn the value of long-term strategic commitments to nonmarket strategy. After the Bhopal disaster in December 1984, when a leak of deadly gases from a Union Carbide pesticide manufacturing plant in India led to the loss of thousands of lives, the global chemical industry took aggressive action to improve its safety and environmental practices. The Responsible Care initiative, launched by the Canadian Chemical Producers' Association in 1985, has grown into a worldwide program with a membership of more than 50 national manufacturing associations. It works toward continual improvement in health, safety, and environmental performance, and promoting transparent risk communication at thousands of chemical sites.[3] Individual companies, such as Dow Chemical, have gone beyond these protocols and used environmental safety and sustainability to further differentiate their products from those of their competitors and garner positive support from government regulators and customers around the world. This example underscores the need for—and potential benefits of—long-term strategic commitments to nonmarket strategy and the range of mechanisms at multiple levels—individual company, national association, and global coalition—through which these strategies become operationalized.

Why do you Need Nonmarket Strategy?

Business managers have an extensive array of tools and techniques to help them make sense of their industry and market environments. Analysis of such inputs is reasonably clear and unambiguous, and resulting strategy decisions can be pursued with relative confidence in the outcomes. No such confidence exists when moving beyond the market into the gray area that many academic commentators refer to as the nonmarket arena.[4] Here managers begin to resemble 15th-century European explorers sailing west: they have little or no knowledge of their destination, are unaware of many of the trials that will inevitably complicate their journey, and fear that they may ultimately reach the horizon of comprehension, beyond which lies uncharted and potentially dangerous territory.

Managers trained in a specific discipline, such as finance, marketing, engineering, or human resources, may face particular challenges understanding and working with nonmarket actors and influences. Unfortunately, despite some research advances,[5] the nonmarket strategic environment remains relatively uncharted territory for both scholars and practitioners of strategic management. This is particularly true in emerging economies. Indeed, the literature on strategic management lacks a consistent conceptual framework to identify and incorporate nonmarket forces into basic management theory. In particular, the influence of government, a subset of the nonmarket context, is a largely unexplained and indeterminate variable within companies' strategic decision-making processes. Although there is research on state–business relations[6] and, more specifically, the influence of firms on public policy formulation,[7] less work has been done on how top-management teams factor the external political environment into their strategic decisions and actions.[8]

What do we mean by strategy for the nonmarket? Bach and Allen emphasize that nonmarket strategy recognizes that businesses are social and political beings, not just economic agents.[9] Nonmarket strategy considers how managers anticipate, preempt, and respond to actors, influences, and actions emanating from the cultural, social, political, and regulatory arenas. A basic premise of this orientation is that these nonmarket actors affect the strategic direction and market objectives of businesses. Indeed, the rapidly changing global environment of the early 21st century has demonstrated that governments and social actors exert significant—and in many instances increasing—influence over the economic and business environment.[10] Yet many companies are ill-prepared to manage a resurgent state and civil society.[11]

What is Alignment?

The word *alignment* has its origins in the French verb meaning "to put into line." This notion of corrective positioning is how we approach aligning. We emphasize the need for business managers to place their market and nonmarket strategies in parallel, equally informed and guided by corporate vision, values, and objectives. In other words, if the overarching purpose and intent of an organization are to be effectively and consistently acted upon, what is done in terms of market positioning and industry competition needs to be synchronized with what happens in terms of social engagement and political activism. When, at a corporate level, a company emphasizes the strategic importance of people development, social impact, or sustainability, alignment of the market and nonmarket will be a key determinant of advantage in competitive arenas. Similarly, in certain industry, national, or cultural contexts, the prominence of nonmarket influences and actors may be greater than (or different from) that in others, and these differences must be reflected in market strategy if a company is to achieve and sustain a competitive advantage.

A way to approach and manage this alignment is through the concept of strategic fit. This concept has a variety of interpretations within the field of management. The most widely shared is that fit describes the appropriateness of a company's strategy in terms of its match with the environmental or organizational contingencies facing the business.[12] In other words, business strategy is rooted in the concept of aligning organizational resources with environmental threats and opportunities.[13] Some interpret strategic fit as the degree of alignment that exists between the competitive position, corporate strategy, organizational culture, and leadership style of an enterprise.[14] These interpretations are similar to our approach but do not capture the external nonmarket dimensions. Nor do they explicitly broach the issue of how to align these dimensions with competitive positions and market choices. Therefore, we concur that strategic fit is about the optimal alignment of a company's resources, culture, governance, and positions with the opportunities and threats that exist externally to the business. But we argue that these external threats and opportunities can emanate from both market and nonmarket contexts. The ability to align with and across both the market and the nonmarket is a key determinant of competitive advantage in the modern, multipolar world economy. Previous research indicates that the pursuit of strategic fit has advantageous performance implications.[15] Ensuring fit between market and nonmarket strategies and with the overall corporate strategy and culture can separate the winners from the losers in a business context.

Aligning Corporate Strategy in the Nonmarket Environment

It is important for business executives to distinguish between corporate strategy and corporate policy. Strategy is about vision, direction setting, marshaling of resources, and aligning business practice with environmental realities. Policy, on the other hand, is generally focused on implementation—the delivery of results and adding value. Understanding and internalizing this distinction will help strategic managers to deal more effectively with contextual complexity and successfully implement an aligned strategy.

In this book we examine and explain the management and mechanisms of nonmarket strategy by identifying and teasing out the process through which senior executives factor the nonmarket environment into their strategic decisions and actions. In doing so, we explore a variety of concepts and techniques and draw on research from economics, sociology, political science, and international relations. For instance, we argue that corporate executives who adapt and apply a structural realist approach from international relations[16] may be better equipped to understand and respond to what Gilpin describes as the reciprocal and dynamic interaction in the world economy between the pursuit of wealth and the pursuit of power.[17] These twin forces complicate and often confound the decision-making process of corporate leaders, as they involve variables outside of the control of the organization and beyond the scope of rational economic actor analysis. As Gilpin further argues, both economics and political science, as separate, compartmentalized disciplines, are inadequate to explain the state–market nexus: economics does not integrate power analysis into its explanatory models, and political science often treats economics as external to or even dependent on the political setting.[18] In short, the autonomy of market forces is missing. Strange argues for a structural approach that seeks to integrate the Marxist concern with production and the realist concern with security into a wider analysis of the world political economy around a concept of structural power.[19] The structural power approach, discussed further in Chapter 3, is a useful conceptual lens for top management teams seeking to make sense of the political nonmarket context of their organizations. Understanding power, its main conduits in the world, and the forces that determine it in international business allows strategic leaders to understand and factor nonmarket forces into corporate strategy.

Diverse Perspectives on Nonmarket Strategy and the Need for Synthesis

The development and sustainability of competitive advantage constitute a core challenge for all strategic leaders but political and social arenas are often underestimated as a setting for creating and capturing value for the firm and its stakeholders. Research by business scholars on corporate political activity (CPA) and corporate social responsibility (CSR) is the principal mechanism through which academics and other experts explore the ways in which firms pursue their political and social strategies. The literature has contributed greatly to our understanding of the processes and outcomes of companies' interactions with nonmarket environments and has called attention to the effectiveness and impact of various strategies and tactics. In addition, scholars from the fields of political science, international relations, sociology, and economics have long studied the role and impact of the state in its many forms, including the interactions between the state and other civil society actors, such as firms. These core disciplines have laid the groundwork for the CPA and CSR literatures, providing them with rigorous conceptual and theoretical foundations and placing them within broader understandings of social and behavioral science. Here we provide a brief summary of our motivation for writing this book, which stems from some of the unanswered questions in the existing literature.

The Scholarly and Practical Relevance of the Nonmarket Environment

There is increasing attention[20] being paid to nonmarket strategy and firm-level experiences. Indeed, there is a growing appreciation of the contribution that a nonmarket strategy may play in the development of a firm's overall competitive advantage. For example, literature on political environmental scanning,[21] the resource-based view of politics,[22] and discussions of the potential of business-to-business political strategy as a competitive weapon[23] underscore the growing attention to social and political forces—and the strategies that respond to them—in the academic literature. We are especially motivated by calls that suggest that there is still a need for work that explicitly explores the relationship between a firm, its political stakeholders, and its more traditional strategic management activity,[24] and, in particular, the search for value creation from strategic political management.[25]

At the same time, the number of companies affected by government action or oversight is increasing. Adding to the list of industries for which regulation of activity is already an everyday reality (such as utilities, health, education, airlines and other transport services, and extractive industries covered by ecological regulations) or in which government actors are at the forefront of boundary forming or rule setting (such as biotechnology, pharmaceuticals, and many high-technology and defense sectors), the post-2008 international economic crisis increased the number and range of sectors in which government actively intervenes to re-regulate, stimulate, or support. Banking and finance in particular, as well as automobiles and other heavy manufacturing, are increasingly under government control or influence. Therefore, for a growing number of companies, governmental or oversight bodies are active stakeholders that are interested in the strategy-making process and, hence, able in some form to affect a company's financial performance.

Given these circumstances, businesses need to understand how they can manage such important influences on their strategic directions. This is a challenging area, as the concept of "managing" political—or social—actors and institutions tends to have negative and pejorative associations. A starting point for a more neutral understanding of the role and value of nonmarket strategy is the work of David Baron and his colleagues and disciples.

Baron, writing in 1995, argued that firms should integrate their market and nonmarket strategy in a way that leverages the complementary contributions of each to the process of competitive effectiveness and value creation.[26] Since he made that seminal contribution, the literature on CPA, CSR, and strategy has contributed a great deal to our understanding of how, when, and to what effect business enterprises pursue initiatives and activities that advance their interests with governments and other stakeholders.[27] Relatively little of this literature, however, has expressly considered the importance of aligning strategy directed toward the competitive commercial environment with strategy focused on the political and social arenas.

Corporate Political Activity as Nonmarket Strategy

The CPA literature has, among other objectives, sought to explain the frequency, variation, and performance impacts of firm-level political action. A wide variety of firms are involved in political activities, in industries as varied as oil and gas, air transport, information technology, tobacco, and pharmaceuticals. These firms have long influenced governments through campaign contributions, direct lobbying, government representatives on company boards, voluntary agreements, political action committees (PACs), and at times even bribery.[28]

Hillman and Hitt made a basic distinction between relational political action—those strategies that seek to use personal connection, networks, and formal lobbying to advance a firm's interests—and financial CPA—providing donations to political campaigns or other kinds of financial support to political actors.[29] But the nonmarket environment has become much more complex and multidimensional, and as research in the nonmarket becomes more multifaceted and fractured, it requires some basic synthesis to understand its various dimensions. Hence, scholarly research in the area of CPA—defined as corporate attempts to shape government policy in ways favorable to the firm[30]—has not kept pace with the prevalence of CPA practice in industry or across political systems. Important progress in understanding CPA has been made, derived from disciplines as diverse as strategic management, marketing, economics, sociology, finance, and political science.[31] However, to some extent, Vogel's observation that the study of corporations and their interaction with government has yet to realize its potential remains valid today.[32] When Vogel wrote those words, the collapse of the Soviet Union and the embrace of more market-led forms of capitalism in the developed world signaled the need to understand a greater role for business in the development and implementation of public policy. But the dominant approach in responding to this need has been to import methods and perspectives that mirror the natural and formal sciences and to relegate ethics and (irrational) human behavior to matters of secondary importance. Fuchs and Lederer similarly note that management studies often adopt a functionalist perspective in regard to CPA, seeing firm political involvement as apolitical and primarily concerned with regulatory compliance.[33]

Another reason for the greater interest in the political activity of firms is that the business–government landscape has changed dramatically. The emergence of new market economies—including those with a significant element of state-led capitalism, such as China or the Gulf states—demonstrates the need for greater comparative understandings of firms and governments in a range of institutional contexts.[34] In the Western context, CPA, while controversial, is largely about legal, firm-level engagement with institutionalized political actors and structures. However, in many countries, weak or incomplete institutionalization can lead to the development of informal—and potentially corrupt—political engagement by firms.[35] As these states develop, their institutional structures may change and, consequently, so too may their patterns of corporate political behavior. But any convergence with Western practices cannot be assumed; the area requires more studies to establish the extent, if any, of convergence.[36]

Overall, the end of the first decade of the new millennium presented CPA scholars with a business–government landscape that was transformed in ways scarcely imaginable ten years earlier. Governments had reasserted their authority relative to markets and seized controlling stakes in firms across a range of industries. The forces of globalization were in disarray and the "runaway world" described by Giddens had lost its momentum.[37] Catching up with events and making sense of this rebalancing of business–government relations is a challenge for management and CPA scholars alike.

Corporate Social Responsibility as Nonmarket Strategy

The literature on CSR has similarly provided powerful insights into why, how, when, and to what effect firms contribute to the social arena above and beyond what might be required by law. While the literature is extensive, it is also still evolving. Beginning as a normative commentary on the broader role of business in society, the CSR literature has developed in a number of distinct but complementary directions.[38]

In his review of the history of CSR literature, Carroll cites Bowen's work as the basis for modern definitions of CSR, asking "What responsibilities to society may businessmen reasonably be expected to assume?"[39] Bowen proposed an initial definition that was founded on assumptions of the moral and ethical obligations of individuals. These early perspectives on CSR were firmly lodged in broader philosophical and ethical ideas about individual responsibility and obligation, and defined much of the early research and writing on CSR.[40]

Carroll notes another trend in the 1960s and 1970s in which definitions and research focused on managers' obligations beyond what would otherwise be expected. For example, he cites Davis's contention that CSR refers to "businessmen's decisions and actions taken for reasons at least partially beyond the firm's direct economic or technical interest,"[41] with Frederick arguing that social responsibilities required businesspeople to oversee the operation of an economic system that fulfills the expectations of the public.[42] Finally, Carroll offered perhaps the most comprehensive and holistic definition of CSR when he suggested:

> In my view, CSR involves the conduct of a business so that it is economically profitable, law abiding, ethical and socially supportive. To be socially responsible…then means that profitability and obedience to the law are foremost conditions to discussing the firm's ethics and the extent to which it supports the society in which it exists with contributions of money, time and talent. Thus, CSR is composed of four parts: economic, legal, ethical and voluntary or philanthropic.[43]

While the concept of CSR continued to evolve through the 1970s and 1980s, a critical development occurred when the concept of stakeholder management appeared in the 1960s and 1970s. According to one interpretation, there are four essential elements of stakeholder theory, which are interrelated and complementary: (1) the corporation has relationships with many constituent groups or actors ("stakeholders") that affect and are affected by its decisions; (2) the theory focuses on the nature of these relationships in terms of both processes and outcomes for the firm and its stakeholders; (3) the interests of all (legitimate) stakeholders have intrinsic value, and no set of interests is assumed to dominate the other; and (4) the theory focuses on practical and actionable managerial decision-making.[44]

One interpretation of stakeholder theory is that it is concerned with a broader and more expansive view of CSR. For example, stakeholder theory centers on the overall obligations of corporations to society. Various applications of stakeholder theory have addressed its normative and instrumental dimensions. More recently, scholars have sought to establish a "convergent" perspective that considers both these normative and instrumental underpinnings.[45] Further, scholars attempted to develop highly actionable frameworks of stakeholder theory that would allow managers to classify stakeholders according to their relative salience.[46] Throughout this period, the conceptualization of CSR as part of stakeholder theory reaffirmed the instrumental view of stakeholder management and fully included shareholders as a key stakeholder, going so far as to identify them as one of the most critical primary stakeholders of the firm.

Most recently, CSR has evolved even further to be viewed as a strategic or instrumental tool of the corporation. Strategic theories of CSR[47] assert that a company's social practices can be integrated into its business- and corporate-level strategies.[48] Baron, who coined the term "strategic CSR," argued that companies compete for socially responsible customers by explicitly linking their social contribution to product sales.[49] The strategic view of CSR has generated a series of studies (well over a hundred) that have sought to link various aspects of corporate social performance (CSP) to corporate financial performance (CFP).[50] A meta-analysis found that the overall effect of CSP on CFP was positive but small and that as much evidence exists for reverse causality (CFP leading to CSP).[51] These authors concluded that the exhaustive and never-ending efforts to establish a CSP–CFP link would be better directed at understanding why companies pursue CSP, the mechanisms connecting prior CFP to subsequent CSP, and how companies manage the process of pursuing both CSP and CFP simultaneously.

Insights from the Social Sciences

Finally, we would be remiss not to mention the many insights and contributions from the core social science disciplines of political science, international relations, sociology, and economics, among others. In relation to our discussion, scholars in these fields have focused especially on the role of the state and its constituent institutions;[52] the interactions among states in contributing to national, regional, and global governance;[53] the interactions among states and civil society actors, including corporations;[54] and the dynamic exchanges among policymakers and those who have sought to influence the development of laws, regulations, and other policies by local, national, and international governmental organizations.[55] Given that multinational enterprises (MNEs) have a choice regarding how they want to respond to host government institutions—a point often ignored by mainstream theory—a research program has been conducted to explore how MNEs adapt to and, in some instances, seek to shape their environments.[56]

In fact, scholars of what has been termed "the new institutionalism" highlight that institutional systems vary widely across cultures and geographies.[57] As MNEs operate in different countries around the world, they experience different types and intensities of institutional pressures, and it may be difficult for them to accurately assess and comprehend the needs of these differing entities.[58] The new institutionalism and its variants may be helpful in revealing the appropriate responses based on these conditions.[59]

In addition, an emerging research stream that integrates traditional studies of regulation and governance with more recent attention to CSR has explored the emergent phenomena of growing private regulation (such as voluntary codes, standards, and third-party ratings) and the interaction of these private regulatory initiatives with public regulations.[60] Historically, the state was viewed as the main vehicle through which the regulation of business activity was conducted. Increasingly, however, private regulation is viewed as a supplement or complement to public regulation. As firms become more global, public regimes cannot oversee their increasingly multinational presence. At the same time, there are concerns that private regimes may supplant or even replace public regimes, undermining the role of the state.[61]

Our Approach

We approach this subject from the perspective of management theory and practice. We draw upon and integrate relevant insights from our own research work and that of our many colleagues within and outside academia. In addition, we leverage our executive engagement, drawing on formal and informal interviews with senior managers, entrepreneurial leaders, and industry experts. We also employ publicly available data from companies, trade publications, and industry databases and associations to compile a rigorously researched book. Representative businesses discussed include airlines (such as British Airways, Lufthansa, and Virgin), carmakers (BMW and Tata), food and beverage producers (Ben & Jerry's, Coca-Cola, Danone, Diageo, Grupo Balbo, Heinz, Nestlé, and PepsiCo), consumer and industrial products companies (DuPont, Johnson & Johnson, Lexmark, Masisa, Saint-Gobain, and Unilever), insurance and banking, and financial service providers (Bank of America Merrill Lynch, Barclays, Equity Bank Kenya, ICICI Bank, and Swiss Re), information and communication technology providers, media giants, electronic equipment manufacturers (Apple, Dell, Google, MCI, Microsoft, Samsung, and others), relief organizations (Doctors Without Borders/Médecins Sans Frontières, and Oxfam America), and extractive or building materials multinationals (BP, CEMEX, and Shell). Furthermore, our own backgrounds in public policy research and practice have informed our analysis, and we have consulted with local, national, and supranational governmental bodies and officials on a range of questions and issues described in the book.

Many authors have made extensive use of case material, but the approach taken in *Aligning for Advantage* is distinct in two respects. The first is a recognition of the differing traditions and contexts of business and management across the world. Company and contextual examples are drawn from North and South America, Europe (including non-EU countries), Russia,

Asia-Pacific, and Africa, rather than exclusively from the United States and Western Europe, as is so often the case. This more measured and textured approach to case selection is the source of numerous original and revealing insights. The second is the incorporation of business history cases and illustrations—particularly in Chapter 2—alongside contemporary examples. Doing so provides an opportunity and a challenge: the opportunity is to exploit existing historical examples to test and exemplify the core propositions of *Aligning for Advantage*, while the challenge is to demonstrate the essential timeless nature of the logic and practice of corporate political and social strategy. What emerges is a more compelling and well-founded piece of work.

The perspective we bring as authors of this book is based on many years of studying corporate strategy and business context not only in academic settings but also through active engagement with managers and leaders in private-sector—and public-sector—organizations in many parts of the world. Our roles have included executive educator, consultant, and trusted adviser. It was through listening carefully to, and exchanging ideas with, these entrepreneurs and executives that the perspectives and concepts presented in this book began to take shape.

Overview of the Book

In Section I and Chapter 1 we provide the motivation for the book, survey the key literature that provides its foundations, and describe what we mean by alignment. In Chapter 2 we consider the roots of modern corporate engagement in the political and social spheres, exploring the historical premises and examples of nonmarket strategy. We also reflect on the contrasting philosophical perspectives on the role of business in society and articulate our own view on this issue. In Chapter 3 we engage especially with the changing regulatory context of nonmarket strategy and theoretical perspectives from political science and international relations in order to discuss the ensuing conceptual complexity of nonmarket strategy. We focus on relevant power constructs and their ability to cut through the intellectual intricacies surrounding nonmarket strategy. We also consider the difference between corporate strategy and corporate policy, and how this distinction can inform our understanding of the distinction between strategy formulation and implementation.

In Section II we build on this discussion, focusing especially on the pathways and mechanisms by which firms can influence the political and social arena and how these activities lead to aligned strategies. Looking at a variety of companies, we discern patterns, teasing out common strategic and leadership characteristics that are the hallmark of aligned companies. In Chapter 4 we address how managers and companies deal with uncertainty around political and social issues and propose a framework for managing in such uncertain environments. In Chapter 5 we explore a longstanding debate about when firms should address public policy and social issues individually or through collective initiatives such as trade associations or other ad hoc coalitions. In Chapter 6 we deal explicitly with the organizational architecture needed to best respond to nonmarket challenges, reviewing different ways firms can organize—and have organized—their approach to public and social policy, and the advantages and disadvantages of these options.

In Section III we introduce a political and social strategy development and delivery framework. Political and social strategy making is depicted as iterative and ongoing, embracing four main processes—sensing, shaping, aligning, and actioning (SSAA). Chapter 7 focuses on the process of sensing to incubate interest. Chapter 8 explores how firms can shape information value, and Chapter 9 details the advantages of—and processes for—aligning with stakeholders. All three chapters consider actioning or executing nonmarket strategy, which is also discussed more explicitly in Section IV.

Section IV addresses issues of balanced implementation, new institutional challenges (particularly in emerging economies), and ideas and insights for the practice of nonmarket strategy leadership. A wide body of thought is brought to bear on the context for choices in leadership and governance, and how this can help design and deliver political and social strategies. The main objective of Section IV will resonate with existing and aspiring leaders intent on improving their corporate political and social principles and practices. Chapter 10 explores the delicate balance necessary in aligning commercial and political/social strategies and objectives. Chapter 11 incorporates the challenges and opportunities posed by emerging and transitioning economies and markets for political and social strategy. In Chapter 12 we conclude the book by underscoring the need for a distinct kind and level of leadership to successfully manage and align political and social strategy with basic competitive strategy.

Together, the four sections of *Aligning for Advantage* provide a complete system for designing and implementing aligned strategies.

Notes

* Portions of this chapter have been adapted from Lawton, T., McGuire, S., and Rajwani, T. (2013). Corporate political activity: a literature review and research agenda. *International Journal of Management Reviews*, 15(1): 86–105.

1. Tzu, S. (2002). *The art of war: complete text and commentaries*. Translated by T. Cleary. New York: Shambahala Publications: 167.

2. Thomas, K. (2012). Johnson & Johnson to remove formaldehyde from products. *The New York Times*, August 16: B1.

3. International Council of Chemical Associations, Responsible Care Initiative. <http://www.icca-chem.org/en/home/responsible-care> (accessed February 10, 2013).

4. Baron, D.P. (1995a). The nonmarket strategy system. *Sloan Management Review*, 37(1): 73-85; Baron, D.P. (1995b). Integrated strategy: market and nonmarket components. *California Management Review*, 37(2): 47–65.

5. For example, Baron, 1995a; Baron, D.P. (1997). Integrated strategy in international trade disputes: the Kodak-Fujifilm case. *Journal of Economics & Management Strategy*, 6(1): 291–346; Baron, D.P. (2001). Private politics, corporate social responsibility, and integrated strategy. *Journal of Economics & Management Strategy*, 10(1): 7-45; Baron, D.P. (2007). Introduction to the special issue on nonmarket strategy and social responsibility. *Journal of Economics & Management Strategy*, 16(3): 539–545; Baron, D.P. and Diermeier, D. (2007). Strategic activism and nonmarket strategy. *Journal of Economics & Management Strategy*, 16: 599–634; Pearce, J.L. (2001a). How we can learn how governments matter to management and organization. *Journal of Management Inquiry*, 10(2): 103–112; Shaffer, B. and Hillman, A.J. (2000). The development of business–government strategies by diversified firms. *Strategic Management Journal*, 21: 175–190.

6. Boddewyn, J.J. (1988). Political aspects of MNE theory. *Journal of International Business Studies*, 19(3): 341–363; Boddewyn, J.J. (1993). Political resources and markets in international business: beyond Porter's generic strategies. In A. Rugman and A. Verbeke (eds.). *Research in global strategic management.* Greenwich, CT: JAI Press: vol. 4: 162–184; Boddewyn, J.J. and Brewer, T.L. (1994). International-business political behavior: new theoretical directions. *Academy of Management Review*, 19(1): 119–143; Brewer, T.L. (1992a). An issue-area approach to the analysis of MNC-government relations. *Journal of International Business Studies*, 23: 295–309; Brewer, T.L. (1992b). MNC-government relations: strategic networks and foreign direct investment in the United States in the automotive industry. *The International Executive*, 34: 113–129; Coen, D., Grant, W., and Wilson, G. (eds.) (2010). *The Oxford handbook of business and government.* Oxford: Oxford University Press; Czinkota, M. and Ronkainen, I. (1997). International business and trade in the next decade: report from a Delphi Study. *Journal of International Business Studies*, 28(4): 827–844; Lenway, S. and Murtha, T. (1994). The state as strategist in international business research. *Journal of International Business Studies*, 25(3): 513–535; Murtha, T. and Lenway, S., (1994). Country capabilities and the strategic state: how national political institutions affect multinational corporations' strategies. *Strategic Management Journal*, 15 (supplement S2): 113–129; Ring, P., Lenway, S., and Govekar, M. (1990). Management of the political imperative in international business. *Strategic Management Journal*, 11: 141–151; Rugman, A. and Verbeke, A. (1998). Multinational enterprises and public policy. *Journal of International Business Studies*, 29(1): 115–136.

7. Richardson, J. and Jordan, A. (1979). *Governing under pressure: The policy process in a post-parliamentary democracy.* Oxford: Martin Robertson; Mazey, S. and

Richardson, J. (1993). *Lobbying in the European Community*. Oxford: Oxford University Press; Streeck, W. and Schmitter, P. (eds.) (1984). *Private interest government: beyond market and state*. London: Sage; Coen 1998; Green-Cowles, M. (1995). Setting the agenda for a new Europe: the ERT and EC 1992. *Journal of Common Market Studies*, 33(4): 501–526; Lawton, T. (1997). *Technology and the new diplomacy: the creation and control of EC industrial policy for semiconductors*. Aldershot: Avebury.

8. Hambrick, D.C. (1981). Environment, strategy, and power within top management teams. *Administrative Science Quarterly*, 26(2): 253–275.

9. Bach, D. and Allen, D.B. (2010). What every CEO needs to know about nonmarket strategy, *MIT Sloan Management Review*, 51(3): 41–48.

10. McWilliams, A., Van Fleet, D., and Cory, K. (2002). Raising rivals' costs through political strategy: an extension of resource-based theory. *Journal of Management Studies*, 39(5): 707–723; Baron 2001.

11. Oliver, C. and Holzinger, I. (2008). The effectiveness of strategic political management: a dynamic capabilities framework. *Academy of Management Review*, 33: 496–520.

12. Andrews, K.R. (1971). *The concept of corporate strategy*. Homewood, IL: Dow Jones Irwin; Hofer, C. and Schendel, D.E. (1978). *Strategy formulation: analytical concepts*. St. Paul, MN: West.

13. Andrews 1971; Chandler, A.D. (1962), *Strategy and structure: chapters in the history of American industrial enterprise*. Cambridge, MA: MIT Press; Zajac, E.J., Kraatz, M.S., and Bresser, R.K.F. (2000). Modeling the dynamics of strategic fit: a normative approach to strategic change. *Strategic Management Journal*, 21(4): 429–454.

14. Chorn, N.H. (1991). The "alignment" theory: creating strategic fit. *Management Decision*, 29(1): 20.

15. Ginsberg, A. and Venkatraman, N. (1985). Contingency perspectives of organizational strategy: a critical review of the empirical research. *Academy of Management Review*, 10: 421–434; Miles, R.E. and Snow, C.C. (1994). *Fit, failure and the hall of fame*. New York: Macmillan.

16. Strange, S. (1985). Protectionism and world politics. *International Organization*, 39(2): 233–259; Strange, S. (1987). The persistent myth of lost hegemony. *International Organization*, 41(4): 551–574; Strange, S. (1988). *States and markets: an introduction to international political economy*. London: Pinter; Strange, S. (1996). *The retreat of the state: the diffusion of power in the world economy*. 2nd ed. Cambridge: Cambridge University Press; Rosecrance, R. (1986). *The rise of the trading state: commerce and coalitions in the modern world*. New York: Basic Books; Waltz, K.N. (2000). Structural realism after the Cold War. *International Security*, 25(1): 5–41.

17. Gilpin, R., (1975). *US power and the multinational corporation: the political economy of foreign direct investment*. New York: Basic Books: 40.

18. Gilpin, R. (1987). *The political economy of international relations*. Princeton, NJ: Princeton University Press.

19. Strange 1988.

20. Bonardi, J.P., Holburn, G.L.F., and Vanden Bergh, R.G. (2006). Nonmarket strategy performance: evidence from U.S. electric utilities. *Academy of Management Journal*, 38: 288–303; Pearce II, J.A., and Doh, J.P. (2005). The high impact of collaborative social initiatives. *Sloan Management Review*, 46(3): 30–39.

21. Barrows, D.S. and Morris, S. (1989). Managing public policy issues, *Long Range Planning*, 22(6): 66–73; Keim, G.D. and Hillman, A.J. (2008). Political environments and business strategy: implications for managers. *Business Horizons*, 51(1): 47–53.

22. Dahan, N. (2005a). Can there be a resource-based view of politics? *International Studies of Management & Organization*, 35(2): 8–27.

23. Capron, L. and Chatain, O. (2008). Competitors' resource-oriented strategies: acting on competitors' resources through interventions in factor markets and political markets. *Academy of Management Review*, 33: 97–121; McWilliams et al. 2002.

24. Baron 1995a, 1995b; Bonardi, J.P., Hillman, A.J., and Keim, G.D. (2005). The attractiveness of political markets: implications for firm strategies. *Academy of Management Review*, 30: 397–413; Hillman, A. J., Keim, G. D., and Schuler, D. (2004). Corporate political activity: a review and research agenda. *Journal of Management*, 30(6): 837–857.

25. Oliver and Holzinger 2008.

26. Baron 1995a.

27. For a review of CPA research, see Hillman et al. 2004; and Lawton et al. 2013.

28. Austen-Smith, D. and Wright, J.R. (1996). Theory and evidence for counteractive lobbying. *American Journal of Political Science*, 40: 543–564; Delmas, M.A. and Montes-Sancho, M.J. (2010). Voluntary agreements to improve environmental quality: symbolic and substantive cooperation. *Strategic Management Journal*, 31: 575–601; Hansen, W. and Mitchell, N. (2000). Disaggregating and explaining corporate political activity: domestic and foreign corporations in national politics. *American Political Science Review*, 94(4): 891–903; Okhmatovskiy, I. (2010). Performance implications of ties to the government and SOEs: a political embeddedness perspective. *Journal of Management Studies*, 47(6): 1020–1047; Ring et al. 1990; Spiller, P.T. (1990). Politicians, interest groups, and regulators: a multiple-principals agency theory of regulation, or "let them be bribed." *Journal of Law and Economics*, 33: 65–101; Yoffie, D. and Bergenstein, S. (1985). Creating political advantage: the rise of the corporate political entrepreneur. *California Management Review*, 28(1): 124–139.

29. Hillman and Hitt 1999.

30. Hillman and Hitt 1999.

31. Hillman et al. 2004.

32. Vogel, D. (1996). The study of business and politics. *California Management Review*, 38: 146–165.

33. Fuchs, D. and Lederer, M. (2007). The power of business. *Business and Politics*, 9(3): 1–17.

34. Barron, A. (2010). Unlocking the mindsets of Government Affairs Managers: cultural dimensions of corporate political activity. *Cross Cultural Management: an International Journal*, 17(2): 101–117; Sun, P., Mellahi, K., and Thun, E. (2010).

The dynamic value of MNE political embeddedness: the case of the Chinese automobile industry. *Journal of International Business Studies*, 41(7): 1161–1182.

35. Adly, A. I. (2009). Politically-embedded cronyism: the case of post-liberalization Egypt. *Business and Politics*, 11(4): 1–26.

36. Gould, J. and C. Sickner (2008), Making market democracies? The contingent loyalties of post-privatization elites in Azerbaijan, Georgia and Serbia. *Review of International Political Economy*, 15: 745–769.

37. Giddens, A. (2000). *The Third Way and its critics*. Cambridge: Polity Press.

38. See McWilliams, A. and Siegel, D. (2000). Corporate social responsibility and financial performance: correlation or misspecification? *Strategic Management Journal*, 21: 603–609; Preston, L.E. and O'Bannon, D.P. (1997). The corporate social-financial performance relationship: a typology and analysis. *Business and Society*, 36: 419–429; Stanwick, P.A. and Stanwick, D. (1998). The relationship between corporate social performance and organizational size, financial performance, and environmental performance: an empirical examination. *Journal of Business Ethics*, 17: 195–204; Griffin, J.J. and Mahon, J.F. (1997). The corporate social performance and corporate financial performance debate: twenty-five years of incomparable research. *Business and Society*, 36: 5–31; Roman, R.M., Hayibor, S., and Agle, B.R. (1999). The relationship between social and financial performance: repainting a portrait. *Business and Society*, 38: 109–125; Ruf, B.M.K., Muralidhar, R.M., Brown, J.J., and Paul, K. (2001). An empirical investigation of the relationship between change in corporate social performance and financial performance: a stakeholder theory perspective. *Journal of Business Ethics*, 32(2): 143–157; Margolis, J.D. and Walsh, J. P. (2003). Misery loves companies: rethinking social initiatives by business. *Administrative Science Quarterly*, 48: 268–305; Margolis, J.D. and Walsh, J. P. (2001). *People and profits? The search for a link between a company's social and financial performance*. Mahwah, NJ: Lawrence Erlbaum Associates; Balabanis, G., Phillips, H., and Lyall, J. (1998). Corporate social responsibility and economic performance in the top British companies. *European Business Review*, 98(1): 25–44; Moore, G. (2001). Corporate social and financial performance: an investigation in the U.K. supermarket industry. *Journal of Business Ethics*, 34(3/4): 299–315.

39. Bowen, H.R. (1953). *Social responsibilities of the businessman*. New York: Harper & Row: xi; Carroll, A.B. (1979). A three-dimensional conceptual model of corporate social performance. *Academy of Management Review*, 4(4): 497–505.

40. Bowen 1953.

41. Davis, K. (1960). Can business afford to ignore corporate social responsibilities? *California Management Review*, 2: 70.

42. Frederick, W.C. (1960). The growing concern over business responsibility. *California Management Review*, 2: 54–61.

43. Carroll, A.B. (1991) The pyramid of corporate social responsibility: toward the moral management of organizational stakeholders. *Business Horizons*, 34(4): 39–48; Carroll, A.B. (1983). Corporate social responsibility: will industry respond to cutbacks in social program funding? *Vital Speeches of the Day*, 48(19): 604.

44. Schwartz, M.S. and Carroll, A.B. (2008). Integrating and unifying competing and complementary frameworks: the search for a common core in the business and society field. *Business and Society*, 47(2): 160.

45. Jones, T.M., and Wicks, A.C. (1999). Convergent stakeholder theory. *Academy of Management Review*, 24(2): 206–221.

46. Mitchell, R.K., Agle, B.R., and Wood, D.J. (1997). Toward a theory of stakeholder identification and salience: defining the principle of who and what really counts. *Academy of Management Review*, 22(4): 853–886.

47. McWilliams, A., Siegel, D.S., and Wright, P.M. (2006). Corporate social responsibility: strategic implications. *Journal of Management Studies*, 43: 1–18.

48. McWilliams, A. and Siegel, D.S. (2001). Corporate social responsibility: a theory of the firm perspective. *Academy of Management Review*, 26(1): 7–127.

49. Baron 2001.

50. See for instance Margolis and Walsh 2003; Ruf et al. 2001; McWilliams and Siegel 2000; Preston and O'Bannon 1997; Stanwick and Stanwick 1998; and Griffin and Mahon 1997.

51. Margolis, J.D., Elfenbein, H.A., and Walsh, J.P. (2007). Does it pay to be good? A meta-analysis and redirection of research on the relationship between corporate social and financial performance. Working paper. Boston, MA: Harvard Business school.

52. Strange 1988; Strange 1996.

53. Prakash, A. (2002). Beyond Seattle: globalization, the nonmarket environment and corporate strategy. *Review of International Political Economy*, 9: 513–537.

54. den Hond, F. and de Bakker, F.G.A. (2007). Ideologically motivated activism: how activist groups influence corporate social change. *Academy of Management Review*, 32(3): 901–924; Djelic, M.-L. and Quack, S. (2003). *Globalization and institutions: redefining the rules of the economic game*. Cheltenham, U.K.: Edward Elgar.

55. Ramamurti, R. (2001). The obsolescing "bargaining model"? MNC-host developing country relations revisited. *Journal of International Business Studies*, 32(1): 23–39.

56. Dahan, N., Doh, J., and Guay, T. (2006). The role of multinational corporations in transnational institutional building: a policy-network perspective. *Human Relations*, 59(11): 1571–1600; Tsebelis, G. (1991). *Nested games: Rational choice in comparative politics*. Berkeley, CA: University of California Press; Oliver, C. (1991). Strategic responses to institutional processes. *Academy of Management Review*, 16: 145–179; Djelic and Quack 2003.

57. Dahan, Doh, and Guay 2006; Bulmer, S. (1994). The governance of the European Union: a new institutionalist approach. *Journal of Public Policy*, 13(4): 351–380; Levy, D.L. and Egan, D. (2003). A neo-Gramscian approach to corporate political strategy: conflict and accommodation in the climate change negotiations. *Journal of Management Studies*, 40(4): 803–829; Pollack, M. (1996). The new institutionalism and EC governance: the promise and limits of institutional analysis. *Governance: an international journal of policy, administration, and institutions*, 9(4): 429–458.

58. Dahan, Doh, and Guay 2006; Hillman, A.J. and Wan, W. (2005). The determinants of MNE subsidiaries' political strategies: evidence of institutional duality. *Journal of International Business Studies*, 36(3): 322–340; Kostova, T. and Roth, K. (2002). Adoption of an organizational practice by subsidiaries of multinational corporations: institutional and relational effects. *Academy of Management Journal*, 45(1): 215–233.

59. Dahan, Doh, and Guay 2006; Levy and Egan 2003. Egan, M. (2002). Setting standards: strategic advantages in international trade. *Business Strategy Review*, 13(1): 51–64.

60. Scott, C., Cafaggi, F., and Senden, L. (eds.) (2011). *The challenge of transnational private regulation: conceptual and constitutional debates*. Wiley-Blackwell: London; Graham, D. and Woods, N. (2006). Making corporate self-regulation effective in developing countries. *World Development*, 34(5): 868–883.

61. Vogel, D. (2003). The hare and the tortoise revisited: the new politics of consumer and environmental regulation in Europe. *British Journal of Political Science*, 33: 557–580.

2

Origins of Engagement*

Study the past if you would divine the future.[1]

Confucius

History has a way of repeating itself, and few human actions lack historical precedent. Although terms such as *corporate social responsibility* and *corporate political activity* have entered the management lexicon only quite recently, enterprises and those who lead them have practiced these activities for much longer. From the time of the Industrial Revolution, business history is replete with examples of good deeds and noble causes conducted and funded by captains of industry. Evidence also abounds of business leaders leveraging their economic and financial power to gain political influence that would help to defend and extend their commercial interests. For instance, in response to accusations in the early 20th century that slave-grown cocoa was being used in his manufacturing facilities, the well-known British chocolatier William Cadbury lobbied the Portuguese monarchy to end the policy of contract labor (de facto slavery) in Portuguese Africa.[2]

Yet despite this rich history, much of modern management theory and practice is ahistorical. Before we progress to the ideas of, and approaches to, nonmarket strategy and subsequently the management and mechanisms of nonmarket influence, it is important to first consider the roots of modern corporate engagement in the political and social spheres. In this chapter we therefore set out to engage with the origins of strategic alignment by examining historical examples of nonmarket strategy—before it became labeled as such—and the business leaders who executed it. We also reflect on contrasting philosophical perspectives about the role of business in society and develop our philosophy for this book, seeking to avoid the normative attitude and approach often found in other books on nonmarket strategy or its subthemes. Instead of advocating that managers and firms *do the right thing,* we endeavor to identify how they can *do things right.* Our interest is not in proselytizing or converting readers to a specific way of thinking or course of action, as every manager, business, and supply chain is unique and faces its own challenges and opportunities. Instead, we aim to use our research findings and experience to illuminate and integrate nonmarket strategy processes and practices. Our intent is simply to provide ideas and options that can be used by managers and leaders to align market and nonmarket strategies both inside a company and within a value chain.

Going Back to the Future

We begin by touching on past relationships between business and government, and the historical evolution of the state–company nexus. Corporate-like organizations conducted private commerce in the Mauryan Empire of ancient India as early as the 3rd century B.C.E., and similar entities managed state-driven public projects during the Roman Empire.[3] In the centuries before the emergence of modern capitalism in Europe, the interests of states and corporations were difficult to separate. Companies, if not owned outright by the state or the church, usually operated under the aegis of government or of a political or religious patron. This interconnection endured into the Late Middle Ages; for example, the Casa di San Giorgio, one of the world's oldest chartered banks, acted as an instrument of the Republic of Genoa's mercantile power. Likewise, the global expansion of European empires from the 16th through 18th centuries relied heavily on state-backed enterprises such as the Dutch East India Company and the Hudson's Bay Company.

The notion of nonmarket strategy did not really gain traction until the Age of Enlightenment and the subsequent Industrial Revolution, when large-scale private enterprise, free of state control and patronage, first emerged. Modernity encouraged new types of commercial enterprises, often founded by individuals with a strong moral compass and acute political sense. Philanthropists such as Andrew Carnegie and John Rockefeller in the United States, John Cadbury (grandfather of William) and Joseph Rowntree in England, Arthur Guinness in Ireland (whose approach we examine in detail later in this chapter), and Jamsetji Tata in India understood both the need for a nonmarket strategy and the importance of aligning this with their commercial interests and market strategies. In many instances, their purpose and approach was informed by religious beliefs, underlining the moral dimension that has often pervaded nonmarket strategy.

Nonmarket Activism, Past and Present

To illustrate this point, reflect for a moment on the phrase "The man who dies thus rich dies disgraced." These words—which might have come from an early Fabian Society pamphlet or even a modern socialist activist—were in fact written[4] by U.S. steel magnate Andrew Carnegie toward the close of the 19th century, at the high point of an era of industrialization dominated by "the robber barons." This term—most likely derived from the practices of medieval lords who charged tolls on ships navigating the Rhine but offered neither security nor service in return—was popularized during the Great Depression, most notably by U.S. author and commentator Matthew Josephson, who argued that America's big businessmen, like their German forerunners, had amassed enormous fortunes through immoral and unethical means.[5] Just as in the anticapitalist backlash that followed the Great Recession of 2008–2012, the press, public, and politicians pilloried big business during the Depression, demanding justice for those who languished on unemployment lines. Of course, the truth is rarely so black and white, and, then as now, capitalism and philanthropy were never far apart. Consider for instance that the names of Carnegie and fellow "robber barons" Andrew Mellon and Leland Stanford today are all associated with renowned U.S. universities.

There have always been those who view the achievement of personal success and the accumulation of wealth as an implicit obligation to give money, time, or expertise to worthy social causes. We can easily trace a line from a Bill Gates or a Richard Branson of today back to an Andrew Carnegie or a Henry Wellcome of yesterday. (See Tables 2.1 and 2.2 for additional illustrations of the continuity in corporate philanthropy and the nonmarket activism of business leaders over time.) Similarly, there are those in business who forge corporate cultures that encourage and even incentivize "doing good" within their communities. One example is Lorenzo Zambrano, chairman and chief executive of Mexican corporate giant CEMEX, one of the world's largest producers of building materials. Not long after taking on the chief executive role of his family's business in 1985, Zambrano began to imbue the corporation with the values of environmental responsibility and social progress. Today CEMEX is viewed around the world as a leading example of a company that actively engages with, and gives back to, the communities and environments in which it does business. It also values and invests in its employees, which makes jobs at CEMEX highly desirable in many countries.

Through some examples since the mid-19th century, Tables 2.1 and 2.2 illustrate the continuity over time in corporate philanthropy and the nonmarket activism of business leaders.

As we can see from the two eras emphasized in Tables 2.1 and 2.2, the practice of philanthropic giving is not new. Many successful entrepreneurs and industrialists then and now have accumulated vast wealth and subsequently decided to give something back to society. There is, of course, a significant difference between benignly funding disparate social and environmental causes and actively engaging with specific nonmarket issues and agendas that

Table 2.1. Early industrialists and nonmarket impact

Andrew Carnegie (1835–1919)	Made his fortune in steel. Funded public libraries, swimming baths, music halls, universities, and schools across Scotland (his country of birth) and the U.S.A. (his adopted home), giving away the equivalent of more than U.S.$300 million.
John D. Rockefeller (1839–1937)	Founder of Standard Oil, now Exxon Mobil. Gave away half his fortune, about U.S.$450 million. His legacy includes Rockefeller University in New York and the Rockefeller Foundation, which works globally to promote the well-being of humanity through social, health, environmental, and related initiatives.
Joseph Rowntree (1836–1925)	A British Quaker, chocolate magnate, and champion of social reform. He set up a model village for the poor with public libraries and free schools. His factories were among the first to introduce occupational pension schemes. Trusts in his name to fund poverty studies and effect social reform still exist in the U.K.
Henry Ford (1863–1947)	The inventor of the world's first affordable automobile, the Model T. Together with his son Edsel, he set up the Ford Foundation, committed to social change in developing countries. When Ford died, the foundation owned 90 percent of non-voting shares in the Ford Motor Company, estimated to be worth U.S. $500 million to U.S. $700 million. It is the second-largest private foundation in the world, with assets today in excess of U.S. $10 billion.
W.K. Kellogg (1860–1951)	An American industrialist, Seventh-day Adventist, and founder of the Kellogg Company, producer of well-known breakfast cereals. During the Great Depression he set up the W.K. Kellogg Foundation and transferred U.S. $66 million of company stock to it. Kellogg and his foundation placed an emphasis on children's education, nutrition, and health, as well as racial equity and civic engagement.

Source: Adapted from <http://studyfundraising.info/page12.php> and *The Week* magazine, June 27, 2006.

Table 2.2. Nonmarket activism in the modern era

William H. Gates (1955–)	The Bill and Melinda Gates Foundation was founded in 1999 with U.S. $16 billion of Microsoft stock. It focuses on health and education, and has spent U.S. $10 billion on vaccines. By many measures Gates is the world's largest giver, having donated U.S. $28 billion (half of his net worth) to charity.
Warren Buffett (1930–)	The famed investor and CEO of Berkshire Hathaway pledged in 2006 to give more than U.S. $30 billion over 20 years to the Gates Foundation. He has donated U.S. $2.7 billion to support education, medical research, and family planning.
George Soros (1930–)	The Hungarian-born international investor has given more than U.S. $8 billion to a variety of education, human rights, and social causes. Most notably in terms of nonmarket activism, he established the Open Society Foundations to help countries transitioning from communism.
Li Ka-shing (1928–)	The Hong Kong tycoon and chairman of Hutchison Whampoa started a foundation in 1980. Regarded as Asia's most generous philanthropist, he has pledged to give U.S. $10 billion to charity. To date he has donated U.S. $1.5 billion to children's centers, churches, universities, and health initiatives across Asia and North America.
Pierre Omidyar (1967–)	Together with his wife, Pam, the French-born eBay founder and chairman established the Omidyar Network in 2004. It invests in social enterprises, particularly in developing countries. The idea is to use the power of business to address global poverty. By late 2012, the network had invested more than U.S. $550 million through grants, loans, and equity.

Source: The good Samaritans: Buffett and Gates, *The Week*, June 27, 2006 and <http://www.therichest.org/most-influential/the-worlds-biggest-givers/> (accessed May 8, 2013).

strategically affect a company. Moreover, the examples given have an important common characteristic: they all gave back *after* they had made their fortunes. This differs from the approach of successful businesspeople like Ben Cohen and Jerry Greenfield of Ben & Jerry's ice cream and the late Anita Roddick of the Body Shop, who gave back *while* they were accumulating their wealth. However, benevolence, strategy, and business success are not mutually exclusive. We will return to this issue later in the chapter, after we delve more deeply into the intellectual and moral underpinnings of alignment.

Guinness: an Early Example of the Art of Alignment

Arthur Guinness, founder of the brewery and brand that has become intertwined with Irish identity around the world, was an astute business leader who managed to be accepted by both sides in the tumultuous politics of pre-independence Ireland. While building his company during the second half of the 18th century, he followed a political strategy that allowed the company to successfully court the nationalist cause through supporting Henry Grattan and the Irish Patriot Party, which advocated self-government, although not outright independence, for Ireland. Coincidentally (or not), Grattan also supported reducing the tax on beer. The strategy also leveraged Guinness's membership in the Protestant Ascendancy[6] ruling class and avowed support of the empire to facilitate the company's entry into the much larger English market. The result was a brilliant alignment of business imperatives and political expediency: positioning himself as a Protestant businessman with sympathy for, and understanding of, the Catholic and Dissenter cause of Irish Home Rule,[7] Guinness appeared to his customers to support Ireland's autonomy from England *while at the same time* appearing to the British government to be a resolute advocate of the status quo.

On social strategy, Guinness again acted pragmatically but was also most likely shaped by religious sentiment. He was known to have attended sermons in Dublin given by John Wesley, the noted theologian and co-founder of Methodism. Wesley's message can best be summarized by his rule:

> *Do all the good you can. By all the means you can. In all the ways you can. In all the places you can. At all the times you can. To all the people you can. As long as ever you can.*

Arthur Guinness appears to have taken this message to heart and acted on it. His contribution to the social development of working-class Dublin was significant, with investments in his workers, in the community adjacent to his brewery at St James's Gate, and in Irish society at large. At a time when government relied on private munificence to provide many public services,

Guinness built public parks and housing for Dublin's poor. Through such acts of social responsibility, Guinness not only consolidated his company's reputation as being in touch with the common man, but also rapidly built a brand as Ireland's preeminent brewer. Furthermore, Guinness Brewery became one of the most sought-after employers in Ireland. The company paid high wages; created a range of social, leisure, and educational programs for its workers and their families; and even allowed every worker to take home two pint bottles of Guinness each day. The loyalty and productivity of Guinness workers were unrivalled. His heirs honored this ethos and continued these activities as the company grew to become the largest brewery in the world by the late 19th century. These principles survive, even after the 1997 merger of Guinness and GrandMet to create the global drinks giant Diageo. The Arthur Guinness Fund, set up by Diageo, supports social entrepreneurs in Ireland and around the world. The Fund is innovative in that it provides not only financial support, but also expertise, advice, and networks from Diageo and partners such as Social Entrepreneurs Ireland. In 2010, the year after the Fund was set up, €1 million was awarded to ten Irish social entrepreneurs, along with practical support and mentoring. A further €3 million was awarded to programs in Ghana, Indonesia, Nigeria, and the U.S. It is probably not a coincidence that all four countries are important Guinness markets. More than 40 percent of all Guinness sales are in Africa. Guinness Ghana Breweries Ltd. is regularly a top-five-performing stock on the Ghana Stock Exchange. The Guinness brewery in Lagos, Nigeria, was the first outside of Ireland and Great Britain, and Nigeria is the second-largest market in the world for Guinness consumption. As sales in Ireland and across Europe have declined, sales in the U.S. and Indonesia have increased, and Diageo has focused on growing markets in Africa, Asia Pacific, and Latin America. As in the time of Arthur Guinness, pragmatism and alignment are at the forefront of Diageo's corporate strategy.

Moral and Spiritual Disconnectedness

An aligned approach to corporate strategy may often be linked to the spirituality and religiosity of company founders and leaders. By examining the lives of well-known business figures since the beginning of the industrial age, we can glean insights into how their faith has shaped their approach to corporate vision and values, organizational culture, and strategic alignment. In addition to the examples already cited, a further illustration can be found in the culture and ethos of the respected and highly successful British retailer, the John Lewis Partnership. John Spedan Lewis forged the employee-owned enterprise from the company left to him by his father. Although he was not overtly religious, his admiration of Quaker traditions prompted him to relinquish his claim to an income greater than that of his entire workforce. Lewis introduced a profit-sharing scheme in 1928, and in 1950 he transferred control of the company to the employees. The partnership's long-held opposition to Sunday trading was shaped by its Quaker traditions[8] and intent to honor the Christian Sabbath. John Lewis was the last of the large U.K. retailers to open its stores seven days a week.

In the world of 21st-century capitalism, do faith and religion still play a role in influencing some business organizations and corporate strategies? More specifically, can we discern any connection between spirituality and strategy alignment? The growing moral and spiritual challenge of "disconnectedness" can be seen in the modern era of business.[9] While globalization has made the world smaller by easily and rapidly connecting people everywhere, it has also accelerated a disconnectedness of firms from their communities and nations, and most profoundly from themselves. This is particularly true within publicly traded firms, where the intense pressure to maximize shareholder wealth disconnects the firm from other goods, particularly any understanding of the common good.[10]

This disconnectedness is formed in various ways, but we will highlight two elements of it. The first is disconnected wealth. While more and more leaders find themselves looking at stock markets and the expansion of personal stock options and other retirement programs, such ownership tends to be valued on one metric alone—price. Wealth is becoming increasingly impersonal and separate from firm strategies in markets and nonmarkets. This is because the ownership of equity shares of publicly traded companies is found within capital markets, which leads to a lack of connection between the owners of capital and the society in which they work. In the past, the founders and leaders of companies had some local or at least some national connection to what they owned and where they resided. Today wealth is characterized by disconnection from any value except financial value.[11]

Second, in the past, religious beliefs overtly determined the ethics and practices of many companies in countries from India to the United States. These beliefs, translated into managerial principles, were frequently at the heart of culture and enterprise. They enabled strategic managers to approach their tasks with a sense of higher purpose and wider influence. Their beliefs continually reminded them of where they had come from (origins), what their purpose was (present), and where they were going (destiny). However, in the modern age, the disconnection caused by capital markets, technology, and cultural forces is not universal. Consider the lending practices of Islamic banks such as Dubai Islamic Bank or the Islamic Bank of Britain. While they are, like conventional banks, operated to earn a profit, they cannot charge interest in accordance with sharia law. To accommodate this religious restriction, they have developed an alternative business model in which, for example, they do not give a buyer a mortgage to purchase a new home, but instead buy the house and resell it to the buyer at a markup. The buyer then pays off that higher amount in interest-free installments.

Apart from specific examples such as Islamic banking, most modern enterprises purposefully avoid overt religiosity both in principle and in practice. Senior managers prefer to speak of ethical values instead of spiritual values, and of morality in organizational rather than individual terms. As we discuss in the next section, this can precipitate at best moral relativism and at worst a culture of individualism and a corporation that is decoupled from its external communities and natural environment.

Contrasting Views on the Role of Business in Society

A definition of the role and purpose of business in society has long been caught between two contrasting ideological perspectives.[12] The first advocates corporate social responsibility in some or all of its dimensions—social, environmental, cultural, regulatory, and political. Proponents include business leaders who believe that their organizations embody the principles and practices of "good companies," as well as nongovernmental organizations and other advocacy groups that continually pressure business to increase its societal accountability and responsibility. The underlying principle represents a shift from shareholder to stakeholder capitalism. This means not only a corporate emphasis on generating shareholder return, but also on creating viable and well-paid jobs for employees, minimizing harmful impact on the environment, building positive relations with communities and transparent links with governments, and producing reliable products and services for consumers.[13] As discussed earlier in this chapter, this is not a new concept. Business leaders such as Jamsetji Tata—the 19th-century founder of India's Tata Group, for which social responsibility and ethical behavior were at the core of corporate strategy from the outset—provide examples of how companies can be shaped by taking into account the interests of multiple stakeholders.[14] In the post-World War II era of modern capitalism, we can track the evolution of a more concerted and prescriptive approach to, and perspective on, the role of business in society.[15] The core argument is that businesspeople have an obligation to pursue strategies, make decisions, and follow actions that are desirable in terms of the objectives and values of society.[16] More specifically, the objectives, values, and needs of stakeholders must be factored into corporate initiatives and activities. A stakeholder may be defined as any individual who or group that can affect or is affected by the achievement of the organization's objectives.[17] Some commentators even went so far as to argue that the neoclassical theory of the firm be replaced by a broader theory premised on the firm's responsibility to a wider set of stakeholders than just the owners.[18] This normative ethical theory of the firm argued that the firm should be managed for the benefit of *all* of its stakeholders and that management even has a fiduciary obligation to stakeholders to act as their agent.[19] Furthermore, the stakeholder approach suggests that the triple bottom line of "people, planet, and profit"[20] should not only become the norm for companies, but is also a basis on which to build a successful corporate strategy. The argument here is that quantifiable returns on investment need not be divorced from concern for values, ethics, and responsible corporate citizenship.[21]

Those who hold ideological positions contrary to those of the advocates of stakeholder capitalism vigorously dispute this win-win perspective. The contrasting free-market-economics perspective is best exemplified by the well-known saying "The business of business is business." This is generally attributed to Milton Friedman,[22] although it is also claimed to have been first said in the 1920s by U.S. industrialist Alfred Sloan. The position here is clear-cut: the sole legitimate purpose of business is to create shareholder value.[23] A concern with wider societal issues and interests is not only inappropriate but may even detract from a firm's ability to deliver profits. In fact, Friedman explicitly stated that increasing profits is the social responsibility of business.[24] This perspective is frequently misconstrued as being preoccupied with corporate profit at the cost of social and environmental value. Friedman and others did not see it as a zero-sum game. Instead, their initial premise is that only people have responsibilities. As such, businesspeople have individual and specific responsibilities, but these do not extend to the corporation as a whole. In a free enterprise, private property system, the paramount responsibility of a proprietor or corporate executive is to his or her key stakeholders, namely the owners (shareholders) of the business.[25] The manager is, therefore, the agent of those who own the enterprise. As a private individual, the manager has, of course, a much wider set of responsibilities to society. In this personal capacity he or she acts as a principal, not an agent, and is at liberty to spend his or her time, money, and energy on charitable work and other social responsibilities. Therefore, Friedman provocatively argues, "to say that the corporate executive has a 'social responsibility' in his capacity as a businessman...must mean that he is to act in some way that is not in the interest of his employers."[26] This is because they are in fact spending someone else's money—shareholders' or customers'—on what they deem social responsibility. In essence, this approach is rejecting the "bolt-on approach" to corporate responsibility, in which corporations allocate annual budgets and staff resources to specific social or environmental causes. The main intent is reputation enhancement and a desire to be seen to be "doing good." This contrasts with the "built-in approach," in which an enterprise is founded on principles of responsibility and/or sustainability. Friedman views the built-in approach in a more benign light, as it indicates that entrepreneurial founders have consciously chosen to reduce the profit-maximizing potential of their enterprises to fulfill specific social responsibilities. They are spending their own money and not someone else's, which is their right as individuals. What Friedman does not acknowledge is that the built-in approach may in fact be a strategic differentiator, enabling an entrepreneur to build a distinctive brand and in some cases to position his or her company in a high-end market niche. This may ultimately allow the company to generate greater profit than a "less responsible" competitor.

Moving Beyond Ideology and Toward Pragmatism

We are not interested in exploring the ins and outs and pros and cons of built-in versus bolt-on approaches to responsible business specifically and nonmarket strategy more generally. Moreover, unlike the opposing perspectives just outlined, the premise of strategic alignment and its constituent elements is not normative. As such, we are not advancing an ideal standard or specific model that strategic managers *should* adopt. Instead, we discuss different perspectives and approaches and suggest that the top management team of a company will be best served by adopting an approach that is most closely aligned with its strategic vision and values, business objectives, and market positions. Therefore, every company's approach is different, and we see a spectrum of stances in every industry, ranging from those that build a business around social responsibility and political activism (Ben & Jerry's, for instance) to those that perceive their societal obligations solely as wealth creation and begrudgingly meet the minimal regulatory requirements (many low-price competitors). Of course, there are also companies that fall off the spectrum, i.e. those that willfully exploit the social good and purposefully circumvent or undermine their regulatory obligations. These are not the focus of this book. Nonetheless, we offer insights, lessons, and techniques that such organizations can instill, if they choose to alter their strategic positions and market perceptions.

Our intent is to provide strategic leaders with a pragmatic perspective on how to compete in political and social arenas and forge a successfully aligned strategy. The challenge is to do so while refraining from advancing a universal approach to right and wrong attitudes and actions. This does not by default imply a positivist perspective. Intuition and introspection are valid managerial instincts and can often make the difference between strategies that succeed and those that fail. Instead, we lean toward a degree of moral relativism, particularly of a meta-ethical nature, as typified in the work of Friedrich

Nietzsche. Without agreeing with his perspectives *in toto*, we believe that a Nietzschean viewpoint, adapted for business management, can usefully underpin the approach of an executive or entrepreneur to strategic alignment. For instance, Nietzsche argues that there are no moral phenomena, only moral interpretations of phenomena.[27] If there are no moral phenomena or facts at all, nothing is in any way good or evil.[28] According to this line of argument, there are no good or bad companies—it is all down to individual interpretation. We, of course, need to be careful with moral relativism, as there are instances of certainty where most, if not all, observers can find common agreement. Examples of definitive "bad" corporate behavior include the bribing of government officials to obtain public-sector contracts (for example, the British bridge-building firm Mabey & Johnson was convicted in 2009 of having offered large bribes in countries such as Bangladesh, Ghana, and Jamaica) and the fraudulent marketing and sales of products that cause consumer health risks (we can think of Merck's marketing of the painkiller Vioxx, which led to a criminal indictment in 2011). Environmental damage and death caused by managerial or procedural negligence lead us to further question the moral relativism thesis. The 1984 Union Carbide gas leak in Bhopal, India, and the 2010 Deepwater Horizon oil spill in the Gulf of Mexico come to mind.

Unlike nihilists, Nietzsche does not assert that there is no such thing as morality; rather, that there must be a "revaluation of values."[29] Neither does he claim that all interpretations have a moral equivalence. He in fact makes a distinction between those that are emblematic of a noble character and those that are indicative of a decadent being. In a business and managerial context, Nietzsche's perspective indicates that good and bad depend on context and who is interpreting the situation. For example, Ben & Jerry's premium ice cream company gives a portion of profits away and is identified with causes such as homelessness and rain-forest preservation. But it also produces an expensive, high-cholesterol product. In saying that the moral character of qualities is the result of interpretation, Nietzsche was not pursing a radical indeterminacy about reality. Instead, he was making a sober psychological point that facts are never only facts, self-evident and comprehended by all minds in the same way in all circumstances and contexts.[30] Extrapolated to a nonmarket strategy context, interpretations of and approaches to corporate responsibility or political activism vary according to who is accountable and where and why it is occurring. To categorically declare that in 2012, for instance, General Mills was the most reputable company in America and Goldman Sachs was one of the least reputable[31] is both subjective and path dependent. To what extent is the poor ranking of Goldman Sachs determined by events and industry specificities of the past, particularly in the U.S., rather than global strategies and initiatives of the present?

Knowledge is conditioned by the context in which what we call *facts* are encountered and by the mental processes—not all conscious—that we call *interpretation*. There is, of course, the danger that this approach can be reduced to "it's all relative." However, as we previously mentioned, Nietzsche would argue that some interpretations are better than others. Though moral systems are relative and arbitrary, conformity to rules is the beginning of civilization and makes life meaningful and worth living. Like those of Aristotle and the ancients, Nietzsche's ethics are primarily concerned with character, emphasizing individual virtue, rejecting universal moral rights that inhibit character, and treating everyone as equal.[32] Hence, if your impulse is to succeed in business and to make money, the Nietzschean view suggests to do so in a way that has positive externalities and that does not purposefully damage or destroy other individuals.

The integration of opposing impulses and feelings is key to "nobility" and explains the contradictions of extraordinary people. Richard Nixon was a rabid anti-communist and a key supporter of Senator Joseph McCarthy's communist witch-hunt in the 1950s, and yet he forged détente with China in the 1970s. Many successful CEOs are simultaneously inspirational people motivators and perpetual organizational bullies. Thus, in a development of our previous discussion of philanthropy and other forms of nonmarket activism, Nietzsche's concept of the integration of opposing impulses explains why individuals, managers, and entrepreneurs may desire and choose to make money while also serving their fellow human beings. Selfishness and altruism are a false antagonism.[33] These seemingly contradictory human impulses can be found in all of us and may be most pronounced, extreme, and polarized in successful people—whether in business, politics, or other walks of life. Consequently, engaging with, and contributing to, social and political advancement can be at ease and aligned with making profit and building a successful company.

Toward a Philosophy of *Aligning for Advantage*

In addition to these Nietzschean perspectives, we build on the entrepreneurial philanthropy model,[34] in turn based on capital theory,[35] to frame and explain the interconnection between business and benevolence as practiced especially by entrepreneurial leaders past and present. This model demonstrates how investment in philanthropic projects can yield positive returns in cultural, social, and symbolic capital, which in turn can lead to increased economic capital. We also consider how "doing good" converts into wider social networks, status, and influence, conveying increased power, both relational and structural.[36] This in turn can be leveraged to gain political influence. Such influence may be relatively benign—for instance, a situation in which a politician draws on the experience and inspiration of a business leader to advance a specific policy agenda. In a modern context one can think of the tax-reform initiatives jointly championed by President Barack Obama and Warren Buffet, the legendary U.S. investor and philanthropist. The darker side of such influence may be witnessed in the results of Operation Elveden in the U.K., a large-scale police investigation into allegations that journalists paid bribes to public officials in exchange for information. Andy Coulson, the former editor of the *News of the World*, and Rebekah Brooks, the ex-chief executive of the newspaper's parent company, News International (part of media mogul Rupert Murdoch's News Corp International), were charged in 2012 in connection with alleged payments to police and public officials. These cases brought national and international attention to bear on the long-standing and apparently intimate relationships that existed between British politicians and media companies. Coulson was formerly Prime Minister David Cameron's director of communications, and Brooks and her husband were personal friends of the prime minister and his wife. These professional and personal relationships—social capital—were apparently leveraged as part of the nonmarket—and market—strategy of News International. Even if the alleged bribes to gain information are discounted, political access and, potentially, influence were likely leveraged to give News International a market edge relative to its rivals in the media business. It appears to be a clear illustration of strategy alignment, albeit not in a form advocated in this book.

Of particular note in the entrepreneurial philanthropy model is the use of capital theory to forge a symbiotic relationship between for-profit entrepreneurship and not-for-profit philanthropy.[37] Successful entrepreneurs invest economic capital to bring about social (and sometimes political) advancement and change. This may range from building public libraries, as Andrew Carnegie did across the U.S. in the late 19th and early 20th centuries, to supporting global health initiatives and cancer research centers, as Li Ka-shing did a century later. To return to our earlier Friedman-inspired discussion, in both cases these men used their own—not company—money to support social causes. This is often done through a foundation (such as the Li Ka-shing Foundation) set up specifically for such purposes and by leveraging symbolic, cultural, and social capital to increase the scale and impact of the activities. By definition, there is no direct economic return on economic capital invested in philanthropic activities. However, there are potential returns in the form of symbolic, cultural, and social capital, which in turn may yield an economic return.[38] For instance, the reputational enhancement afforded by high-profile philanthropic activities can enhance the brand equity of the entrepreneur's business ventures, particularly when these are closely aligned with his or her name and persona. Richard Branson, founder of the Virgin Group, personifies the enterprising, slightly maverick, and innovative Virgin brand. His more high-profile philanthropic ventures, such as the Branson Centre of Entrepreneurship and Virgin Unite, are likely to bolster the brand and reputation of associated Virgin companies. Both organizations seek to stimulate entrepreneurial thought and action, particularly in developing countries such as South Africa, and to support and encourage entrepreneurship as a force for social and economic development. These kinds of initiatives also provide social capital that can be useful when an entrepreneur wishes to leverage public opinion or political action in favor of his or her commercial activities. An example might be Branson's high visibility in championing the cause of lower U.K. passenger duties and a third runway at London's Heathrow airport. Both issues are of concern to his long-haul airline, Virgin Atlantic, which is based at Heathrow.

Our approach is different from the entrepreneurial philanthropy approach in that our interest is not just in those who make money and then engage in aligning their business strategy with political and social strategies. We are more interested in entrepreneurs, leaders, and companies that build (or rebuild) an aligned strategy from the outset. For instance, what Julius Rosenwald did at Sears, Roebuck and Co. from 1895 onward is a truer example of win-win aligned strategy, since corporate responsibility and societal impact developed hand in hand with the business.[39] In essence, there was a mutual dependency: business success was clearly correlated with stakeholder initiatives. Similarly, these initiatives could not happen without the success of, and funding from, the company, which elicited a state of mutual dependency. An example was the 4-H Club, partially sponsored by Sears and established to promote youth educational initiatives in rural American communities—a key market for the company.

Although Rosenwald was, at a personal level, a leading philanthropist, the approach he adopted at the company he led and brought back from the brink of bankruptcy was a very different one from those of Carnegie, Mellon, Rockefeller, Wellcome, and other great philanthropists. Theirs was a form of post-successful benign paternalism similar to that exhibited by Bill Gates, Warren Buffet, and others today, whereby the rich man gives back to the society that enabled him to become wealthy. Therefore, two different models can be identified: the post-corporate social-benefactor style of Andrew Carnegie or Bill Gates and the executive, integrative-strategist style of Julius Rosenwald or Coca-Cola chairman and CEO Muhtar Kent. The first makes money with little or no recourse to strategic alignment or social responsibility until *after* the fortune is amassed; the second builds a fortune in part *because* of an aligned approach to corporate strategy and recourse to social initiatives that also benefit company interests.

Conclusions and Managerial Implications

The antecedents of business political activism and social engagement can be traced back two hundred years and beyond. An important distinction between then and now is the modern role of professional managers in forging and implementing nonmarket strategy on behalf of transnational corporations. During the Industrial Revolution, nonmarket and market strategy was determined and aligned by philanthropic entrepreneurs, who frequently filled institutional voids, particularly in healthcare and educational provision, at a local and national level. Their motives for doing so most likely had several interlocking sources. For some such as Joseph Rowntree and the Cadburys, social reform was part of their Quaker religious tradition. For others, like Andrew Carnegie, assisting those less fortunate may have stemmed from his own humble origins. In the case of Jamsetji Tata, providing workers with pensions and paid accident compensation may have reflected an element of *noblesse oblige* within the caste-riven society of 19th-century India as well as family religiosity (the Tatas were Parsee priests). Beyond these motives and a desire to leave a legacy by which to be remembered, there was an inherent business logic in the actions of great philanthropists. Tata and Rowntree knew that improving the lot of their factory workers gained them loyal and productive employees. Arthur Guinness realized that playing the roles of supporter of Irish Home Rule and loyal subject of the British monarch ensured that his customers, workers, regulators, and partners were all favorably disposed toward him and his company.

In a modern era dominated by corporations run by managers rather than owners, the dynamic and approach shifted. Formalized strategy and ideology largely replaced entrepreneurial instinct and religion as the determinants of how companies interact with their political and social environments. The consequence has been the long-running rivalry between those who advocate a stakeholder approach to running a company and those who believe that the shareholder is paramount and businesses should not be involved in nonmarket activities. In advancing the notion of strategy alignment we seek to circumvent these polarizing positions. Drawing in part on Nietzschean ideas of meta-ethical moral relativism, combined with insights from capital theory and the entrepreneurial philanthropy model, we suggest that "it depends." The approach and activism of a company in nonmarket strategy depend on its market strategy. The firm's vision and values, market positions, and business objectives determine why, what, how, when, and where it engages in political and/or social arenas. Moreover, there are instances in which proactively leveraging economic, cultural, and/or social capital for a political purpose or charitable cause can generate positive externalities, particularly for the symbolic capital—reputation and brand—of an enterprise.

Although the processes and practices are often clinical, the ideals behind them are driven by human emotions, ranging from compassion to greed. As this book is primarily focused on best practices and constructive methods, we aim to examine and speak more to the higher emotions of business leaders. In doing so, we are, of course, aware that even those with lofty standards and good intentions get it wrong sometimes and that power can corrupt.

The concepts and practices of corporate social responsibility and corporate political activity are not 21st-century phenomena. New issues have arrived on the agenda, particularly environmental protection, sustainable business, and supranational regulation. However, the need to ensure a strategic fit between business objectives, social imperatives, and political challenges has been around at least for several centuries. It may be worthwhile for modern business leaders to reflect on and even emulate the approaches of old to deliver winning strategies in today's economy.

In summary, there are several key learning points in this chapter for strategic managers and business leaders:

- Nonmarket strategy should not be approached as a recent phenomenon that lacks useful templates and tried-and-tested tactics; many of the principles and practices of today are post-Enlightenment in origin.

- Managers must not allow themselves or their companies to be held hostage by the ideologies and interest groups that pervade nonmarket arenas. Instead, they should do what is in their best interest and in accordance with their business strategies.

- Managers should use various forms of organizational capital sparingly and strategically to advance nonmarket causes that also benefit their enterprises.

In the next chapter we move from the historical and philosophical origins of nonmarket strategy and strategy alignment to examine their multidisciplinary theoretical foundations. We consider the various actors and interests in the nonmarket strategy domain and the power dynamics that exist. Taken together, Chapters 2 and 3 constitute the intellectual basis of *Aligning for Advantage*.

Notes

* Portions of this chapter originally appeared in somewhat different form as Lawton, T.C. (2012a). Big business social responsibility is nothing new. *U.S. News*

& *World Report*. Economic Intelligence blog. <http://www.usnews.com/opinion/blogs/economic-intelligence/2012/05/04/socially-responsible-big-business-is-nothing-new>, May 4 (accessed May 7, 2013).

1. Confucius. (2011). *The sayings of Confucius*. Translated by L.A. Lyall (1909). Online reprint: CreateSpace Independent Publishing Platform.
2. Duffy, J. (1967). *A question of slavery*. Oxford: Clarendon Press: 179.
3. Adapted from <http://en.wikipedia.org/wiki/Maurya_Empire#Economy> (accessed May 8, 2013).
4. Carnegie, A. (1889). The gospel of wealth. *The North American Review*, June. Republished 1906, 183(599): 526-537.
5. Josephson, M. (1934). *The robber barons—the great American capitalists, 1861–1901*. New York: Harcourt, Brace and Company.
6. The Protestant Ascendancy refers to the group of landowners, clergy, and professionals, all members of the Established Church (Church of Ireland/Church of England), who dominated Ireland politically, economically, and socially from the 17th to 19th centuries.
7. Griffith, M. (2005). *Guinness is Guinness: the colourful story of a black and white brand*. London: Cyan Books.
8. Wallop, H. (2005). John Lewis opens shutters to rethink on Sunday hours. *The Telegraph*, November 8. <http://www.telegraph.co.uk/finance/2925489/John-Lewis-opens-shutters-to-rethink-on-Sunday-hours.html> (accessed May 8, 2013).
9. Naughton, M. and Cornwall, J.R. (2009). Culture as the basis of the good entrepreneur. *Journal of Religion and Business Ethics*, 1(1): 1-13.
10. Novak, M. (1993). *The Catholic ethic and the spirit of capitalism*. New York: The Free Press: 221–237.
11. Dawson, C. (1960). *The historic reality of Christian culture: a way to the renewal of human life*. New York: Harper & Brothers Publishers: 13.
12. Davis, I. (2005). What is the business of business? *McKinsey Quarterly*, 3: 105–113.
13. Kelly, M. (2006). The methodology behind the 100 best corporate citizen rankings. *Business Ethics*, 20(1): 28.
14. Sivakumar, N. (2008). The business ethics of Jamsetji Nusserwanji Tata—a forerunner in promoting stakeholder welfare. *Journal of Business Ethics*, 83: 353–361.
15. For further insights on this perspective, see for instance Bowen 1953; Carroll, A.B. (1987). In search of the moral manager. *Business Horizons*, 30(2): 7–15; Clarkson, M.B.E. (1995). A stakeholder framework for analyzing and evaluating corporate social performance. *Academy of Management Review*, 20(1): 92–117; Freeman, R.E. (1984). *Strategic management: a stakeholder approach*. Boston: Pitman; Langtry, B. (1994). Stakeholders and the moral responsibilities of business. *Business Ethics Quarterly*, 4(4): 431–442; Mitchell et al. 1997; Stedlmeier, P. (1991). *People and profits*. Englewood Cliffs, NJ: Prentice Hall.
16. Bowen 1953.
17. Freeman 1984.
18. See for instance Evans, W.M. and Freeman, R.E. (1988). A stakeholder theory of the modern corporation: Kantian capitalism. In T.L. Beauchamp and N. Bowie

(eds.). *Ethical theory and business.* 3rd edition. Englewood Cliffs, NJ: Prentice Hall; Langtry 1994; Sivakumar 2008.

19. Langtry 1994: 431.
20. The triple bottom line notion was first alluded to by Spreckley, F. (1981). *Social audit: a management tool for co-operative working 1981.* Leeds, U.K.: Beechwood College. Spreckley argued that companies should measure and report on social, environmental, and financial performance. The principle was more widely disseminated in subsequent work by, most prominently, the UN's Brundtland Commission. United Nations General Assembly (March 20, 1987). *"Report of the World Commission on Environment and Development: Our Common Future*; Transmitted to the General Assembly as an Annex to document A/42/427— Development and International Co-operation: Environment; Our Common Future, Chapter 2: Towards Sustainable Development; Paragraph 1."* United Nations General Assembly. Retrieved on November 25, 2012. However, the phrase "people, planet, profit" was coined by Elkington, J. (1997). *Cannibals with forks: the triple bottom line of 21st century business.* Oxford: Capstone.
21. Sivakumar 2008: 355, citing Tripathi, D. (2006). *Well begun.* <http://www.tata.com/company/articles/inside.aspx?artid=xxlOO43Wmc8=> (accessed May 10, 2013).
22. Friedman, M. (1962). *Capitalism and freedom.* Chicago: University of Chicago Press.
23. Davis 2005: 105.
24. Friedman, M. (1970). The social responsibility of business is to increase its profits. *The New York Times Magazine.* September 13: 32–33.
25. Friedman 1970.
26. Friedman 1970.
27. Nietzsche, F. (1886). *Beyond good and evil: prelude to a philosophy of the future.* First published in German. Translated by R.J. Hollingdale, 1990. London: Penguin Books.
28. Starling, G. (1997). Business ethics and Nietzsche. *Business Horizons*, 40(3): 2–12 (7).
29. Nietzsche, F. (1883–85). *Thus spoke Zarathustra: a book for all and none.* First published in German. Translated by R.J. Hollingdale, 1961. London: Penguin Books.
30. Nietzsche 1883–85: 8.
31. As declared by Forbes Media, in partnership with Reputation Institution, in their 2012 U.S. RepTrak Pulse ranking, an annual study that measures the reputations of the 150 largest U.S. public companies. <http://www.forbes.com/sites/jacquelynsmith/2012/04/04/americas-most-reputable-companies/> (accessed May 12, 2013).
32. Starling 1997: 9.
33. This point was made by Nietzsche (1886): and reinforced by Starling (1997): 9.
34. Harvey, C., Maclean, M., Gordon, J., and Shaw, E. (2011). Andrew Carnegie and the foundations of contemporary entrepreneurial philanthropy. *Business History*, 55(3): 425–450.
35. Bourdieu, P. (1986a). *Distinction: a social critique of the judgment of taste.* London: Routledge; Bourdieu, P. (1986b). The forms of capital. In J.G. Richardson (ed.). *Handbook of theory and research for the sociology of education.*

New York: Greenwood: 241–258; Burt, R.S. (1997). The contingent value of social capital. *Administrative Science Quarterly*, 42(2): 339–365; Finkelstein, S., Harvey, C., and Lawton, T. (2007). *Breakout strategy: meeting the challenge of double-digit growth.* London and New York: McGraw-Hill; Harvey, C. and Maclean, M. (2008). Capital theory and the dynamics of elite business networks in Britain and France. *The Sociological Review*, 56(S1): 105–120; Maclean, M., Harvey, C., and Press, J. (2006). *Business elites and corporate governance in France and the UK.* London: Palgrave Macmillan.

36. See Strange 1988. Notions of power will be discussed further in Chapter 3.
37. Harvey et al. 2011: 431–432.
38. Harvey et al. 2011: 432.
39. Drucker, P. (1984). The new meaning of corporate social responsibility. *California Management Review*, 26(2): 53–63.

3

Rationalizing Complexity*

Out of intense complexities, intense simplicities emerge.[1]

Winston Churchill

The evidence of far-reaching change in the world of corporate capitalism is all around us. Companies from Brazil, China, India, Russia, and other emerging and transitional economies are reshaping global competitive dynamics and international markets once held in check by regulation and statism. In this new order, opportunities abound, but so too do the possibilities for strategic error. Increasing interdependence with respect to supply chains, markets, and finance has made for more complexity, not less, as companies have entered into an abundance of alliances, partnerships, and joint ventures. To survive and prosper in this challenging environment, companies must become ever more strategically clear and adept. Those lacking first-rate strategic capabilities invariably find it difficult to chart a viable course, are more vulnerable to competitive attacks, and are in danger of making costly, sometimes fatal, mistakes.

As strategy researchers and educators, we are often asked by businesspeople how they can formulate and implement a corporate strategy in such a volatile and complex world. An answer to the question requires us to look at a much broader canvas than we conventionally do when we consider strategic management as a process and practice. Conventional approaches to strategy divide conveniently into three parts: what is going on inside the company, what is happening in the external environment in terms of competition in the company's markets, and, by deduction, what both inquiries hold for the company's future in the wider world. Furthermore, we must make a conceptual distinction between the formulation (strategizing) and implementation (policymaking) of strategic management. Although closely related, corporate *strategy* can be distinguished from corporate *policy*.[2] For us, strategy is broadly the means by which leaders create and take control of the future,[3] whereas

41

policy relates more to organizational structures, processes, and routines that cumulatively orchestrate and deliver on strategic objectives. In other words, strategy is about vision, analysis, and configuration, while policy is concerned with implementation and the delivery of results. An approach acknowledging this distinction can help managers to better deal with complexity both inside and outside the organization. It can also facilitate the alignment of market and nonmarket strategy.

To get to this level of clarity and simplicity, we must first delve into the theories and frameworks underpinning strategic management and situate nonmarket strategy within wider strategy research. Therefore, in this chapter, we consider the regulatory parameters of nonmarket strategy and review some of the key literatures that have addressed the nonmarket environment and nonmarket strategy, particularly from a theory of power perspective. This is the starting point in the development of nonmarket strategy as a managerial concept and practice. This literature has approached nonmarket strategy through the logics of micro- and regulatory economics and theories of power and influence, and in so doing helps to lay the foundation for our subsequent inquiry into how managers can develop a deeper understanding of, and greater clarity around, how to manage the interplay and influence of politics, society, markets, and business.[4]

Nonmarket Strategy in Strategic Management Research

A significant body of literature exists that examines the interaction of state policies and corporate strategies in shaping business outcomes. We provided a brief review of this literature in Chapter 1.[5] Baron perhaps provides the simplest description of the nonmarket environment when he described it as "...the social, political and legal arrangements that structure interactions among companies and their public."[6]

In this section, we review some of the foundational logic for why firms should care about the nonmarket environment before moving on to discuss several perspectives on that environment that draw from the economics and political science disciplines.

The Regulatory and Legal Element of Nonmarket Strategy

As Hillman and Hitt noted, the elements described by Baron can be further separated into their respective parts.[7] For example, the law of contract is an important part of the nonmarket environment that enables companies and their public to contract for the exchange of goods, services, labor, and capital.

Variations in contract law between different countries and industries affect the strategic choices of firms. These various social, political, and legal arrangements are collectively referred to as *regulation*. In advanced industrialized nations, regulation pervades the competitive environment within which firms select and execute their strategies.[8] Trade policy, competition policy, employment policy, environmental policy, fiscal policy, monetary policy—government policies in general and the particular regulations to which they give birth—have the ability to alter the size of markets through government purchases and regulations affecting substitute and complementary products; to affect the structure of markets through entry and exit barriers and antitrust legislation; to affect the cost structure of firms though various types of legislation pertaining to multiple factors, such as employment terms and conditions and pollution standards;[9] to affect the demand for products and services by charging excise taxes and imposing regulations that affect consumer patterns;[10] to affect access to scarce resources;[11] and to affect firms' profitability by increasing costs and restricting markets.[12] Consequently, there is substantial interdependence between regulation and the competitive environment within which firms operate.[13]

These issues have taken on increasing importance as the regulatory reach of the state has evolved. Between the end of World War II and the end of the 1970s oil crises, Western governments (particularly in Europe) managed industrial policy by taking direct ownership of certain aspects of the means of production through full or partial nationalization of key firms and industries. However, from the early 1980s, those governments eschewed direct ownership by privatizing formerly nationalized industries and relied instead on regulation to manage their industrial policies. In particular, regulation was used to manage the (inappropriately named) process of deregulation: of creating a framework that encouraged competition among firms and addressed instances of market failure such as price collusion and monopoly. Ironically, deregulation significantly increased the influence of regulation on firm strategy; hence the unexpected phenomenon of "freer markets, more rules."[14] Indeed, the penetration of business strategy by regulation has become so substantial that some argue that it has fundamentally altered the relationship between business and government, and that these changes are tantamount to a second managerial revolution.[15] Weidenbaum contends that the shift of decision-making away from the firm to government regulators (through increased regulation and selected deregulation) is as significant for management as the separation of ownership and control was in the early 20th century.[16]

Since regulation increasingly permeates the competitive environment, nonmarket strategy must be a business priority.[17] The purported objective of firms' nonmarket strategies is to produce outcomes that are favorable to their continued economic survival and success.[18] Firms can use their influence over regulation for a number of strategic ends: to bolster their economic positions, to hinder both their domestic and foreign competitors' progress and ability to compete, and to exercise their right to a voice in government affairs.[19]

Firms, therefore, take an interest in regulation, placing importance on minimizing the cost of existing and proposed regulation upon strategy and business models; an interest in lobbying for regulations that are consistent with, and supportive of, preferred strategy and business models; and an interest in regulation as a source of competitive advantage. The interest that firms take in regulation is captured in management literature as part of their nonmarket strategy. Responding to the nonmarket environment defined earlier, a nonmarket strategy is that component of a firm's business strategy that helps it navigate the nonmarket environment.[20] This is distinct from a firm's market strategy, which is understood as that component of a firm's business strategy that helps it navigate the competitive environment, which consists of the market choices of competitors, customers, distributors, employees, suppliers, and shareholders. The market environment sits within the nonmarket environment: choices in the former are prescribed—to a greater or lesser degree— by the latter.

Strategizing for the Nonmarket

In many industries, the success of firms' nonmarket strategy is no less important than that of their broader market strategy.[21] For example, the initial strategy of communications giant MCI was political. The company successfully created a market opportunity by influencing legislators to deregulate the U.S. long-distance telephone market.[22] Firms also use nonmarket strategies to ensure competitive advantage or possibly even survival. In the late 1990s, PepsiCo, losing ground in a fierce competitive battle for soft drink market share to rival Coca-Cola, turned to the courts for help. Having lost its exclusive franchise in the now defunct Soviet Union, PepsiCo was rapidly losing global market share to its archrival. Litigation became a new competitive weapon, as PepsiCo took legal action four times over a two-year period, in countries as diverse as France, India, Venezuela, and the U.S., claiming that Coca-Cola was using its larger size and supply chain power to unfairly keep PepsiCo out of specific markets.[23] In aircraft manufacturing, Airbus and Boeing pursue overt and elaborate political strategies both in their respective home markets and internationally as each seeks access to markets and public contracts.[24] A 1990s study of the U.S. steel industry found that domestic steel producers used the government's control over access to the U.S. market as a political tool to enjoy stabilized revenues and profits in a declining market and to gain temporary relief from downsizing by lobbying for trade protection.[25] Subsequently, in 2002, indigenous steel producers again persuaded the U.S. government to provide trade protection but failed to simultaneously pursue their nonmarket strategy through the World Trade Organization. As a result, the trade protection was ruled illegal and the political strategy ultimately failed.

Through nonmarket strategy, firms can potentially increase market share and gain a competitive advantage. This in turn enables them to reduce the threats from rivals, substitutes, and new entrants, and even increase their bargaining power relative to suppliers and customers. However, a challenge persists: how can a top management team gain, leverage, and retain nonmarket power?

The Power Dynamic

Nonmarket power remains a difficult variable to factor into strategic management processes. Exogenous power is not easy to define unequivocally and is impossible to measure convincingly. As Strange argues, "Anything as messy as power simply cannot be included in an economic equation, or even a purely economic analysis."[26]

Nevertheless, to remove it from the analysis of corporate decision-making or state–firm bargaining renders research incomplete, if not inaccurate. Attempts by economists to explain politics and power through the prism of rational choice may not be entirely useful for practical purposes.[27] In the real world, the strong may not always wield power in a rational manner. For instance, an industry leader may choose to forgo profit to enable price reduction in order to drive new entrants out of the market. Such action is not rational if we apply the strict economic logic of firm action being motivated by profit maximization. Of course, the rebuttal of the scenario just mentioned is that forgoing profit in the short term can result in greater profit in the long term. However, this is not assured, and there is risk associated with such action—for example, regulatory authorities may deem such action illegal or the new entrant(s) may successfully resist predatory behavior and subsequently use it to undermine the dominant firm's market position. Witness, for instance, the clash between British Airways and Virgin Atlantic when Virgin first entered the airline business. British Airways attempted to undermine Virgin Atlantic's market entry into lucrative transatlantic routes by engaging in price competition and negative advertising. Virgin Atlantic weathered the storm, won a court ruling against British Airways' practices, and subsequently subverted its archrival through appealing to airline customers as the David to British Airways' Goliath.

The notion of bounded rationality potentially offers a more plausible per-spective.[28] It advances the argument that governments and corporations have multiple—and not always obvious—objectives when they make decisions. They are not always seeking the optimal outcome, but are looking for a result that satisfies multiple objectives. Again, rational action—bounded or not—does not always determine the actions of actors in the international political economy. The main drawback of the bounded rationality concept is its static nature: it assumes that the objectives to be satisfied remain the same over time.[29] This does not always happen, as markets can rise or fall, new technologies can emerge, and so forth. These events will often cause a shift in actor objectives. From a cor-porate strategy perspective, power within organizations has long been a focus of management research.[30] However, less emphasis has been placed on power as an exogenous variable or on the state–firm power dynamic and its impact on corporate strategy. This is where the structural power approach, borrowed from international relations, can prove useful to top management teams.

Adapting Structural Power Theory to Strategic Management

The concept of structural power advances a framework for analyzing the who-gets-what of world society based on four basic structures.[31] In these, power over others and over the mix of values in the system is exercised within and across frontiers by those who are in a position to offer *security*, or to threaten it; by those who are in a position to offer, or to withhold, *credit*; by those who decide what to *produce*, where, and on what terms and conditions; and by those who control access to *knowledge* and information and who are in a position to define the nature of knowledge.[32]

Of the four kinds of structural power outlined, the state takes the lead role in only one—security—and even there it needs the support of other systemic agents. In all the other structures, nonstate authorities—primarily firms—play a large part in determining the allocation of resources. Therefore, structural power is the unevenly distributed systemic ability to define the basic struc-tures of the world economy: security, credit, production, and knowledge.[33] All other elements of the international political economy (for example, global matters such as trade or more specific sectoral items such as integrated circuits) are secondary structures, being molded by the four fundamental power struc-tures. Moreover, structural changes in finance, information and communi-cations systems, defense equipment, and production methods have together played the most important role in redefining the relationship between author-ity (government) and market (firms). To clarify the determinants of change at a systemic level, it is accepted that the state and the market (through its corporate agents) together comprise the broad vehicles of transformation.[34]

Each of these systemic players shapes the nature of the four pillars of structural power. A corporate actor that understands this systemic dynamic and gains first-mover advantage in bringing about structural change can wield considerable power, both relative to government and to other companies.

Definitions of power vary greatly across academic disciplines, and the term's meaning changes slightly in different languages. A well-known conceptual dichotomy distinguishes between *hard* and *soft* power.[35] The former corresponds approximately to coercive, relational power, and the latter is indirect power or influence over the four structures of the global economy mentioned earlier.[36] A straightforward definition is that "power is simply the ability of a person or a group so to affect outcomes that their preferences take precedence over the preferences of others."[37] This definition avoids attaching the concept of power to the pursuit of the highly subjective notion of "interest" (national, corporate, and so on).

The real challenge is establishing who has power. How do you measure power? Resources and capabilities often emerge as key determinants. Australia is a more powerful country than New Zealand because it has a larger army. The U.S. is more powerful than Australia because it has greater technological competence and armament production capacity. However, resource size and technological capability do not always triumph. To continue our military analogy, consider how, in Afghanistan, the mighty Soviet Red Army was defeated by a much smaller but more zealous group of mujahideen fighters (much as NATO forces have been fought to a stalemate by the Taliban). Similarly, with firms, the largest does not necessarily win; it is the leanest, most responsive, and most innovative that can often triumph over large, long-established competitors that may have greater financial and knowledge power.

An Economic Model of the Nonmarket Environment

Some scholars have advanced an unambiguously economically motivated approach to understanding and engaging with the nonmarket context of business. This rational economic approach is generally seen as the progenitor of academic research on why and how companies choose and execute a nonmarket strategy.[38] This approach predicts that firms will engage in nonmarket strategies to the point at which the marginal benefit of intervening in the regulatory process equals the marginal cost.[39] The marginal benefit is broadly calculated as the impact on firm profitability of achieving the nonmarket strategy—for instance, the increase in profits following regulation that reduces the cost of inputs, increases the price of outputs, increases market share, and so on. The marginal cost is calculated as the cost to the firm of implementing the nonmarket strategy—for example, the cost of lobbying or otherwise influencing regulators and policymakers.

This one-firm nonmarket strategy equilibrium model is further elaborated by looking at how multiple firms' nonmarket strategies interact.[40] The argument is that proposed regulations are asymmetric, affecting the profitability of some firms more than others. Depending on the degree of asymmetry, this model mathematically predicts whether firms are likely to form coalitions in pursuing a joint nonmarket strategy (perhaps to oppose regulations that increase costs) or whether one firm is likely to attempt to free-ride on the nonmarket strategy of another.[41] Consequently, this approach predicts prisoner's-dilemma type scenarios, in which firms are unable to form effective coalitions against proposed regulations.[42]

The economic approach also considers the payoff to regulators and policymakers. Regulators have preferences that reflect the interests of their constituents and their own policy interests. The more congruent a proposed regulation is with such preferences, the lower the marginal cost to the firm of buying support from such regulators. By calculating the total amount of support required (for example, in a majority-voting legislature), one can predict the marginal cost of pursuing a nonmarket strategy.[43]

This analysis of nonmarket strategy is firmly based on concepts drawn from the market environment. In both the market and the nonmarket, scarce resources (goods, services, labor, and capital on the one hand and regulation on the other) are allocated by the interaction of producers (regulators) and consumers (firms). An equilibrium is thus predicted between demand (by firms for regulation) and supply (by regulators of regulation) at a point where the lobbying costs to firms equal the political needs of regulators for campaign contributions, reelection support, and so on.[44]

Analyses of nonmarket strategy from Baron's work in the mid-1990s onward are not incorrect, but they are incomplete.[45] It is true, for instance, that firms in the U.S. lobby legislators with campaign contributions and reelection support, but that does not comprise the entirety of the relationship between legislators and firms. By modeling nonmarket strategy using market concepts, scholars fail to explore other, perhaps more irrational, aspects of the relationship between the market and the nonmarket, and ultimately fail to provide a convincing account of how the market and nonmarket environments interact. Consequently, it is necessary for executives to also reflect on the less transactional and often more indirect and informal context in which they formulate nonmarket strategy.

Conclusions and Managerial Implications

In this chapter, we have considered perspectives on nonmarket strategy that draw particularly from economics and political science. Our focus has been primarily on micro-theories of actors, their interests, and the power dynamics and interactions among these players in the nonmarket environment. More recently, researchers have become interested in a range of institutional perspectives on various business phenomena, including nonmarket strategy. We explore these institutional views later in the book and also reflect on comparative capitalism perspectives and its increased relevance in framing a multipolar world.

The ideas we have reviewed here offer a rigorous foundational logic for the examination of nonmarket strategy and its relevance for the commercial actions and orientations of the firm in a complex world. To rationalize this complexity and more clearly align nonmarket conditions with market objectives, we advance several takeaways for business practitioners:

- For nonmarket purposes, it is useful to conceptually separate formulation (the *strategy* of vision, analysis, and configuration) from implementation (the *policy* of execution, delivery, and performance measurement).

- All aspects of regulatory engagement and compliance can be understood through a nonmarket strategy lens, which thus rationalizes and reduces the complexity that companies encounter.

- Market influence and competitive advantage can accrue to managers who understand power and influence, both structural and relational, and how to leverage it relative to other companies and nonmarket actors such as government agencies.

In the next chapter we will explore how firms respond to uncertainty and volatility in their business environment. We will begin by looking at the dynamics of uncertainty and the best available options. The chapter will explore uncertainties in different international markets and the resultant challenges that emerge.

Notes

* Portions of this chapter have been adapted from Story, J. and Lawton, T. (2010). Business studies: The global dynamics of business–state relations. In D. Coen, W. Grant, and G. Wilson (eds.). *The Oxford Handbook of Business and Government*. Oxford: Oxford University Press: 89–120.
1. Churchill, W. (2007). *The world crisis 1911–1918*. London: Penguin Classics.
2. Story and Lawton 2010: 104.
3. Finkelstein, Harvey, and Lawton 2007: 13.
4. Story and Lawton 2010.

5. For instance see Schuler, D.A., Rehbein, K., and Cramer, R.D. (2002). Pursuing strategic advantage through political means: a multivariate approach. *Academy of Management Journal*, 45(4): 659–672.
6. Baron, 1995a.
7. Hillman and Hitt 1999.
8. Shaffer, B. (1995). Firm level responses to government regulation: theoretical and research approaches. *Journal of Management*, 21: 495–514.
9. Gale, J. and Buchholz, R.A. (1987). The political pursuit of competitive advantage: what business can gain from government. In A. Marcus, A. Kaufman, and D. Beam (eds.). *Business strategy and public policy*. New York: Quorum: 31–42.
10. Hillman and Hitt 1999: 826; Wilson, G.K. (1990a). *Business and politics: a comparative introduction*. London: Chatham House.
11. Boddewyn 1993.
12. Schuler, D.A. (1996). Corporate political strategy and foreign competition: the case of the steel industry. *Academy of Management Journal*, 39(3): 720–737.
13. Baron, D.P. (1997) Integrated strategy and international trade disputes: The Kodak–Fujifilm case. *Journal of Economics & Management Strategy*, 6(1): 291–346.
14. Vogel, D. (1996). The study of business and politics. *California Management Review*, 38(3): 146–165.
15. Weidenbaum M. (1980). Public policy: no longer a spectator sport for business. *Journal of Business Strategy*, 1(1): 46–53.
16. Hillman and Hitt 1999: 826; Weidenbaum 1980: 46; Bearle, A. and Means, G. (1932). *The modern corporation and private property*. London: Transaction Publishers.
17. Yoffie, D.B. (1988). How an industry builds political advantage. *Harvard Business Review*, 38(3): 80–89.
18. Baysinger, B.D. (1984). Domain maintenance as an objective of business political activity: an expanded typology. *Academy of Management Review*, 9: 248–258; Keim, G. and Baysinger, B.D. (1988). The efficacy of business political activity: competitive considerations in a principal-agent context. *Journal of Management*, 14: 163–180.
19. Hillman and Hitt 1999: 826; Keim, G.D. and Zeithaml, C.P. (1986). Corporate political strategy and legislative decision making: a review and contingency approach. *Academy Management Review*, 11: 828–843.
20. Baron 1995a: 73; Baron 1995b: 73.
21. Baron 1995a.
22. Yoffie and Bergenstein 1985.
23. Hillman and Hitt 1999: 826; Light, L. and Greising, D. (1998). Litigation: the choice of a new generation. *Businessweek*, May 25: 42.
24. Lawton, T. and McGuire, S. (2002). Constraining choice: exploring the influence of WTO regulation and domestic politics on US trade policy for steel. *Academy of International Business*. Conference Proceedings, San Juan, Puerto Rico.
25. Hillman and Hitt 1999: 826; Schuler 1996.
26. Strange 1996: 20.

27. Frey, B. (1984). The public choice view of international political economy. *International Organization*, 38(1): 199–207.

28. Simon, H.A. (1982, 1997). *Models of bounded rationality, vols 1–3*. Cambridge, MA: MIT Press.

29. Strange 1996.

30. French, J. and Raven, B. (1959). The basis of social power. In D. Cartwright (ed.). *Studies in social power*. Ann Arbor, MI: University of Michigan Press; Emerson, R. (1962). Power dependency relationships. *American Sociological Review*, 27: 31–41; Hambrick 1981.

31. Strange 1988.

32. Strange 1996: ix.

33. Strange 1988: 15.

34. Stopford, J. and Strange, S. (1991). *Rival states, rival firms: competition for world market share*. Cambridge: University of Cambridge Press.

35. Nye, J.S. (1990). *Bound to lead: the changing nature of American power*. New York: Basic Books.

36. Strange 1988.

37. Strange 1996: 17.

38. Baron 2001.

39. Baron 1995b.

40. Baron 1995b: 74.

41. Baron 1995a: 73.

42. Baron 1995a: 73.

43. Baron 1995b.

44. Baron 1995b.

45. Baron 1995a and 1995b.

Section II
Pathways to Influence

4

Responding to Uncertainty*

Although our intellect always longs for clarity and certainty,
our nature often finds uncertainty fascinating.[1]

Carl von Clausewitz

In the mid-1980s, Microsoft made its initial entry into the Greater China region. By the close of 2007, it had a global support center in Shanghai, a major research lab (the China Research & Development Group) in Beijing, and more than 3,200 employees across the country. Throughout this period, however, Microsoft faced significant tests. These included widespread piracy of its products, governmental pressures to transfer technology, domestic governmental support of competitors, discrimination in public procurement, and direct and indirect pressure to enter joint ventures (JVs) with local firms. As a response to these challenges, Microsoft's management established relationships with top Chinese leaders, entered into partnerships with regional and municipal governments, invested heavily in China, and established alliances with Chinese technology suppliers. Despite these efforts, uncertainty surrounding the Chinese government's policies toward foreign investors and the future direction of those policies has been trying and challenging. Indeed, Microsoft senior counsel Fred Tipson said in November 2006, "We have to decide if the persecuting of bloggers reaches a point that it's unacceptable to do business there." Yet, Microsoft's sales and revenue grew more rapidly in the Greater China region than in any other market in the world. This success resulted, in part, from Microsoft's ability to maintain a complementary relationship between its market and nonmarket strategies in the face of an uncertain and changing business and political environment—which, in China, are inextricably linked.[2]

In May 2006, India's Tata Motors announced that it would build a plant in Singur, West Bengal, to produce the Nano, its low-cost "people's car." To launch the project, Tata depended on the West Bengal government to cede land it did not own outright, which sparked violent protests from local farmers. After a series of confrontations, Tata ceased production at the factory—in which it had already invested $350 million—in the summer of 2008. A few months later, the company formally accepted an invitation from the Gujarat government to relocate the project there. As part of the agreement, the company was assured that no *bandh* (a form of political protest used in some South Asian countries) or labor unrest would delay the project. Tata, arguably the most powerful, politically influential, and well-respected corporation in India, would appear ideally positioned to manage its interactions with government policymakers and other stakeholders. Yet it misread and misjudged the deep-seated mistrust and skepticism among a minority in West Bengal and was forced to make a difficult and costly about-face.[3]

Most research on strategy formation has been dedicated to the economic effects of market forces on corporate strategy and competitive advantage.[4] These two examples, however, underscore the impact that uncertain and dynamic *nonmarket* forces such as government regulation, activism, and interest-group pressure have on the competitive landscape—an impact that is increasingly causing firms to alter their corporate strategies[5] and providing material for a growing body of literature that examines how multinational enterprises can utilize such nonmarket conditions to their advantage.

In this section of *Aligning for Advantage*, we explore the interaction between the market and nonmarket environments and the strategic actions firms undertake to respond to that interaction. As many scholars and analysts have documented, businesses tend to imitate one another.[6] While it is true that a "follow the leader" rule may in many contexts lead to suboptimal returns for the followers and, more broadly, stifle innovation and creative solutions, managing effectively in the political and social arenas can nonetheless present opportunities to shape policies and shift social expectations in a manner that transforms an industry or market. Companies that become innovative rule-changing agents can use political and social influence to alter policy in the defense of current market positions and in the creation of new market possibilities.[7]

Political and social integration on this scale requires systemic changes in an organization and the command of substantial resources.[8] For example, scholars have explored how opportunities shape policy initiatives by spurring the development of standards that are later adopted by an entire industry[9] or by influencing the construction of institutional conditions in emerging markets[10] that can generate real and lasting value for firms with a first-mover advantage.[11]

In this chapter, we explore several frameworks that classify and derive implications for nonmarket strategy. We begin by explicating the importance and dynamics of uncertainty and then describe and define the different levels and types of policy and regulatory uncertainty in the political and social environment. We show how companies can make the most of available options by building on research into strategy under uncertainty to classify different types of policy uncertainty and the strategies best tailored to those situations,[12] including scenario planning, real options modeling, and others. The chapter also explores how uncertainties in international markets—particularly in emerging markets—present especially challenging situations. We draw upon diverse examples to reveal what works and what does not work when a business expands its geographic horizons.[13]

Risk and Uncertainty: Definitions and Extensions

Managers continually face an uncertain and volatile global business environment, and the nonmarket arenas we discuss in this book in particular are increasingly characterized by sudden change.[14] The first years of the 21st century featured a series of difficult-to-anticipate events, such as the dot-com bust of 2000, the 9/11 terrorist attacks on the United States, prolonged and polarizing wars in Iraq and Afghanistan, the global financial and economic crisis that commenced in 2008, the "Arab Spring" movements of 2011 and their aftermath, and many others. At the same time, ethics, corruption, and environmental scandals plagued some of the largest and most respected companies in the world. Consider the April 2010 explosion and fire on Transocean's Deepwater Horizon drilling rig, which had been licensed by BP. The resulting oil spill in the Gulf of Mexico had profound and lasting effects on BP's market and nonmarket performance, including its share value and operations elsewhere in the world, and quickly reverberated in a number of energy and environmental policy reversals in many jurisdictions around the world. In a similar vein, the March 2011 Fukushima Daiichi nuclear disaster in Japan, precipitated by an earthquake and accompanying tsunami, affected economies and industries around the world, including a range of automotive- and electronics-related businesses that faced shortages of critical supplies. As its short-term effects began to wane, the disaster's long-term impact loomed in Germany's decision—the first among the major industrial powers—to close down all of its nuclear power plants by 2022.

Various forms of risk and uncertainty may be present in a particular market, especially in unpredictable emerging economies. A brief description of the challenges present in these economies and a classification of the differences between types of risk will add insight into the strategic choices firms make when deciding how to enter these markets.

Of course, a thorough assessment of a country's risk profile does little good when management does not recognize and accept its strategic implications and limitations. Pierre Wack of Royal Dutch Shell Petroleum, legendary for anticipating the oil shock of the 1970s, used to warn managers that predictions are generally wrong when you need them most.[15] For a company to be prepared, Wack argued, uncertainty must not only be measured, but embraced: in light of senior management's view of the future, corporate resources should be allocated in the present. Assessing and preparing for the future, therefore, lies at the heart of corporate strategy, just as sensitivity to context lies at the heart of corporate policies.

Uncertainty in the Nonmarket Context: Political Risk

The term *political risk* has various interpretations in the literature.[16] Broadly, it has been defined as unanticipated government actions that have an impact on business operations.[17] Although political risk has been seen to include country-level risks such as currency inconvertibility, civil strife, violent conflict, and other macro-level developments and shocks, we are more concerned here about the specific contractual and transactional manifestations of political risk as they affect specific investors. Two fundamental sources of political risk that affect private investors are the expropriation by national governments of foreign-owned assets[18] and the repudiation of contractual obligations by host governments.[19]

Expropriations were widespread in the 1970s—particularly in Latin American countries, where socialist or populist leaders in Argentina, Chile, Venezuela, and elsewhere seized assets, often in sensitive financial, natural resource, and especially infrastructure operations—chilling the atmosphere for investment throughout the world. In the 1980s and early 1990s, however, *outright* expropriations in developing countries virtually disappeared, falling from 83 cases in 1975 alone to only 11 cases from 1981 to 1992.[20] As Doh and Ramamurti[21] point out, however, there was a commensurate rise in "voluntarily" renegotiated contracts throughout this period: "Governments continue to engage in a pervasive practice of selective and disruptive ex-post recontracting of legally binding agreements, especially when there are shifts in political parties or ruling governments."[22] Such respecification of legislation or regulation could require MNEs to dilute their equity holdings in foreign subsidiaries, which, coupled with pressures for host government involvement, constitutes a form of "creeping expropriation."[23] For example, the dramatic (and forced) renegotiation in 2008 of Shell's massive petrochemical facility in northeast Russia, the Sakhalin II project, did not constitute a forced expropriation, nor did the cancellation of a portion of BP's joint venture with its Russian partner TNK as a result of contractual and legal disputes with the Russian conglomerate Rosenoft. Even Hugo Chavez's compulsory divestment by foreign oil and gas companies from Venezuela was "negotiated" in some fashion—further evidence that dramatic changes in the political environment in which firms operate often result in unforeseen and damaging outcomes.

While political risk analysis has historically focused on assessing political instability[24] arising, for instance, from social revolution and indigenous upheaval,[25] such instability increasingly forms only a small portion of the risks faced by business. Instead, issues related to "business as usual" economic nationalism in emerging economies[26]—creating pressures for forced joint ventures, unilateral contract renegotiations, and regulations calling for increased local value-added—constitute the bulk of risks companies routinely encounter.[27] Firms with large fixed investments are particularly vulnerable to the "obsolescing bargain,"[28] in which an enterprise's success is used as a pretext to change or renegotiate its operating agreement. Political risk is further compounded by distinctions between macro dimensions (which affect all business enterprises in general) and micro political risks (which selectively affect specific business activities).[29] In general, investors "incorporate into their investment decisions both the probability of policy change and the extent to which a given change is likely to be inimical or favorable to their interests" to determine the level of investment.[30]

In addition, there are new sources of risk in emerging economies. Growing local business interests may seek to displace foreign firms from their traditional areas of activity by leveraging political connections for preferential treatment.[31] Nationalistic sentiment invoked by local competitors can lead to political pressure on host-country governments to regulate and limit foreign investments as well as their managerial control.[32] Powerful business groups in emerging economies can protect vested interests using informal structures and relationships that are not available to foreign investors, who, in contrast, may have to rely on weak institutional safeguards.[33] An additional source of risk stems from government policies that impose conditions on private-investor activity, such as mandatory local-business participation in foreign investments. Overall, private investments are particularly vulnerable to the threat of opportunism in the form of political actors changing the rules of the game and reneging on contractual obligations, including property rights protection,[34] which leads to increased political risk[35] and the erosion of credible commitment.[36] In sum, in the context of investment in emerging economies, we conceptualize political risk as the risk of expropriation, including creeping expropriation, and contract repudiation emanating from a limited number of political actors, specifically those that interact with private investors and have the authority to enforce policy changes.

Uncertainty in the Nonmarket Context: Institutional Risk

Institutions serve the purpose of reducing both transaction and information costs by mitigating uncertainty and establishing a stable societal structure that facilitates human and organizational interactions.[37] In the context of emerging economies, institutional deficiencies or "voids"[38] that arise from inconsistent rule enforcement,[39] inadequate legal frameworks, and governmental corruption[40] have been sources of risk detrimental to these investments. We argue that the rule of law, low levels of corruption in government, and capital market development can shape the constraints that structure human interaction.[41] The absence of these attributes contributes to higher levels of institutional risk.

Governmental corruption reflects the abuse (or misuse) of public power for private (personal) benefit,[42] with bureaucrats allocating favors in exchange for bribes[43] or, more informally, additional payments "to get things done."[44] Investors may either acquiesce to such practices to avoid angering corrupt officials or exploit the situation to overcome the numerous difficulties associated with entering new foreign markets.[45] Whatever the immediate motivation, corruption often points to contempt on the part of both the corrupter (private citizen or investor) and the corrupted (usually a public official) for the proper form of their relationship,[46] which indicates the presence of weak institutions[47] and leads to reduced investment.[48] Notwithstanding the investor's tacit or explicit compliance, corruption in government remains an unpredictable phenomenon with, to a greater or lesser or extent, unforeseen consequences, and as such contributes to uncertainty in the business environment while also raising transaction costs for private investors. Although specific corrupt transactions could be viewed as more analogous to our definition of political risk, we conceptualize corruption as a system-wide phenomenon that is closely intertwined with the quality and efficacy of institutions.

In addition, institutional capacity is reflected in the level of stock market development and shareholder legal protection.[49] Overall, weak institutions[50] that fail to provide for basic public goods, property rights, capital markets, legal protections, and even free speech[51] result in poor economic performance and instability[52] and contribute to investor perception of risk in emerging economies. In Chapter 11, we explore how these differing institutional contexts require different approaches to nonmarket strategy and how that strategy is aligned with commercial interest.

In sum, we conceptualize institutional risk as arising from a lack of rule of law, the existence of pervasive corruption, and underdeveloped capital markets and regulatory infrastructure. These risks transcend the "few" actors/individuals and reflect a systemic or structural risk. In this conceptualization, corruption is not restricted to political actors but extends far beyond them to include bureaucrats and other economic and business agents with whom investors interact. It is corruption permitted and encouraged by the absence of institutional constraints to curtail it.

In understanding and unpacking different risk types, we extend and broaden a recent conceptualization of corruption that characterizes it as a relatively specific and narrow type of risk.[53] This conceptualization proposes that corruption can be better understood by evaluating how its pervasiveness (how widespread it is) and arbitrariness (its unpredictability) affect entry and ownership strategies.[54] In this framework, however, we go beyond this division to examine government-inspired risk in the broadest categories and seek to develop an analogous but more finely grained understanding of risk, focusing on such important elements as duration, variability, and frequency. In doing so, we provide the basis of knowledge that will serve companies well when deciding how to approach and enter uncertain environments.

Risk and Integrated Strategy in Transitional Policy Environments

According to Doh and Pearce, markets in a state of transition are defined in terms of the *degree of uncertainty* of the future and the *slope* and *inflection of change.* [55] As such, the transitional public policy environment depends on the predicted direction of the policy and the speed at which the change is likely to occur. For example, the unpredictable nature of the North American Free Trade Agreement (NAFTA) during the 1992 U.S. presidential elections left companies in the dark about the future trade environment. Accordingly, they had to create proactive plans to position themselves successfully no matter what the outcome, and many firms were in a strong position to take advantage of the upcoming changes. Given the uncertain nature of government policy, which is often characterized by democratization, privatization, deregulation, regulation, and trade liberalization, to name a few, corporations have the opportunity to exploit changes to their advantage.[56] Therefore, by first identifying the state of uncertainty in conjunction with the likely change and time frame associated with it, corporations can use real options theory to weigh the risks and rewards associated with each potential outcome and enhance their competitive performance.[57]

Real Options Perspectives on Transitional Public Policy

Real options theory is a body of literature involving investments of real assets that entail managerial decision-making rather than financial investments.[58]

The real options perspective defines the opportunity for a company to continue investing in a particular asset rather than the responsibility to invest in it,[59] allowing it to view the risks and rewards associated with an uncertain future while both minimizing losses and retaining the potential to increase future rewards.[60] The cost of the real option is limited to the initial cash outlay, but if future conditions are positive, further investment in the project can occur.[61]

This framework has been shown to be extremely successful in terms of entrepreneurship in a transitional public policy environment because of its ability to exploit potential future returns with minimal capital outlay. The possible future benefits can be extremely strong if the strategy is utilized correctly, which is key in terms of uncertainty in the nonmarket. Therefore, firms have many options in exploiting the opportunities available to them in a vague nonmarket environment, and how they decide to enter these dynamic environments can have significant strategic impacts.

Response Speed and Competitive Dynamics

In conjunction with the real options perspective, the speed at which a company responds to the dynamism of the public policy environment can have enormous implications for subsequent gains or losses. [62] A "follow the leader" approach rarely results in optimal results for any company in a particular industry. In essence, real options theory allows for entrepreneurial strategic initiatives that could create various positive outcomes depending on the approach taken, the speed of the response, and competitor responses. Specifically, the response time is measured by how quickly a firm changes its original course of action to meet customer demands or to benefit from changing tides.[63]

Two approaches stand out in transitional public policy environments. One option is to gain a first-mover advantage that puts the entering company in a winner-takes-all position.[64] This is usually the most beneficial strategy when "one-time discontinuities create generous rent streams for the early entrant, with little left for followers," such as in the case of privatization.[65] Doh describes these strategies as "big bang" or "shock therapy" approaches to reform that may allow these early entrants to gain advantages if there is a lag between privatization and ensuing liberalization.[66] For example, when Southwestern Bell together with its strategic partners bought a minority (20.4 percent) but controlling interest in Telefonos de Mexico for $1.757 billion in the early 1990s and later bought additional shares, it derived a powerful combination of first-mover and incumbency advantages that guaranteed it a dominant position in the Mexican market for decades to come.[67]

Another response to the volatile nonmarket environment is to take a laggard approach characterized by "gradualist, measured, and incremental" steps.[68] In these situations, the company or MNE will be in a strong position to learn from a first-mover's mistakes and exploit opportunities in a more economic fashion once the way has been paved. Such a strategy may be appropriate when the conditions appear to be moving in a positive direction but early movers have "locked in" to an investment when conditions were less favorable.[69]

By contrast, a firm may pursue a strategy previously employed, learning from its own mistakes.[70] This self-mimicking approach has proven to be not only successful but very common, as firms tend to trust their own prior experiences and often follow similar strategies over time out of habit.[71] Firms may even take past experiences in one nonmarket and duplicate them as successful strategies in entirely new nonmarkets.[72]

The overall purpose of creating an advantageous response is to use a firm's entrepreneurial insight in a dynamic nonmarket environment to create value for customers in a new way or timely manner. As we have represented, various strategies can exploit opportunities in different ways depending upon the hypothesized environmental outcome and competition. Firms must decide on an entrepreneurial strategy that will have the most positive impact, given these pertinent forces.

Corporate Entrepreneurship and Real Options in Transitional Policy Environments

The main question firms need to answer is how to actually deploy strategies that successfully respond to these changes in public policy.[73] According to Timmons,[74] entrepreneurship is a way for firms to rise against the competition in spite of available resources. Another definition of entrepreneurship is "the degree of proactivity, risk tolerance, and innovation of a given firm or strategy."[75] However, Doh and Pearce go so far as to say that corporate entrepreneurship encompasses the range of strategies employed by a firm to secure a competitive position regardless of firm size or age.[76]

In terms of a changing nonmarket environment, firms will have the option of shifting previously held strategies to new ones that take advantage of market opportunities by changing the way they organize and use resources.[77] Research in corporate political strategy suggests that, because government policies can have a significant impact on business activities, corporations adopt various strategies both to affect government policy and to respond to competitor efforts to influence that policy.[78]

Prior literature on corporate political strategy has focused on working with the government in a way that emphasizes "compliance, avoidance, circumvention, conflict, or partnership," which is typically defined as bargaining versus non-bargaining strategies.[79] However, an entrepreneurial strategy seeks to complement these previously held approaches and offer new insight into ways to influence public policy by narrowing the range of likely outcomes to come up with the best-case scenario from a wide range of influencing efforts.[80]

Entrepreneurial opportunities are "those situations in which new goods, services, raw materials, and organizing methods can be introduced and sold at greater than their cost of production."[81] Hence, combining this definition with the idea of responding to changes in public policy, Doh and Pearce define corporate entrepreneurship activities as the "innovative, proactive, or risk-seeking behavior that seeks to exploit knowledge or relationships regarding present and future developments in the public policy arena, specifically legislative and regulatory policy."[82] Therefore, on the basis of the types of changes occurring and the pace at which these changes are taking place, companies have many options available to them when deciding which entrepreneurial strategy to take on.

Nonmarket Strategies in Response to Uncertainty and Change

Porter's five forces model has been widely adopted as a broad framework for understanding the industry environment in which strategy is conducted.[83] However, given that this book focuses on strategies in response to stimuli and changes in the nonmarket, it may be more useful to suggest "viewing nonmarket strategies as complements to market strategies that in some cases can be used to address directly the five market forces Porter identifies."[84] Another way to look at it is to simply use nonmarket strategy to address the five forces and evaluate it in terms of threats or potential advantages.[85]

As we mentioned earlier, to create and/or evaluate a strategy, knowledge of the types of nonmarket environmental changes taking place, as well as the pace of these changes, is essential. According to Courtney, this creates a level of uncertainty that, in terms of strategic management, can be characterized as four levels of ambiguity: a clear future around which probabilities can be established, alternate paths, a range of possible futures, and true ambiguity.[86] Doh and Pearce have added to Courtney's framework, suggesting that the pace of change can also be characterized as having three possible levels: slow, continuous change; rapid, high-velocity change; and uneven, discontinuous change.[87] Given these classifications of policy change and pace of change,

Doh and Pearce identified four types of entrepreneurial corporate strategies that apply to transitional policy environments: preemptive, optioned, synchronous, and adaptive.[88]

Preemptive strategies are defined by those firms that make a "first strike," i.e. they take a first-mover advantage that typically requires a large initial outlay of resources.[89] They naturally involve an aggressive, "preemptive" attack designed to garner a strong, defensible competitive position. Preemptive strategies are especially attractive when the level of uncertainty is relatively low and when market lockout opportunities are well defined. A specific example of this strategy occurred in 2000, when Deutsche Telekom purchased VoiceStream, a Washington-based cellular provider, to gain access to the growing U.S. wireless market. Opposition to the deal came from members of Congress concerned about market access reciprocity, given the German government's 58 percent stake in Deutsche Telekom, although the Federal Communications Commission (FCC) could reject the merger only if it proved to be a clear violation of the public interest. In this case, Deutsche Telekom chose to exercise a definitive strategy in the face of a public policy environment characterized by relatively low uncertainty (at least over the long term) with reasonably predictable outcomes.

Optioned strategies require a large initial investment intended to reserve a limited position that will help in terms of future access to limited resources.[90] Optioned strategies are most appropriate when the level of uncertainty is moderate and when clear alternate paths can be identified. They will generate the highest returns when the inflection profile is uneven, allowing for temporal entry barriers that may be powerful for a period of time but may abruptly disappear when the policy environment is suddenly altered. Optioned strategies allow the firm to hedge the preemptive bet and reserve the right to participate in a more influential manner later. A specific example of a preemptive optioned strategy came in the midst of the 1990s North American Free Trade Agreement (NAFTA) negotiations when Corning, the largest U.S. glassmaker, initiated a joint venture (JV) deal with Vitro Sociedad Anónima, the $3 billion Mexican glassmaker, in which each company took an equity stake in the JV and agreed to a series of marketing, sales, and distribution relationships. Corning had initially opposed the rapid reduction of tariffs on glass imports and lobbied vigorously to delay or slow these reductions because of concerns that cheap imports from its Mexican competitor, Vitro, would swamp the U.S. market. By linking with Vitro, Corning took an optioned approach to an uncertain policy environment characterized by uneven and discontinuous change but for which clear alternate paths could be identified—glass tariffs would either come down or they would not.

It should be noted that uneven, discontinuous change is hard to estimate in the short run. After seeing long-serving dictators fall in the 1990s and 2000s, first in Central and Eastern Europe and then in a number of Asian countries, the "Arab Spring" of 2011 saw autocrats who had been in power for decades toppled in Egypt, Libya, and Tunisia. While some of these developments seem likely over the long term (all leaders eventually relinquish rule through one means or another), the timing of such events is often quite unexpected.

Synchronous strategies afford firms the right to move in conjunction with the changing environment, deploying resources as the changes occur. This in turn eliminates the riskiness of a first-mover or laggard approach.[91] The high-risk option of choosing proactive or laggard strategies can be eliminated when a firm plans to synchronize its investments with the progress of policy change. A synchronous strategy directs the firm to match its resource commitments with post-decision, pre-activation policy changes. The goal of a synchronous strategy is to help the company establish a position as a mainstream player with solid prospects for industry-comparable profits. It does so by increasing its investments in competitive options as the likelihood of occurrence and the consequence (payoff) of each path become more certain. Microsoft's previously mentioned entry into the Chinese market reflects this approach. Its strategy toward the Chinese government and the overall policy environment evolved in tandem with the opening and liberalization of that environment, beginning with partnerships with local governmental entities to facilitate its entry and growth. When progress stalled, Microsoft pursued a more aggressive approach, always calibrating its actions with the state of play and with government policy and ensuring alignment between its market and nonmarket strategies.

With *adaptive strategies*, the firm constantly and continuously changes its strategy in tandem with the public policy environment.[92] It has proven to be most appropriate when the level of uncertainty is extremely high, creating a dangerous environment in which to lock in a strategy, or when change is occurring at an abnormally rapid pace, necessitating flexibility as a strategic element.[93] Tata Group initially adopted a "big bet" preemptive strategy in its decision to invest heavily in West Bengal but was forced to adapt to the changing environment in India by abandoning its investment in favor of the alternative in Gujarat. It is possible that Tata misjudged the degree of uncertainty around the initial investment and should have taken a more deliberate, staged investment that more easily allowed for reversal and consideration of other options when its initial choice became problematic.

Table 4.1 summarizes these combinations of uncertainty type and speed of change. While there are many other frameworks that can be used to classify and explicate uncertainty, this approach offers a simple, comprehensible, and flexible approach to incorporating risk and uncertainty in policy environments into an integrative strategy.

Table 4.1. Inflection profile, degree of uncertainty, and political strategy in transitional public policy environments

Degree of uncertainty	Pace/Inflection profile		
	Slow, continuous change	Uneven, discontinuous change	Rapid, high-velocity change
Level 1 uncertainty: clear future	Preemptive-measured	Preemptive-moderate	Preemptive-accelerated
Level 2 uncertainty: alternate paths	Optioned-measured	Optioned-moderate	Optioned-accelerated
Level 3 uncertainty: range of paths	Synchronized-measured	Synchronized-moderate	Synchronized-accelerated
Level 4 uncertainty: true ambiguity	Adaptive-measured	Adaptive-moderate	Adaptive-accelerated

Source: Adapted from Doh, J.P. and Pearce, J.A. II. (2004). Corporate entrepreneurship and real options in transitional policy environments: theory development. *Journal of Management Studies*, 41 (4): 645–664.

Conclusions and Managerial Implications

Managing uncertainty and risk is an ongoing and inexorable reality in the contemporary global business environment. With the advent of technology, social media, dramatic political and social change, and general volatility in markets and systems, uncertainty and risk are ever-present elements of managing in market and nonmarket environments. Managers must assess the type and degree of uncertainty and risk, chart a strategic response, and continually evaluate and re-evaluate that response to ensure the firm is reasonably insured against adverse events and, more importantly, is in a position to leverage elements of uncertainty for competitive advantage.

In this chapter we have explored the challenges of managing risk and uncertainty in the nonmarket environment. As the two examples at the beginning of the chapter illustrate, there are no sure recipes for addressing these challenges. Facing serious and persistent challenges in China, Microsoft has pursued a dual strategy alternating between aggressive posturing (lobbying the U.S. government to pressure China to enhance its protection of foreign company intellectual property (IP) rights, filing IP lawsuits in Chinese courts, and suing Chinese firms using pirated software) and working closely with the Chinese government in an effort to be seen as a legitimate local player in the market. Despite Tata's status as the ultimate "insider" in India, it appeared to misjudge the level and intensity of uncertainty in states such as West Bengal and was forced to retreat and redeploy its investment elsewhere. Others firms have had more success, sometimes by employing the strategies described above that are tailored to the particular nature, degree, and timing of uncertainty.

Therefore, companies should consider the following when seeking to align market and nonmarket strategies in the face of uncertainty and change:

- Change and uncertainty are endemic to all business environments, and it is better to embrace these forces than to try to ignore or avoid them.

- As they are influenced by political and social actors that reflect latent and nonobvious interests and constituencies, nonmarket environments may be subject to less "rational" and more volatile change.

- Notwithstanding this volatility, uncertain environments can be classified and categorized in a manner that can reveal and limit some of that variability, which enables firms to tailor strategies—both market and nonmarket—to the specifics of those changing conditions.

- Strategies targeted to the political and social arenas should reflect the type and pace of uncertainty and change, and should be revisited as those conditions evolve.

In the next chapter, we will see from various studies how cultural, institutional, industry, and firm-specific factors might inform a company's decision to lobby individually or as part of a collective. Moreover, we will explore different strategic behaviors used to engage with political and social actors in ways that can shape and influence social and political decisions. Subsequently, we will explore future opportunities in social technologies to create individual or collective influence in the nonmarket. Therefore, chronologically and systematically, we will emphasize the increasing value of collective versus individual action in the process of political and social strategy development and its associated value-creation process.

Notes

* Portions of this chapter have been adapted from Doh, J.P., and Pearce, J.A. II. (2004). Corporate entrepreneurship and real options in transitional policy environments: theory development. *Journal of Management Studies*, 41(4): 645–664.

1. Clausewitz, C. von. (1976). *On War*. Edited and translated by M. Howard and P. Paret. Princeton, NJ: Princeton University Press: Book One: 75–89.

2. Blanchard, J-M. (2012). Microsoft opens the gates: patent, piracy, and political challenges in China. In F. Luthans and J.P. Doh (eds). *International management: culture, strategy and behavior*. 8th ed. Boston, MA: McGraw-Hill Irwin: 388–392.

3. Azarova, T. (2012). Tata "Nano": the people's car. In F. Luthans and J.P. Doh (eds.). *International management: culture, strategy and behavior*. 8th ed. Boston, MA: McGraw-Hill Irwin: 399–407.

4. Bach and Allen 2010.

5. Baron 1995a; Boddewyn and Brewer 1994.

6. Lu, J.W. (2002). Intra- and inter-organizational imitative behavior: institutional influences on Japanese firms' entry mode choice. *Journal of International Business Studies*, 33(1): 19–37.

7. Baysinger 1984.

8. Dahan 2005a; Dahan, N. (2005b). A contribution to the conceptualization of political resources utilized in corporate political action. *Journal of Public Affairs*, 5(1): 43–54.

9. Cummings, J.L. and Doh, J.P. (2000). Identifying who matters: mapping key players in multiple environments. *California Management Review*, 42 (2): 83–105.

10. Khanna, T., Palepu, K., and Sinha, J. (2005). Strategies that fit emerging markets. *Harvard Business Review*, 83(6): 63–76.

11. De Figueiredo, J.M. and Tiller, E.H. (2001). The structure and conduct of corporate lobbying: how firms lobby the Federal Communications Commission. *Journal of Economics & Management Strategy*, 10(1): 91–122.

12. Doh and Pearce 2004; Delios, A. and Henisz, W.J. (2003a). Policy uncertainty and the sequence of entry by Japanese firms, 1980–1998. *Journal of International Business Studies*, 34(3): 227–241; Delios, A. and Henisz, W.J. (2003b). Political hazards, experience, and sequential entry strategies: the international expansion of Japanese firms: 1980–1998. *Strategic Management Journal*, 24(11): 1153–1164.

13. Delios, A. and Henisz, W.J. (2001) Uncertainty, imitation, and plant location: Japanese multinational corporations, 1990–1996, *Administrative Science Quarterly*, 46(3): 443–475.

14. Delios and Henisz 2001.

15. Wack, P. (1985). Scenarios: uncharted waters. *Harvard Business Review*, 63(5): 73–89.

16. A simple (but quite broad) definition of political risk offered by Kobrin (1979: 67) is "government interference with business operations." For further details, see Kobrin, S. (1979). Political risk: a review and reconsideration. *Journal of International Business Studies*, 10(1): 67–80. Weston and Sorge propose a more specific definition (Weston, V.F. and Sorge, B.W. (1972). *International Managerial Finance*. Homewood, IL: Richard D. Irwin, as cited in Kobrin, 1979: 67): "Political risks arise from the actions of national governments which interfere with or prevent business transactions, or change the terms of agreements, or cause the confiscation of wholly or partly owned foreign business operations." Simon provides a more elaborate explanation, suggesting political risk is "governmental or societal actions and policies, originating either within or outside the host country, and negatively affecting either selected groups of, or the majority of foreign business operations and investments" (1982: 62).

17. Moran, T.H. (1985). Risk assessment, corporate planning and strategies. In T.H. Moran (ed.). *Multinational Corporations: the political economy of foreign direct investment*. Lexington, VA: Lexington Books: 107–117.

18. Sethi, S. and Luther, K.A.N. (1986). Political risk analysis and direct foreign investment: some problems of definition and measurement. *California Management Review*, 28(2): 57–68.

19. Levy, B. and Spiller, P.T. (eds.) (1996). *Regulations, institutions, and commitment: comparative studies of telecommunications.* Cambridge, MA: Cambridge University Press.
20. Minor, M.S. (1994). Demise of expropriation as an instrument of LDC policy, 1980–1992, *Journal of International Business Studies*, 25(1): 177–188.
21. Doh, J.P. and Ramamurti, R. (2003). Reassessing risk in developing country infrastructure, *Long Range Planning*, 36(4): 342.
22. Doh and Ramamurti 2003: 342.
23. Encarnation, D.J. and Vachani, S. (1985). Foreign ownership: when hosts change the rules. *Harvard Business Review*, 63(5): 152–160.
24. We use the term "risk" to reflect unpredictability in the business environment of a host country. In this sense, political upheaval, which may reflect instability, will not be considered a risk, since the investor can conceivably factor such disturbances into associated investment decisions.
25. Poynter, T.A. (1993). Managing government intervention: a strategy for defending the subsidiary. In R.Z. Aliber and R.W. Click (eds.). *Readings in international business: a decision approach.* Cambridge, MA: MIT Press: 473–492.
26. Moran 1985.
27. Poynter 1993.
28. Vernon, R. (1971). *Sovereignty at bay: the multinational spread of U.S. enterprises.* New York: Basic Books.
29. Robock, S. (1971). Political risk identification and assessment. *Columbia Journal of World Business*, 7: 6–20.
30. Henisz, W.J. and Zelner, B.A. (2004). Political risk management: a strategic perspective. In T.H. Moran (ed.). *International political risk management: the brave new world.* Washington, DC: The World Bank: 154–170.
31. Wells, Jr., L.T. (1998). God and fair competition: Does the foreign direct investor face still other risks in emerging markets? In T.H. Moran (ed.). *Managing international political risk.* Boston, MA: Blackwell: 15–43.
32. Encarnation and Vachani 1985t.
33. Markwick, S. (1998). Trends in political risk for corporate investors. In T.H. Moran (ed.). *Managing international political risk.* Boston, MA: Blackwell: 44–56.
34. Lenway and Murtha 1994.
35. Sethi and Luther 1986; Zelner and Henisz 2000; Robock 1971.
36. Levy and Spiller 1996; Laban, R. and Wolf, H.C. (1993). Large-scale privatization in transition economies. *American Economic Review*, 83: 1199–1210; Murtha and Lenway 1994.
37. North, D.C. (1990). *Institutions, institutional change and economic performance.* New York: Cambridge University Press; North, D.C. (1993). Institutions and credible commitment. *Journal of Institutional and Theoretical Economics*, 149: 11–23.
38. Khanna, T. and Palepu, K. (1997). Why focused strategies may be wrong for emerging markets. *Harvard Business Review*, 75(4): 41–51.
39. Wells 1998.
40. Doh, J. P., Rodriguez, P., Uhlenbruck, K., Collins, J., and Eden, L. (2003). Coping with corruption in foreign markets. *Academy of Management Executive*, 17(3): 114–127.

41. North 1993.

42. Doh et al. 2003.

43. Shleifer, A. and Vishny, R. (1993). Corruption. *Quarterly Journal of Economics*, 108(3): 599–617.

44. Kaufmann, D., Kraay, A., and Zoido-Lobaton, P. (1999). Governance matters. *Policy Research Working Paper 2196*. Washington, DC: The World Bank.

45. Doh et al. 2003.

46. Kaufmann, D. and Kraay, A. (2002). Governance matters II: Update indicators for 2000/2001. *Policy Research Working Paper 2772*. Washington, DC: The World Bank.

47. Brunetti, A. and Weder, B. (1998). Investment and institutional uncertainty: a comparative study of different uncertainty measures. *Weltwirtschaftliches Archiv*, 134: 513–533.

48. Mauro, P. (1995). Corruption and growth. *Quarterly Journal of Economics*, 110(3): 681–712.

49. La Porta, R., López-de-Silanes, F., Shleifer, A., and Vishny, R. (1998). Law and finance. *Journal of Political Economy*, 106: 1113–1155; La Porta, R. and López-de-Silanes, F. (1999). Benefits of privatization—evidence from Mexico. *Quarterly Journal of Economics*, 114(4): 1193–1242; Modigliani, F. and Perotti, E. (1990). The rules of the game and the development of security markets. MIT, mimeo; Modigliani, F. and Perotti, E. (1996). Protection of minority shareholders and the development of security markets. MIT, mimeo; Bortolotti, B., Fantini, M., Siniscalco, D., and Vitalini, S. (1998). Privatizations and institutions. Working paper, FEEM, Milan.

50. North, D.C. (1986). The new institutional economics. *Journal of Institutional and Theoretical Economics*, 142: 230–237; North 1993.

51. Levy and Spiller 1996.

52. Olson, M. (1993). Dictatorship, democracy, and development. *American Political Science Review*, 87: 567–76; Henisz, W.J. and Williamson, O.E. (1999). Comparative economic organization—within and between countries. *Business and Politics*, 1: 261–277.

53. Uhlenbruck, K., Rodriguez, P., Doh, J., and Eden, L. (2006). The impact of corruption on entry strategy: evidence from telecommunications projects in emerging economies. *Organization Science*, 17(3): 402–413.

54. Uhlenbruck et al. 2006.

55. Doh 2004. Op cit.

56. Doh and Pearce 2004: 1–2.

57. Doh and Pearce 2004: 10.

58. Doh and Pearce 2004: 10; Bowman, E.H. and Hurry, D. (1993). Strategy through the opinion lens: an integrated view of resource investments and the incremental-choice process. *Academy of Management Review*, 18: 760–782; Dixit, A. and Pindyck, R. (1994). *Investment under uncertainty*. Princeton, NJ: Princeton University Press.

59. Doh and Pearce 2004:10.

60. Doh and Pearce 2004: 10–11.

61. Doh and Pearce 2004: 11; Dixit and Pindyck 1994; Mitchell, G.R. and Hamilton, W.F. (1988). Managing R&D as a strategic option. *Research-Technology Management*, 27(3): 15–22; Roberts, K. and Weitzman, M.L. (1981). Funding criteria for research, development and exploration projects. *Econometrica*, 49: 1261–1288.

62. Doh and Pearce 2004: 12.

63. Doh and Pearce 2004: 12.

64. Doh and Pearce 2004: 12; Kerin, R.P., Varadarajan, P.R., and Peterson, R.A. (1992). First-mover advantage: a synthesis, conceptual framework, and research propositions. *Journal of Marketing*, 56(4): 33–52; Lieberman, M. and Montgomery, D. (1988). First mover advantages. *Strategic Management Journal*, 9: 41–58; Mascarenhas, B. (1992). Order of entry and performance in international markets. *Strategic Management Journal*, 13: 499–510.

65. Doh and Pearce 2004: 12; Doh, J.P. (2000). Entrepreneurial privatization strategies: order of entry and local partner collaboration as sources of competitive advantage. *Academy of Management Review*, 25: 551–572.

66. Doh, J.P., Teegen, H., and Mudambi, R. (2004). Balancing private and state ownership in emerging markets' telecommunications infrastructure: country, industry, and firm influence. *Journal of International Business Studies*, 35: 233–250.

67. Doh et al. 2004; Debraj, R. (1998). *Development economics*. Princeton, NJ: Princeton University Press; Rodrik, D. (1996). Understanding economic policy reform. *Journal of Economic Literature*, 34: 9–41; Ramamurti, R. (ed.). (1996). *Privatizing monopolies: lessons from the telecommunications and transport sectors in Latin America*. Baltimore, MD: The Johns Hopkins University Press.

68. Doh and Pearce 2004: 5.

69. Doh and Pearce 2004: 12; Smith, K.G., Grimm, C.M., and Gannon, M.J. (1992). *Dynamics of competitive strategy*. Newbury Park, CA: Sage; Tellis, G. and Golder, P. (1996). First to market, first to fail? Real causes of enduring market leadership. *Sloan Management Review*, 37(2): 65–77.

70. Doh and Pearce 2004: 7; Tallman, S.B. (1992). A strategic management perspective on host country structure of multinational enterprises. *Journal of International Business Studies*, 25(1): 91–112.

71. Doh and Pearce 2004: 8.

72. Doh and Pearce 2004: 7; Tallman 1992.

73. Doh and Pearce 2004: 4.

74. Timmons, J.A. (1994). *New venture creation*. Homewood, IL: Irwin.

75. Doh and Pearce 2004: 4; Timmons 1994; Covin, J.G. and Slevin, D.P. (1989). Strategic management of small firms in hostile and benign environments. *Strategic Management Journal*, 10(1): 75–87.

76. Doh and Pearce 2004: 4; Nielsen, R.P., Peters, M.R., and Hisrich, R.D. (1985). Intrepreneurship strategy for internal markets—Corporate, nonprofit, and government institution cases. *Strategic Management Journal*, 6(2): 181–189; Pinchot, G. (1985) *Intrapreneuring: why you don't have to leave the corporation to become an entrepreneur*. New York: Harper and Row.

77. Doh and Pearce 2004: 5.

78. Doh and Pearce 2004: 5; Hillman, A.J. and Keim, G. (1995). International variation in the business–government interface: institutional and organizational considerations. *Academy of Management Review*, 20: 193–214; Keim and Baysinger 1988; Keim and Zeithaml 1986; Marcus, A., Kaufman, A., and Beam, D. (eds.). (1987). *Business strategy and public policy*. New York: Quorum; Mitnick, B. (1993). Choosing agency and competition. In B. Mitnick (ed.). *Corporate Political Agency*. Newbury Park, CA: Sage: 1–12; Weidenbaum 1980.

79. Boddewyn and Brewer 1994; Doh and Pearce 2004: 6.

80. Doh and Pearce 2004: 6.

81. Doh and Pearce 2004: 6; Shane, S. and Venkataraman, S. (2000). The promise of entrepreneurship as a field of research. *Academy of Management Review*, 25(1): 217–226.

82. Doh and Pearce 2004: 7.

83. Baron 1995b; Porter, M.E. (1980). *Competitive strategy: techniques for analyzing industries and competitors*. New York, NY: The Free Press.

84. Baron 1995b: 55; Gale and Buchholz also discuss the relationship between political strategies and Porter's five forces: Gale and Buchholz 1987; Yoffie, D.B. (1987). Corporate strategies for political action: a rational model. In A. Marcus, A. Kaufmann, and D. Beam (eds.). *Business strategy and public policy*. New York: Quorum: 60.

85. Baron 1995b: 57.

86. Doh and Pearce 2004: 8; Courtney, H. (2001). *20/20 Foresight: crafting strategy in an uncertain world*. Boston, MA: Harvard Business School Press; Courtney, H., Kirkland, J. and Viguerie, P. (1997). Strategy under uncertainty. *Harvard Business Review*, 75(6): 66–79.

87. Doh and Pearce 2004: 9; Bourgeois III, L.J. and Eisenhardt. K.M. (1988). Strategic decision processes in high velocity environments: four cases in the microcomputer industry. *Management Science*, 34: 816–835; Newman, K.L. (2000). Organizational transformation during institutional upheaval. *Academy of Management Review*, 25(3): 602–619; Newman, K.L. and Nollen, S.D. (1998). *Managing radical organizational change*. Thousand Oaks, CA: Sage; Brown, S. and Eisenhardt, K.M. (1997). The art of continuous change: linking complexity theory and time-paced evolution in relentlessly shifting organizations. *Administrative Science Quarterly*, 42: 1–34; Gould, S.J. (1989). Punctuated equilibrium theory in fact and theory. *Journal of Social Biological Structures*, 12: 117–136; Gersick, C.J.G. (1991). Revolutionary change theories: a multilevel exploration of the punctuated equilibrium paradigm. *Academy of Management Review*, 16(1): 10–36; Romanelli, E. and Tushman, M.L (1994). Organizational transformation as punctuated equilibrium: an empirical test. *Academy of Management Journal*, 37: 1141–1167.

88. Doh and Pearce 2004: 15; Lieberman and Montgomery 1988; Smith, Grimm, and Gannon 1992.

89. Doh and Pearce 2004: 16; Kerin et al. 1992; Lieberman and Montgomery 1988; Mascarenhas 1992; Doh 2000; Patterson, W.C. (1993). First-mover advantage: the opportunity curve. *Journal of Management Studies*, 30: 759–777; Sarkar, M.B., Cavusgil, S.T., and Aulakh, P. (1999). International expansion of

telecommunication carriers: the influence of market structure, network characteristics, and entry imperfections. *Journal of International Business Studies*, 30(2): 361–382.

90. Doh and Pearce 2004: 17.
91. Doh and Pearce 2004: 18.
92. Doh and Pearce 2004: 18; Axelrod, A. and Cohen, M.D. (2000). *Harnessing complexity: organizational implications of a scientific frontier*. New York: Free Press.
93. Doh and Pearce 2004: 21; Newman 2000.

5

Individual versus Collective Action*

Ten people who speak make more noise than ten thousand who
are silent.[1]

Napoleon Bonaparte

In January 2012, competing versions of legislation aimed at limiting piracy
by foreign Internet sites were poised to be voted out of relevant committees and considered by the full chambers of the U.S. Senate and House of
Representatives. Supporters—including leaders of both houses and both
political parties, large entertainment conglomerates such as NBCUniversal,
and powerful trade associations such as the Motion Picture Association of
America (headed by former senator Christopher Dodd)—expected some form
of the legislation, known as the Stop Online Piracy Act, or SOPA (the Senate
version was known as the Protect Intellectual Property Act, or PIPA), to pass
without major objection. However, a viral wave of protests, including black-
outs or partial masks of such major websites as Wikipedia and Google, somewhat spontaneously and explosively emerged. This caused several of the bill's
sponsors to withdraw their support. Google, which had operated with a black
bar over its logo throughout the protest, collected 4.5 million anti-SOPA sig-
natures in just one day. Its powerful reputation as the largest search site in
the world and its ability to mobilize grassroots responses were instrumental
in forcing reconsideration of the legislation.

The Alliance for Healthcare Competitiveness (AHC), representing manufacturers, health services firms, health IT providers, caregivers, and educators,
came together to advance a collective agenda for pushing U.S. governmental and nongovernmental efforts to further liberalize and open markets for
U.S. healthcare exports. According to the AHC, the American health ecosystem includes hospitals and clinics, labs and researchers, doctors, dentists,
nutritionists and nurses, insurers, manufacturers of medicines and medical

devices, health IT managers, and many other professions and industries. As a whole, the health ecosystem is unique in the world for its scale, technical sophistication, and capacity to serve diverse populations. Interestingly, AHC members operate their own public policy offices directed at trade liberalization and are also members of other, more specialized trade associations. For example, the pharmaceutical industry, members of which are active in AHC, also has it own powerful trade association, the Pharmaceutical Research and Manufacturers Association (PhRMA). Indeed, PhRMA is larger and arguably much more influential than AHC, which is more of an ad hoc coalition with no permanent staff or office; its secretariat is staffed by Fontheim International, LLC, a government relations and lobbying firm.

These examples underscore the changing nature of public policy advocacy, sometimes termed "lobbying," and the different forms and levels it can take. They also highlight the broadening dimensions of such advocacy and the different forms, modes, and mechanisms through which it can take place. In this chapter we will explore the various direct and indirect mechanisms by which firms identify and leverage channels of influence and will consider the circumstances under which companies must make the basic choice of "going it alone" or working collaboratively through a trade or industry association or broader social engagement coalition that may include NGOs and other actors to advance political, social, and economic interests.

Research into the process of individual versus collective action, including corporate political activity (CPA) scholarship, has explored the conditions

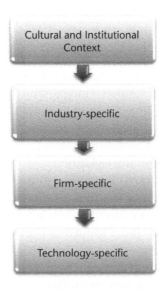

Figure 5.1 A hierarchy of individual versus collective nonmarket factors

under which nonmarket strategy (NMS) is more effective when pursued by the firm in isolation as opposed to as part of a broader coalition. Accordingly, we will draw on research on cultural, institutional, industry, and firm-specific factors to show how firms, alone and in conjunction with a formal or informal coalition, can engage broader political and social actors in ways that can shape and influence social and political decisions. Subsequently, we will explore future opportunities in social technologies to create individual or collective influence in the nonmarket. Building on previous studies, Figure 5.1 captures the key constructs vital in deciding between individual and collective-led nonmarket strategies. Therefore, chronologically and systematically, we will emphasize the increasing value of collective versus individual action in the process of political and social strategy development and its associated value-creation process.

Collective versus Individual Action: Cultural and Institutional Factors

Scholars have long been interested in the conditions under which groups come together to advance some shared goal or interest. In his seminal book, *The Logic of Collective Action*, Mancur Olson challenged conventional wisdom that common interests will beget common (and equivalent) actions and that the majority would always dominate and subjugate the minority.[2] Instead, Olson argued, individuals in any group seeking collective action will have incentives to "free-ride" on the efforts of others if the group is working to provide public goods (those that are generally available without the ability to restrict to some subset), but will be disincentivized to do so if the group provides benefits only to contributing participants.[3] Olson also suggested that large groups face relatively high costs when attempting to organize for collective action, while small groups face relatively low costs. Also, individuals in large groups will gain less individually from successful collective action; individuals in small groups will gain more per capita through successful collective action. Hence, in the absence of specific incentives, the incentive for group action diminishes as group size increases, so that large groups are less able to act in their common interest than small ones. (See Figure 5.2, which builds on Olson's ideas.) In the public affairs and CPA literature there are numerous examples of successful efforts by individual companies, trade associations, grassroots political networks, and other group activities. The lobbying matrix outlined in Figure 5.2 can be used to understand the incentives and number of firms engaged in an issue of common interest. There are also many cases in which firms elect to pursue individual action, which can often produce better outcomes than collective action.[4] But what factors lead firms to choose one

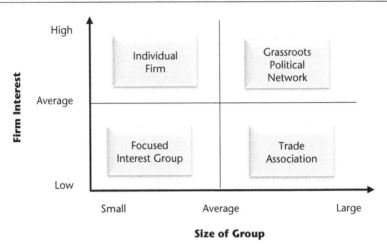

Figure 5.2 The lobbying matrix

avenue over another? One overarching set of variables is the broader cultural, economic, and policy environment within which political and social strategy takes place.

Barron interviewed governmental affairs managers (EU political representatives at several large French and British companies) about how they negotiated with the EU, and more specifically whether they negotiated individually through their representatives in Brussels or collectively through their affiliated European trade associations.[5] He concludes that the French representatives, enmeshed in a more collectivistic culture, tend to favor collaborative approaches to negotiation, otherwise known as "integrative bargaining."[6] For instance, one of the French interviewees said that "a common position of European banks carries more weight than a single position defended by our institution."[7] In contrast, British representatives, who tend to be more individualistic and competitive, prefer to negotiate alone in what the author labeled as "distributive bargaining."[8] One interviewee described this preference succinctly: "There is a community and we share information on matters of common concern, but I do the really important political work, such as lobbying for research budgets or on environment issues, on my own."[9]

Hart argues that regional cultural identities in the U.S. influence corporate political strategies.[10] Basing his research on federal political action committee (PAC) contributions of 120 successful high-tech companies during election cycles from 1977 to 1996, he found evidence that corporations operating in "traditionalistic" states were more inclined to establish or join a PAC than those operating "elsewhere" in the United States. The author also found that firms operating in "individualistic" states—compared with those operating in "moralistic" states—were, contrary to his hypothesis, not more likely to establish or join a PAC.[11]

Jacomet argues that collective action through trade associations is a more successful political strategy for international trade policy negotiations. Examining two case studies in the textile industry, the author identified two values necessary for collective action: unity and trade-offs.[12] Regarding collective versus individual action, Jacomet cites the example of how the American Textile Manufacturers Institute, the main textile industry trade association in the U.S., was able to foster unity among competing manufacturers during negotiations over multifiber international agreements and, in the process, to protect the U.S. domestic textile market. Regarding trade-offs, the author cites a second example of how COMITEXTIL, one of the main textile industry trade associations in the EU, negotiated a trade-off during the Uruguay Round of the General Agreement on Tariffs and Trade (GATT) by promoting stricter international regulations on intellectual property rights and antidumping in exchange for liberalizing the market of developing countries.[13]

Tucker analyzed how mimetic behavior influences the political strategies of a firm.[14] Having interviewed the representatives of the leading trade associations in the U.K. (the Association of the British Pharmaceutical Industry, the U.K. Petroleum Industry Association, and others) on whether their respective member firms chose to join or to remain in various trade associations, Tucker observes that some companies decided to act collectively "simply because other successful firms do so."[15] Referring to the mimetic isomorphism of DiMaggio and Powell to explain such behavior,[16] the author argues that reputational considerations motivate firms to imitate other firms, and by extension, to join trade associations at the collective level.[17]

Schuler, Rehbein, and Cramer also explored this imitative behavior in the context of aggressive competition between corporations over access to policymakers.[18] Drawing on a survey of 1,284 manufacturing firms, they observe that corporations in competitive industries often adopted multiple political strategies—in-house lobbying, outside lobbying, and campaign contributions—to achieve their political objectives if other successful competitors in the industry had already done so. That is, in the crowded and competitive environment of political lobbying, firms may imitate other firms to gain competitive advantage and to establish or uphold legitimacy.[19]

Hillman and Hitt explored how various political systems influence corporate behavior and argue that firms operating within corporatist/centralized political systems—social democracies that favor consensus on public policy—tend to act collectively. Conversely, firms operating within pluralist/fragmented political systems—liberal democracies with diverse and often competing interest groups, many of which do not have to or even want to compromise—tend to act alone and to compete for their own interests.[20]

Moreover, the nature of a given political issue matters, as firms are more inclined to act collectively on the following grounds: first, when they seek to mitigate their visibility on, or responsibility for, unpopular or unsuccessful policies that they either support or are presumed to support (a common example is a pharmaceutical company lobbying against healthcare reform), and secondly, when a successful electoral campaign requires the financial, human, or influential support of diverse interest groups.[21]

Building on this previous research, Hillman investigated the impact of Western European political systems on the corporate behavior of 169 U.S.-based corporate subsidiaries and reached the same conclusion: firms tend to favor collective political strategies in corporatist countries and individual political strategies in pluralist countries. [22] Although the study hypothesized first that industry composition would be more relevant in the conformist corporatist countries and, secondly, that micro-factors specific to individual firms would be more relevant in the competitive pluralist countries, neither prediction was supported in the data.[23]

Lord surveyed key congressional offices and leading corporations, observing that when public policies are not solely business-related and potentially affect numerous stakeholders, corporations can obtain access to policymakers indirectly by collaborating with employees, suppliers, customers, and community members on shared concerns or interests—a practice known as "corporate constituency building."[24] Such community advocacy often attracts U.S. congressional representatives, given the potential for "direct 'grassroots' feedback from [their most politically engaged] constituents."[25]

Industry-Specific Factors

In addition to broad, country-level institutional and cultural factors, research has also pointed to industry-specific factors and inter-firm dynamics, including imitative behavior, as causal factors that contribute to firm decisions to advance their agendas singularly versus pooling their resources and taking collective action. Factors such as firm size, market concentration, degree of unionization, intensity of political competition, and trade association effectiveness have all been shown to influence choices firms make about how they organize and deploy their nonmarket resources.

Research has suggested that industry concentration matters. Grieg, Munger, and Roberts investigated corporate campaign contributions to U.S. congressional candidates who ran for office between 1978 and 1986, finding evidence that, in highly concentrated industries, firms tend to favor collective and concerted action using PACs. Their statistical survey, which sampled 124 representative industries, revealed a strong correlation between industry concentration and corporate willingness to join a PAC. However, as the authors later caution, the correlation turned negative when the level of concentration grew beyond a certain threshold, which implies that when highly concentrated companies dominate an industry they may no longer see the need to join a PAC.[26]

Building on the preceding research on industry concentration, Schuler, Rehbein, and Cramer found that, in addition to industry concentration, variables such as corporate political competition and congressional industry caucuses motivate firms to explore a combination of political tactics—funding PACs, lobbying Washington offices, and hiring outside political consultants—to both break away from the herd and cultivate the attention of busy policymakers.[27]

Drawing conclusions similar to those of Schuler, Rehbein, and Cramer, Gray and Lowery assert that when companies aggressively compete to gain access to a limited number of policymakers, such companies will be more inclined to use multiple political avenues.[28] Surveying registered interest groups in six states (Arkansas, South Dakota, North Carolina, Pennsylvania, Michigan, and Minnesota), the authors found that, to be heard in a crowded legislative room, companies tend to act collectively through their affiliated trade associations as well as individually through PACs—which, oddly enough, often compete directly with the interests of trade associations.[29]

Masters and Keim explored the impact of industry unionization on corporate political activities.[30] Having investigated the PAC contributions of the largest and most politically active firms in the 1981–1982 congressional elections, the authors suggest that because unions, especially those that are "substantially organized," often have established contacts and connections with the government, firms stand to benefit if they take advantage of existing networks and organize hybrid PACs and other collaborative political lobbying campaigns that combine the interests of both firm and union.[31]

Tucker interviewed representatives of the major trade associations in the U.K. and found that companies derive numerous advantages from acting collectively through a trade association. Not only do the most effective trade associations protect the reputation of their respective industries, but they also create an environment of trust and credibility for various stakeholders and offer professional expertise to their members and other community or governmental parties.[32] Wilson, however, warns in another study that if a trade association (or any other business organization) does not carry out its mission effectively, firms may be inclined to revert to more individual political strategies. When the author asked 250 large corporations, each drawn from a sample of representative industries, about their degree of involvement in a business organization, he found that ineffective trade associations—that is, those with a weak mandate or an excessively large, heterogeneous membership—motivate corporations to break away and operate alone through firm-level PACs or in-house lobbying efforts. Moreover, such secessionist tendencies are even more probable if dissatisfied firms are already skeptical of their involvement in a given trade association—or, as the author put it, "Business executives will sometimes compare joining the Chamber of Commerce to attending church in Victorian times—a sign of social conformity and not necessarily conviction."[33]

Examining three case studies, Shaffer and Hillman explore how companies reconcile their broader political preferences with those of their individual business units. They find that the degree of diversification matters, as highly diversified companies tend to adopt comprehensive and "centralized" political strategies, while less diversified companies tend to encourage their business units to remain autonomous and modular.[34] Compare these two examples: A business unit of Acme Motors approached individual congressional representatives to request R&D subsidies for a project. However, because such a modular approach went against the firm's centralized corporate political strategy—one that opposed government funding—the business unit had to later withdraw its request. In contrast, Appalachian Energy, a less diversified corporation, saw no conflict in allowing its transportation business units to directly lobby the U.S. Department of Transportation on truck safety matters.

Firm-Specific Factors

A number of studies have focused on how the particular characteristics of individual firms, including firm size and resources, government dependence, institutional ownership, and types of generic nonmarket strategy patterns, influence the configuration of nonmarket strategies.

Size and Resources Characteristics

The first dominant factor in need of further attention in nonmarket literature is firm size and resources as measured by turnover. Some robust empirical findings of the literature are that large firms experience higher survival probabilities than smaller firms.[35] Size can provide several reasons to explain how firms can affect the policies in their industry. We suggest that industry size moderates the relationship between the nonmarket and the performance of the largest firms in that industry, expecting that if the relationship between nonmarket strategies and performance is positive, this effect will be more pronounced when firm size is larger. For example, Schuler's study of the U.S. steel industry finds that firm size positively affects firms' political involvement in trade protection.[36]

We propose that large firms in highly competitive industries have greater incentives to participate in political action, as they have both market share to defend from new entrants and greater internal resources to devote to non-market strategy. Firm resources also matter, as nonmarket strategy is likely to produce little payoff unless sustained over a period of time. To build on Porter, larger firms, because of the long-term orientation of their nonmarket strategy, face higher exit costs and must therefore adopt a more sustained approach to lobbying.[37] The long-term value creation from their investments in nonmarket strategy deters them from tolerating uncertainties in their competitive environment. It is, therefore, crucial for them to reduce uncertainties and costs and secure their nonmarket environment, and a nonmarket strategy may help to reduce any uncertainty.[38] Also, large firms attempt to establish ongoing ties with government to stay informed about upcoming government policies that may be critical and cumbersome for their business strategy.

Developing some of the ideas above, Lenway and Rehbein examined whether, during the 1976 to 1985 period, individual firms, trade associations, or labor unions filed petitions with the U.S. International Trade Commission to protect their domestic industries from foreign competition. Drawing from the collective-action perspective, they distinguish between "free riders" (companies that did not contribute), "followers" (companies that filed collective petitions via trade associations), and "leaders" (companies that filed individual petitions). Their conclusion: successful firms with greater resources can afford lobbying offices in Washington, DC, and, as such, enjoy existing political networks and easy access to legal and financial experts. Consequently, they are more likely to be leaders and to act alone when filing trade protection petitions.[39] Building on their previous research, Rehbein and Lenway elaborate on the effectiveness of political strategies when, as is the case for trade protection petitions with the U.S. International Trade Commission, a whole industry is the beneficiary. The authors suggest that because trade associations often lack authority (their political actions could be "diluted" if major firms within the industry do not back their petitions; they might not have enough industry-specific information to support their petitions), petitioning industries tend to be more successful if they instead file through an individual firm (or through a few firms).[40]

Hillman and Hitt emphasize that differences in financial and human resources are likely to influence the participation mode of an individual company.[41] Larger firms have greater financial resources and more human capital—including inside knowledge, expertise, and influence—and, as a result, tend to lobby alone. In contrast, to provide a "forceful voice" in the legislative arena, smaller firms with limited financial resources, experience, and authority tend to negotiate collectively, sharing their resources and lobbying costs with other members of a trade association.[42]

In a later study, Cook and Fox reiterate the significance of firm size and resources by comparing the political tactics used by medium-sized firms (100 to 499 employees) and smaller firms (fewer than 100 employees). The authors found that, because of limited resources, smaller firms tend to lobby collectively through trade associations or business chambers. More importantly, firm size is a predictor of success, as smaller firms are not as effective in their lobbying efforts as larger firms.[43] The authors temper their findings, however, and emphasize that the level of government matters for smaller firms, as they will be more inclined to act collectively at the state and federal levels and individually at the local level.[44]

Government Dependency Characteristics

The second main characteristic in nonmarket strategy scholarship is government dependency. Ozer and Lee suggest that the dependency of firms on government contracts or on outsized R&D investments will also govern corporate political behavior. Basing their research on federal-oriented PAC contributions of more than 2,000 U.S. manufacturing companies from 1999 to 2002, the authors argue that firms will be more inclined to act alone and more competitively when they are primarily reliant on government contracts or on potentially lucrative and risky long-term R&D expenditures, even when involved in a highly concentrated industry. Such firms tend to favor individual corporate PACs as opposed to industry-affiliated PACs.[45]

Fear of disclosing unique and competitive proprietary information will encourage a firm to act individually. After investigating the activities of corporations lobbying the Federal Communications Commission, the authors conclude that such companies are reluctant to collectively lobby via a trade association if they have to disclose and share sensitive proprietary information—such as future pricing or market penetration strategies—and, as a result, are more inclined to act individually.[46]

Ownership Characteristics

The third dominant factor that helps shape nonmarket strategy is ownership, a perspective that different scholars in the international business field have explored. Zingales's typology of ownership models of the firm helps to pin down the origins of different views about the role ownership plays.[47] Government ownership was an important governance structure in industries such as air transport, oil, pharmaceuticals, and banking in most parts of the world until the post-Cold War proliferation and adoption of capitalist values.

In many emerging markets, governments continue to exert high levels of control—including outright ownership—over large swaths of the economy.[48] Despite this global phenomenon, few nonmarket studies have explored how publicly listed firms with divergent ownership structures—consisting of mainly private investors or mainly government ownership—affect the development of nonmarket strategy across different industries.

For instance, Hadani does explore the impact of institutional ownership on corporate political strategies. Investigating the political activities of S&P 500 founding-family firms in the 1997 to 2000 U.S. federal election period, the author found that such family firms were more inclined to adopt a "relational" political approach, one that emphasizes building trusting, long-term relationships with policymakers. Under this relational approach, family firms tend to favor the use of more interpersonal political avenues, with a preference for soft-money contributions—especially those that help them cultivate long-term ties with a political party rather than with a specific legislator who may not be reelected.[49]

Despite the lack of ownership perspectives in the nonmarket and, more specifically, in CPA research, we suggest that industries that have more government-owned companies have smaller governmental affairs departments. On the one hand, a government-owned firm may have little need of a governmental affairs department, since its relationship with government authority is essentially symbiotic. On the other hand, government ownership may lead the firm to neglect the nonmarket environment, which ultimately leads to less information optimization and poorer performance. To build on the work of Lawton and Rajwani, ownership affects the size of governmental affairs departments, ultimately affecting firm performance.[50] However, the types of nonmarket strategies also need further attention here.

Types of Generic Nonmarket Strategies and Activities

The value and belief systems of management teams also tend to govern the participation level of firms. Meznar and Nigh develop two corporate political models: *bridging*, a firm's active role in promoting intra-industry change, and *buffering*, a firm's resistance to change. Their conclusion: high-level managers who value collaborative relationships with various stakeholders—competitors, customers, governmental institutions, or local community members—will be more inclined to "bridge" and thus collaborate with competitors and policymakers to gain legitimacy and credibility.[51]

Despite many multinational corporations using buffering and bridging political strategies, fear of exposure will also affect the political strategies of many foreign corporations. When comparing U.S. Fortune 500 companies to the largest foreign-owned firms operating in the U.S., Hansen and Mitchell found that while U.S. affiliates of foreign firms tend to use the same political strategies as their domestic counterparts, they also tend to favor more low-profile and indirect political activities, such as in-house lobbying, and to refrain from any direct contributions to a candidate, such as those through PACs, or from any participation in congressional hearings.[52]

Even the individual actions of corporate officers can influence the choices of how to configure nonmarket activities. Studying personal political contributions of executives from S&P 1500 corporations, Gordon, Hafer, and Landa found that such executives tend to contribute to an individual candidate or to a PAC if their compensation is closely related to, or dependent on, the performance and profitability of their firms, especially if their firms are indirectly vulnerable to unfavorable government policies. Moreover, this research found that, on many occasions, such executives simply contribute personally because it is easier, more flexible, and faster than corporate lobbying.[53]

Technology-Specific Factors

In addition to the conventional choice between individual and collective advocacy, there are new opportunities for engaging and influencing public policy and social actors using technologies. For example, many companies are increasingly engaging in grassroots action that bypasses traditional public policy interactions through innovative social technologies. A new form of lobbying, the currency of which is social connections via social networks rather than corporate donations or individual donations, is providing another avenue for advancing interests.[54] The way firms develop their offline nonmarket strategy is underpinned by financial, structural, knowledge, and relational resources, but the online nonmarket strategy is all about social relationships.[55] Indeed, the offline world is being complemented by emerging online networking strategies that amplify social interactions using what we call *online social lobbying*.

The earlier SOPA/PIPA example is an illustration of both of these trends. In this instance, the traditional forms and mechanisms for resolving differences over a legislative initiative were effectively bypassed by a grassroots campaign that leveraged the power of informational and communications technology and effectively upended the traditional legislative process. Building on this example and others, we see lobbying is fueled not only by money but also by social networks, despite these online relationships still being in their early stages and including different stakeholders at the grassroots level. Academic research currently lags in this area, but we believe that social lobbying will cut into the mainstream nonmarket research field in the future, especially as more firms in democratic countries around the world look at different ways to influence policymakers. It is hard to predict the kind of social lobbying that will emerge from the confluence of new social technologies and different stakeholders but it seems certain that advancing interests in this manner could benefit a greater number of people than those who are affected at the grassroots level. We are aware that lobbying firms use social media but because this can backfire, specific lobbying approaches and issues will always remain shielded from the general public, while broader campaigns may be used to influence majoritarian concerns.[56]

The Power of Grassroots

As we have maintained throughout this book, there is a strong rationale for firms to direct increasing attention—and increasing resources—to cultivating nonmarket strategies. While, in the past, these efforts have often targeted the legislative or regulatory environment, firms have lately become more cognizant of the perceived or explicit concerns, expectations, and demands of a broader group of stakeholders—nongovernmental organizations, community groups, employees, suppliers, and trade associations—and have frequently initiated community relations or CSR strategies to respond to these demands. Most recently, firms have begun pursuing a dual strategy directed at both political and social actors, sometimes engaging in collaborative relationships with those actors to advance a particular interest or set of interests.[57] One approach to managing interactions with stakeholders encompasses corporate grassroots and constituency building.

In addition to using relational and financial CPA, as described by Hillman and Hitt, firms can supplement in-house efforts to engage stakeholders through the campaign-building efforts of professional grassroots lobbying firms (PGLFs). Walker undertook a study of CPA[58] directed at a better understanding of the structural sources of firms' engagement in grassroots efforts used as a complement to (not a substitute for) traditional lobbying and other CPA engaged in grassroots efforts. He found that firms with an in-house external affairs office were also more likely to engage in grassroots efforts. In addition, firms in particular industries—information and communications, arts and entertainment, and taxation and government appropriations—were more likely to engage the public directly. He used the example of Phillip Morris employing multiple tactics—including engaging PGLFs to help mobilize individuals and other collectives (such as restaurant workers)—in its attempt to thwart efforts by public health advocates and others to eliminate or limit smoking in various settings. In this instance, Phillip Morris was ultimately unsuccessful because public health advocates were able to use their own grassroots efforts and coalition building with organized labor and others to push the legislation forward.

Tapping into Traditional and Social Media

Grassroots social lobbying—also called indirect lobbying—is a form of lobbying that focuses on growing awareness of a particular issue or cause at the local level. This approach is intended to reach a legislature or executive branch official through intermediate pressure on civil society or other local groups. Grassroots social lobbying is distinct from direct lobbying because it focuses on the *general society* or *firms who engage with society* to connect with legislators and political actors, as opposed to conveying the message directly to the government. Many companies are engaging in grassroots lobbying using social media to influence a change in legislation or affecting society as a whole in a responsible way.

In the era of Facebook, Reddit, Twitter, YouTube, blogs, tablets, and smartphones, the way firms use communities to interact with governments is crucial to maintaining their competitive advantage. Along with traditional print and broadcast campaigns, firms have used several social media-related tactics to promote and advocate different issues politically. In this way, they engage both offline and online communities to influence political actors to take notice of an issue, a tactic that is particularly prevalent in debates on energy.

Other firms are using these social technologies to generate social movements around CSR issues to help generate social value. For instance, PepsiCo describes the Pepsi Refresh Project on their webpage as follows: "Pepsi is giving away millions each month to fund refreshing ideas that change the world, one community at a time." If someone has an idea to refresh their community, they invite people to support the idea and vote for it. If the idea is approved, Pepsi will help fund it from a Pepsi Refresh Project grant.[59] The project aims to provide funding for those who have identified a problem and solution within their local community. These ideas range from community centers to funding for dance groups to costumes for Halloween for those who cannot afford them. There are specific grant cycles, and the funding categories range from $5,000 to $50,000. In total, PepsiCo is awarding up to $1.2 million each grant cycle to change society in a positive way.[60] The project uses crowdsourcing for both the idea generation and the idea selection, which creates two filters for submissions. This use of modern communication channels is expected to accelerate and will help to shape policy opinion and affect society as a whole. Firms that develop online nonmarket strategies using social media in conjunction with offline nonmarket strategies will not only create enhanced nonmarket positions, but can also defend themselves from different opponents in the nonmarket environment.

Conclusions and Managerial Implications

Companies are increasingly dealing with pressures from governmental and civil society stakeholders. Traditional companies require proactive collective and/or individual strategies directed toward both political and social actors. In our review of the collective action, CPA, and CSR literatures, we conclude that most firms would be well served to recognize the cultural, industry, firm, and technological factors in approaching individual or collective nonmarket strategies. We see that corporations like PepsiCo are using innovative ways to engage with political and social actors to develop their nonmarket strategies. Therefore, companies that understand the costs and benefits of both collective and individual action in the process of political and social strategy development and alignment will not only maintain their competitive advantage, but may also flourish in this environment. To summarize, the managerial implications of this chapter include:

- Companies should carefully consider when to pursue an individual versus collective approach to social and political strategy.

- Geographic and regional context, industry considerations, organizational scope and structure, and the specifics of a particular issue are all elements that will determine whether individual or collective action is more appropriate and likely to be more effective.

- In addition, the interest of the firm and the overall size of the group affected by the issue or challenge are also key determinants.

- In general, companies may underestimate the value of collective efforts because of concerns about competitive effects. Broad-based coalitions that include government agencies and NGOs can be especially influential and effective because they underscore the salience of, and support for, the issue. This is a topic we explore further in Chapter 9.

In the next chapter, we build on this chapter by drawing on the organizational design literature to inform questions and decisions about the organizational architecture for advancing nonmarket strategy. We will explore the development of internal structures of nonmarket strategy, identify the managerial responsibilities for political and social strategy, describe where it sits in the strategy process, offer examples of comparative structures, and synthesize this discussion to propose optimal managerial NMS architecture under varying environmental conditions.

Notes

   * Portions of this chapter have been adapted from Lawton, T., Rajwani, T., and Doh, J. (2013). The antecedents of political capabilities: a study of ownership, cross-border activity and organization at legacy airlines in a deregulatory context. *International Business Review*, 22(1): 228–242. Fanny D'Onofrio also provided helpful research assistance, including production of Figure 5.1 and preparation of article summaries from which a portion of the chapter is derived.

  1. Regenbogen, L.S. (2002). *Napoléon a dit: aphorismes, citations et opinions*. Paris: Les Belles Lettres: 16.

  2. Olson, M. (1965). *The logic of collective action: public goods and the theory of groups*. Cambridge, MA: Harvard University Press.

  3. Pure public goods are goods that are non-excludable (that is, one person cannot reasonably prevent another from consuming the good) and have no inherent rivalry (one person's consumption of the good does not affect another's, nor vice-versa). Hence, without selective incentives to motivate participation, collective action is unlikely to occur even when large groups of people with common interests exist.

  4. Hillman, A. J., Zardkoohi, A., and Bierman, L. (1999). Corporate political strategies and firm performance: indications of firm-specific benefits from personal service in the U.S. government. *Strategic Management Journal*, 20(1): 67–81.

  5. Barron 2010.

  6. Barron 2010: 105.

  7. Barron 2010: 109.

  8. Barron 2010: 105.

  9. Barron 2010: 109.

10. Hart, D.M. (2001). Why do some firms give? Why do some give a lot?: High-tech PACs, 1977–1996. *The Journal of Politics*, 63(4): 1230–1249.

11. Hart 2001.

12. Jacomet, D. (2005). The collective aspect of corporate political strategies: the case of U.S. and European business participation in textile international trade negotiations. *International Studies of Management and Organization*, 35(2): 78–93.

13. Jacomet 2005.

14. Tucker, A. (2008). Trade associations as industry reputation agents: a model of reputational trust. *Business and Politics*, 10(1): 1–26.

15. Tucker 2008: 3.

16. DiMaggio, P.J. and Powell, W.W. (1983). The iron cage revisited: institutional isomorphism and collective rationality in organizational fields. *American Sociological Review*, 48(2): 147–160.

17. Tucker 2008.

18. Schuler et al. 2002.
19. Schuler et al. 2002.
20. Hillman and Hitt 1999.
21. Hillman and Hitt 1999.
22. Hillman, A.J. (2003). Determinants of political strategies in U.S. multinationals. *Business & Society*, 42(4): 455–484.
23. Hillman 2003: 477.
24. Lord, M.D. (2000). Corporate political strategy and legislative decision-making. *Business & Society*, 39(1): 76–93.
25. Lord 2000: 82.
26. Grier, K., Munger, M., and Roberts, B. (1994). The determinants of industry political activity, 1978–1986. *The American Political Science Review*, 88(4): 911–926.
27. Schuler et al. 2002.
28. Gray, V. and Lowery, D. (1997). Reconceptualizing PAC formation: it's not a collective action problem, and it may be an arms race. *American Politics Quarterly*, 25(3): 319–346.
29. Gray and Lowery 1997: 326.
30. Masters, M. and Keim, G. (1985). Determinants of PAC participation among large corporations. *Journal of Politics*, 47: 1158 –1173.
31. Masters and Keim 1985: 1166.
32. Tucker 2008.
33. Wilson, G.K. (1990b). Corporate political strategies. *British Journal of Political Science*, 20(2): 281–288 (283).
34. Shaffer and Hillman 2000.
35. Mata, J. and Portugal, P. (1994). Life duration of new firms. *Journal of Industrial Economics*, 42(3): 323–343.
36. Schuler 1996.
37. Porter, M.E. (1980). *Competitive strategy: techniques for analyzing industries and competitors*. New York: Free Press.
38. Schuler et al. 2002.
39. Lenway, S.A. and Rehbein, K. (1991). Leaders, followers, and free riders: an empirical test of variation in corporate political involvement. *Academy of Management Journal*, 34(4): 893–905.
40. Rehbein, K. and Lenway, S. (1994). Determining an industry's political effectiveness with the U.S. International Trade Commission. *Business & Society*, 33(3): 270–292.
41. Hillman and Hitt 1999.
42. Hillman and Hitt 1999: 831.
43. Cook, R. and Fox, D. (2000). Resources, frequency, and methods: an analysis of small and medium-sized firms' public policy activities. *Business & Society*, 39(1): 94–113.
44. Cook and Fox 2000.
45. Ozer, M. and Lee, S.H. (2009). When do firms prefer individual action to collective action in the pursuit of corporate political strategy? A new perspective on industry concentration. *Business and Politics*, 11(1): 1–21.

46. De Figueiredo and Tiller 2001.
47. Zingales, L. (2000). In search of new foundations. *Journal of Finance*, 4: 1623–1653.
48. Bremmer, I. (2009) State capitalism comes of age. *Foreign Affairs*, 88: 48–55.
49. Hadani, M. (2007). Family matters: founding family firms and corporate political activity. *Business and Society*, 46(4): 395–428.
50. Lawton, T.C. and Rajwani, T. (2011). Designing lobbying capabilities: managerial choices in unpredictable environments. *European Business Review*, 23(2): 167–189.
51. Meznar, M.B. and Nigh, D. (1995). Buffer or bridge? Environmental and organizational determinants of public affairs activities in American firms. *Academy of Management Journal*, 38(4): 975–996.
52. Hansen and Mitchell 2000.
53. Gordon, S., Hafer, C., and Landa, D. (2007). Consumption or investment? On motivations for political giving. *The Journal of Politics*, 69(4): 1057–1072.
54. Rose, G. (2011). Opening up secrets: lobbyists and social media. <http://roseon-politics.com/2011/10/18/opening-up-secrets-lobbyists-and-social-media/> (accessed November 1, 2012).
55. Lawton, McGuire, and Rajwani 2013.
56. Rose 2011.
57. Yaziji, M. and Doh, J.P. (2009). *NGOs and corporations: conflict and collaboration*. Cambridge, U.K.: Cambridge University Press.
58. Walker, E.T. (2012). Putting a face on the issue: corporate stakeholder mobilization in professional grassroots lobbying campaigns. *Business & Society*, 51(4): 561–601.
59. PepsiCo. (2011a). Pepsi Refresh Project. <http://www.refresheverything.com> (accessed June 2, 2013).
60. PepsiCo. (2011b). How it works. <http://www.refresheverything.com/howit-works> (accessed June 2, 2013).

6

Designing Nonmarket Architecture*

Design is not just what it looks like and feels like. Design is how it works.[1]

Steve Jobs

In 2010, the Obama administration's $900 billion healthcare reform bill was forged against a backdrop of intense political and societal debate and acrimonious ideological differences. Aware of the legislation's long-term implications for the industry, individual organizations lobbied and engaged with the government on the bill's design and implementation. The input of firms such as Pfizer and GlaxoSmithKline and trade associations such as the Pharmaceutical Research and Manufacturers of America (PhRMA) was discreet but influential.[2] These organizations use external affairs departments to influence government and the general public in accordance with their needs and objectives and to share information within a given industry.[3] They are configured to exert influence in different ways, on a variety of actors, on an ad hoc or continuous basis.

As a consequence of the increasingly bifurcated individual and collaborative nature of nonmarket activity, which we described in Chapter 5, and the growing strategic importance of CPA and CSR, companies are putting in place new structural design configurations to advance their nonmarket interests. In addition to, and in conjunction with, decisions about whether to advance nonmarket strategy individually or with partners and other collaborators, firms must also consider the design of NMS architecture within their organizations. In the past, CSR- and CPA-related activities were often relegated to public affairs, public relations, marketing, or corporate-giving departments. However, increasingly, firms are considering a more managerially elevated (more senior-level decision-making) and organizationally integrated approach to nonmarket architecture.

For instance, in the mid-1990s, Lufthansa, like other major global airlines, faced interrelated challenges from increased pressure to adopt and incorporate greater fuel efficiency, reduce emissions, and develop a comprehensive social responsibility and sustainability strategy.[4] Unlike in previous eras, this pressure came from both governmental and regulatory agents and from community and NGO stakeholders. Consequently, the focus of Lufthansa's director of external affairs shifted from international traffic rights, slot allocations, and engagement with national legislators toward a more integrated approach that transcended the political and social arenas. In Chapter 12, we discuss Lufthansa's NMS architecture in greater detail.

The Lufthansa example shows the importance of an external affairs department and its NMS architecture in creating or defending success. This chapter advocates that large firms consider their nonmarket architecture in relation to external affairs, as many companies still maintain distinct and separate offices for these functions. This structural separation potentially leads to uncoordinated and at times competing—even conflicting—objectives and outcomes. The term *NMS architecture* has been loosely discussed in the management field,[5] and accordingly, building on ideas of Galbraith and Hillman et al.,[6] we define it as *the structure, roles, and reporting relationships in the externally focused nonmarket function within organizations*.

In this chapter, drawing on organization design literature[7] to inform questions and decisions about the organizational architecture for advancing different nonmarket strategies,[8] we suggest that firms with diverse strategic orientations (for instance, low cost or differentiation) may pursue different approaches. We start by looking at the function of external affairs and where it sits in an organization. We then describe how newer issues in the nonmarket environment—notably the increasing pressure on firms to engage in CSR and sustainability activities—have broadened and changed the structural approach to NMS. Finally, we explore the development of internal structures for NMS and managerial responsibility for successful political and social strategy, synthesizing the overall discussion to propose optimal managerial structure.

The Function and Positioning of External Affairs within an Organization

The notion of nonmarket architecture has been implicitly discussed in research into the function, practices, and profession of lobbying.[9] As Grunig argues, external affairs or public affairs is a management function concerned with identifying the stakeholders that firms affect and that affect them. The task of external relations managers is to build and maintain communication with these stakeholders.[10] In most large companies, the development of non-market practices is, therefore, not an individual management process but instead occurs under the aegis of a broader external affairs or public relations function. Pinkham perceives this function as a subset of corporate communications and public affairs.[11] In this view, external affairs focuses on the creation and maintenance of a specific set of external stakeholder relationships and policy outcomes, from which lobbying emerges as a primary tool for achieving organizational aims and objectives in political and social spheres.

Accepting that external affairs is a strategic management function rather than simply a publicity or media management exercise, and that most large companies have external affairs departments (sometimes known as industry or government affairs), we concentrate our discussion in this chapter on how to unpack and explain the evolution of political and social strategies within the external affairs resource bundle. Along these lines, Grunig further argues that involvement in strategic management is a critical characteristic of external affairs,[12] saying that it should not be subjugated to marketing or other management functions. Instead, it must be represented in the dominant group managing an organization (or at least have direct access to its most powerful and influential members).[13] We accordingly focus on political and social affairs as a subset of external affairs, noting that companies that are more effective in a nonmarket context are those in which political and social activities are developed as strategic capabilities and reflected in strategic plans developed at senior levels of the organization.

From Market to Nonmarket Architecture

As a prelude to examining nonmarket architecture frameworks to understand firm influence in the nonmarket environment, let us clarify several points deriving from key studies on organizational structure. Chandler provided the canonical reference for the notion of structure in his review of the development of four large U.S. firms[14]—DuPont; Standard Oil; Sears, Roebuck and Co.; and General Motors—finding that each embraced the concept of organizational divisions as it sought to grow. He suggested that modifications in product–market diversification strategies involved structural changes. Specifically, changes in strategy moved from a single-market focus to one that was vertically integrated and from being functionally structured to being structured around divisions.[15] This seminal study and Wasserman's subsequent work paved the way for future studies into strategy, structure, and performance.[16]

Nonetheless, Miles and Snow developed Chandler's work to make a typology of strategies to better understand various structures.[17] Organizations with defender strategies developed functional structures, prospectors operated divisional structures, and analyzers utilized matrix structures.[18] This perspective became the structure view that focused on how organizational characteristics fit with their changing environment.[19] Similarly, Blau and Schoenherr have suggested that structures come from specialization that creates a need for authority and rules.[20] However, criticisms of these studies need to be recognized, as they have focused on market factors without considering the nonmarket. More importantly, further empirical evidence on the relationship between firm nonmarket structures and influence has to be developed in the management literature despite some studies implicitly considering them.[21]

For instance, Lawton and Rajwani have used their work on structure to forge a better understanding of how firms build nonmarket influence.[22] We argue that influence is described as the process of shaping and establishing rules and norms.[23] Rather than seeing each nonmarket architectural factor alone as having an important impact on creating influence, we believe it is the linkage between them that is fundamental to understanding influence in the political and social arenas. Therefore, organizational structure is a natural foundational construct that helps to create influence in the political and social spheres.

As Porter noted,[24] the advantage of an organization is defined mainly by how it structures its value-creating activities in relation to its competitors and stakeholders. Taking an approach that is similar to the market view put forward by Porter, we find that the structure of the nonmarket function determines value activities in the nonmarket environment. An increasing body of research examining these design characteristics supports the shift in the unit of analysis from the market to nonmarket.[25] Research has implicitly or explicitly started to explore the size of external affairs departments, the level of centralization of decision-making, task specialization, and reputation development in the nonmarket environment. We next view and elaborate upon these key characteristics in relation to external affairs functions so as to better understand their influence in the nonmarket.

External Affairs Characteristics: Moving toward a Nonmarket Architecture Framework

Managers need a better understanding of the coordinated activities of the external affairs function. From existing market and nonmarket literatures, we propose an integrated framework using the key contingent constructs of *specialization*, *size*, *centralization*, and *reputation* to understand nonmarket architecture. Our framework is intended to create a better understanding of nonmarket structures in coordinating influence, as depicted in Figure 6.1. This framework provides a summary of key concepts that have been widely

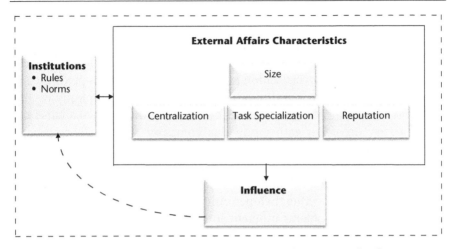

Figure 6.1 An integrated framework for nonmarket architecture and influence

investigated in the management literatures and that describe characteristics of nonmarket architectural variables within the external affairs function.

Size of External Affairs Function versus Firm Size

Research shows that firm size can determine success[26] and that the relative size of the external affairs function may contribute to the influence and power exerted in the nonmarket.[27] Despite the paucity of studies in the nonmarket looking at size, management theory on the market side prescribes that increasing organization size enables incremental advantages through the leveraging of scale to attain higher performance.[28] Scale and functional coordination can provide several reasons to explain how organizations can influence political and social actors. Consequently, larger organizations with specialized departments are more likely to be closer to the minimum efficient scale needed to operate effectively in a market and, therefore, likely to have higher nonmarket cost structures. External affairs departments may be structured differently, not only because of scale, but also because of cash constraints, which force firms to operate and coordinate this function on a smaller scale.[29] The combination of operational issues and organization size (usually measured by the number of employees) plays an important role in determining structure and performance. Therefore, depending on the nonmarket strategy of a given firm, we expect size to be positively related to resources and potential influence. However, influence will also depend on how the external affairs function explores and exploits the nonmarket environment and on the power and influence of the external affairs function and team *within* the organization.

Task Specialization

The tasks undertaken within the external affairs department help to develop more coherent nonmarket strategy through the division of labor. We refer to the notion of task specialization as a configuration of tasks performed by agents who are measured and rewarded in certain ways.[30] Typically we find that the tasks performed by employees or agents for the external affairs function have two steps: first, gather individual company data, usually on production or demand; and secondly, distribute aggregate information to members of the firm and various stakeholders outside the firm.[31] However, we believe that having incorrect structural configurations of tasks and responsibilities can hinder firms in meeting their performance objectives.[32] Previous research has looked at the problems inherent in the performance of organizations, depicting the impetus for the development of staff specializations to maximize efficiency and better coordination through the design of work. Bearing this logic in mind, we believe subfunctions such as external affairs can also maximize efficiency based on task specialization in influencing the political and social spheres.

Management literatures focused on the theme of tasks have tried to research areas such as task complexity, workflow integration, and task interdependence.[33] However, these studies, heavily reliant on design theory, were developed in an era in which manufacturing and production work was the dominant form. As a consequence we find that some of the distinctive characteristics of external affairs functions, such as the intangibility of lobbying, link to task specialization. Therefore, most external affairs functions will have invisible and visible tasks, the measurement of which can allow progress toward the task's completion to be monitored directly by the director of external affairs. More importantly, nonmarket tasks to influence political and social actors can generally be examined, rationalized, and broken down into subelements that can be integrated through the use of two specializations—communications and policy.

We argue that specialization within the external affairs function is done through communications and policy tasks, which are sometimes co-aligned in companies. Scott and Davis illustrate that specialization can lead to increased efficiency and effectiveness.[34] Therefore, we believe that external affairs departments must ensure that the right tools are in the right place at the right time for the work to be performed, and they must continue to improve their communications tasks (media activities via radio, TV, and other outlets) and policy tasks (white-paper writing and information-exchanging activities) to share their interests.

With this rationalization of task design, we begin to see the challenges that specialization can raise in the external affairs department. According to Fredrickson, formalization of structure around a particular function can reduce assertiveness.[35] We argue that handling both of these tasks in the external affairs function can increase nonmarket performance by making it proactive and focused in the nonmarket, by solving problems, monitoring threats, and searching for opportunities. But relying more on one type of task than the other may cause a company to miss potential threats in political or social circles.

Centralization in the External Affairs Function

Firms naturally need to examine their internal coordination mechanisms to deal with issues that arise.[36] Empirical research suggests that firms require a structure that balances the level of democracy with centralization of decision-making to let them move at a pace that is fast enough to deliver results but democratic enough to respond to stakeholder needs.[37] We argue that centralization—some scholars refer to it as centrality—represents the extent to which decision-making and responsibility for aligning interests are shared with support functions such as marketing or finance.[38] In the context of the external affairs function, we can easily distinguish between centralized and decentralized structures. In a centralized structure, a dedicated unit creates and leads the nonmarket strategy, while affiliates remain subordinate to the main function. In a decentralized structure, the responsibility for nonmarket issues might sit in the marketing department or fall to the top management team to handle in a purely reactive way.

Centralization can diminish the perceived need for interaction by inducing conformity of goals and methods through the implementation of specific tasks rather than through discussion.[39] On the other hand, when many managers have authority to make lobbying decisions, as seen in decentralization structures, there is a risk of conflicting perspectives and, consequently, more need to resolve resulting disagreements. Issues arise that clearly involve multiple managers and engender consensus-building interaction.[40] An absence of interaction can in turn foster fragmentation and poor structure at the firm, and result in reduced influence.

In general, centralizing nonmarket strategy through the external affairs function encourages rationality by placing most of the onus of influencing on the director of external affairs and his or her team. We argue that being able to involve other senior executive members democratically in a centralized structure may lead to enhanced performance. Moreover, centralizing the running of external affairs is a key to creating influence. We speculate that this may increase organizational reputation, as the resultant decision-making is more focused and better coordinated.

Reputation

While centralization may be positively correlated with influence, it also undoubtedly affects the reputation of a firm. Large firms command—and attract—attention from various stakeholders. Accordingly, larger external affairs functions, task specialization, and centralization within those functions offer the potential for building reputation with governmental and nongovernmental stakeholders.

The reputation literature in management studies is typically focused on individual organizations.[41] Roberts and Dowling conceptualize reputation as a perceptual representation of a company's past actions and future prospects, describing the firm's overall appeal to key constituents compared with that of leading rivals.[42] Another view of reputation, drawn from an economics perspective, suggests that stakeholders evaluate the organizational attributes of a particular firm or approach it from an institutional viewpoint in which constituents assess the firm's prominence—often via institutional intermediaries and experts—within a broader organizational field. That field may include other firms that comprise a comparative set, so that reputation is made a relative—as opposed to an absolute—calculation.[43] Therefore, building on Bromley and others, we characterize and define reputation here in terms of nonmarket architecture as *a distribution of nonmarket opinions about an organization that results in a collective image about that entity in the political and social spheres.*[44]

King and Whetten note that the concepts of reputation and, broadly, legitimacy are closely intertwined and propose a hierarchical ordering in their effort to develop the relationship between the two. They argue that legitimacy captures an organization's conformity with a *general* set of expected standards, while reputation reflects a view that an organization has achieved a *special, distinctive* standing among its peers.[45] Deephouse and Carter also emphasize that reputation is based on a comparative assessment.[46] Therefore, we believe that external affairs functions must focus on developing and maintaining their reputations using their interrelated variables of tasks, size, and centralization.

Firms increasingly gain reputational enhancement from how their actions are viewed by political and social stakeholders.[47] These include broad rankings and ratings, such as *Fortune*'s "Most Admired" and "Best Companies to Work For," and more specific rankings measuring their efforts at being socially responsible or "good corporate citizens." We believe that external affairs functions that are sufficiently well staffed and centralized and for which tasks are clearly defined, have the potential to support legitimacy and proactively invest in activities that preserve and enhance reputation.

External Affairs Functions: Using Political and Social Strategies in the Nonmarket

Building on the key variables identified above and on our nonmarket architecture framework (Figure 6.1), we next demonstrate how a specific U.K. bank dealt with the issues arising from the banking and financial crisis of 2008. There is evidence to suggest that various firms in the banking industry played a pivotal role in creating new codes of practice in liquidity standards while also managing to avoid regulation that would have reduced their profits.[48]

While securing some bailout funding, Barclays Bank also protected its interests from regulation that would have split its investment banking from its retail banking division.[49] Its influence varied from direct meetings with members of parliament (MPs) to sharing consultation papers with the Bank of England and European Commission on ways to deal with the credit crisis. Moreover, its external affairs department, headed at the time by Howell James, successfully used its centralized functions—a large number of resources, substantial team size, and specialized roles—to lobby key political and social actors on a number of issues.[50] The firm also aided the British Bankers Association (an influential trade association) in developing position documents with regards to securing bailout funding for major financial institutions such as Northern Rock and Royal Bank of Scotland.[51] However, the bank's reputation was subsequently affected by scandals such as the manipulation of interbank lending rates (the Libor scandal) and its high-risk appetite for subprime mortgages. As a result, the company tried to improve its diminished reputation with CSR projects including the funding of charities, aid for start-ups across the U.K., and the development of new codes of practice in trading.

Acknowledging the influence of Barclays and its external affairs function, our nonmarket architectural view of influence in firms suggests that the process and structure of the external affairs function should converge over time. While some scholars believe that structural changes may spread at first for performance reasons,[52] we argue that the external affairs function should focus on creating, enhancing, or protecting reputation rather than on promoting actual performance. We believe that the legitimacy and influence prospects of the external affairs function depend on its structure. Consequently, we see two potential nonmarket strategies that need to be aligned with nonmarket architecture—political orientation and social responsiveness, as shown in Figure 6.2. However, some organizations may adopt both responses or focus primarily on one response, depending on the issue.

As we have seen from the case of Barclays and other examples in previous chapters, companies increasingly face concurrent and coordinated pressures from governmental and civil society stakeholders. The traditional separation

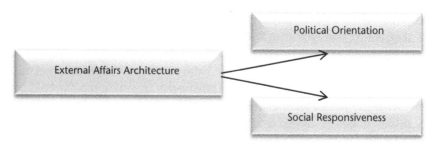

Figure 6.2 Nonmarket architecture and nonmarket strategy

between legal or regulatory affairs functions and corporate activities focused on a broader set of stakeholders (such as NGOs and community groups) may no longer be viable. Issues like climate change, financial regulation and disclosure, cybercrime and terrorism, and the labor and human rights of workers in developing countries all require proactive strategies directed toward both political and social actors and institutions. Some companies are well served to recognize the interdependencies of the political and social environments and those engaged within them, and to consequently unify these managerial functions. Certain companies deploy external affairs functions to respond to both social and political stimuli.

In the next part, we explore the external affairs function in more detail. We argue that an aligned approach to the external political and social arenas will ensure that companies are more effective in nonmarket strategy. We also argue that ensuring functional alignment—if not integration—between CPA and CSR activities within their organizational structures can ultimately serve to protect or promote competitive advantage.

Does Everyone Need an External Affairs Function?

In short, yes. The real question is: How do you configure it? In Figure 6.3 we advance four options for the external affairs architecture of a company, depending on the nonmarket emphasis and related significance.

Political orientation relates to companies that face nonmarket challenges emanating primarily from the political and regulatory arenas and that respond by designating a senior executive to explore or exploit legislative and regulatory affairs. This is common, for instance, in the airline sector (where, at British Airways, the manager of political affairs coordinates lobbying activities to remove or reduce carbon emission taxes) and in the pharmaceuticals sector

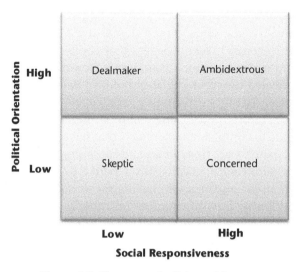

Figure 6.3 The external affairs architecture

(where, for instance, the director of public affairs at Teva Pharmaceuticals campaigned in support of the U.S. Patent Reform Act of 2011).

Social responsiveness relates to companies that explicitly tackle CSR-related issues and have placed executives at relatively senior positions to oversee CSR, sustainability, and community relations. This is particularly pertinent to companies in the extractive and construction industries.[53] For instance, the global building-materials supplier CEMEX has sustainability directors in its country subsidiaries—and a corporate director of sustainability at its headquarters in Mexico—to advance a longstanding strategic commitment to sustainability, biodiversity, and the reduction of CO_2 emissions. Political orientation and social responsiveness help managers and scholars to classify the fundamental methods that businesses use to deal with such issues through developing related nonmarket tasks. Beyond mapping these important issues, our framework serves as an evaluative tool that can enable executives to gauge their current status and form pathways for future changes in executive suite composition and responsibilities.[54]

We next consider each quadrant of Figure 6.3 to understand external affairs design options and choices. The framework does not predict outcomes, but it does advance insights on potential consequences.

High Political Orientation and High Social Responsiveness

In the scenario depicted in the top right-hand quadrant of Figure 6.3 (*ambidextrous*), the fact that a trade-off or compromise is required does not imply that organizations cannot pursue both activities equally within their external affairs function(s). While some empirical evidence highlights the difficulty in achieving this, research acknowledges that combining the roles and the resource weighting can produce advantages.[55] Nonmarket studies have not properly investigated how firms balance political and social activities in an ambidextrous way. But other technology-related studies give us some ideas on how firms can create these balances in other functions.[56] To some extent this might be due to complementary effects that have not received sufficient attention in the past.[57] Cao, Gedajlovic, and Hongping note that the repeated use of existing knowledge may create a better understanding of where resources reside in an organization, facilitating various reconfigurations of knowledge and resources within firms.[58] In other words, a trade-off situation might be inevitable in external affairs departments that are relatively resource-constrained. This also points to a lack of clarity as to what exactly we mean by balancing nonmarket political and social strategies to influence political or social actors and institutions. One dimension of this consideration could be the relative amount of political compared with social, while a second dimension might focus on the combined magnitude of the two. Both of these nonmarket strategies are likely to have an impact on performance in terms of reducing negative externalities or increasing policy attainment.

Low Political Orientation and High Social Responsiveness

In this *concerned* quadrant, we find companies that are more responsibility-focused and less politically fixated and active. CSR is more than a philanthropic add-on in this scenario. Instead, it is embedded within the business model. Firms in this space embody a belief that CSR is a market differentiator and can further lead to sustainable operations that have a positive impact on society. In this regard, the company's CSR function is strategically vital but its political focus is often moderate or low. Moreover, as with any process based on social responsiveness, there is no one approach. In different countries, there are various points of attention and values that will influence how organizations behave. For instance, the Tata Power Company (TPC) has undertaken CSR activities for decades, reflecting the parent group's ethos and the company's promise to deliver sustainable energy without compromising the human and environmental contexts. These actions are assumed by the employees of TPC to be voluntary schemes and not firm-level CSR strategies. However, with large-scale market expansion, the top management team perceived a need to have CSR as a separate function.[59] Therefore, the dilemma for the top management team was whether to go for a separate CSR department or persist with the existing setup. Tata Power eventually decided to focus on developing its CSR function but did not create a politically oriented government affairs department, as management argued that the company could achieve those goals via the CEO or through outsourcing to a third-party consultant if needed.[60]

Low Political Orientation and Low Social Responsiveness

In this situation, neither political nor social activism is given strategic priority. Building on our discussion in Chapter 2 and on research questioning ethical consumerism,[61] we argue that the effectiveness of this approach is contingent on the market position a firm occupies. Consequently, the *skeptics* tend to be price-based competitors. The need for political and social activism is generally more pertinent for firms that compete on the basis of differentiated products or services predicated on service quality, product innovation, reputation, and brand. This is especially true for firms in market segments where customers are highly influenced by corporate reputation and brand image. In contrast, low-cost competitors such as the U.K. food retailer Iceland or European budget airline leader Ryanair have no need to transition from short-term, needs-based CSR and CPA to long-term, values-based advocacy. Their customers and shareholders are concerned about cheap deals and return on investment, and place little value on social and political awareness and activism. The stakeholder requirement to be socially responsible and to have a harmonious long-term relationship with government is not a strategic priority for price leaders. As such, cost leadership competitors are unlikely to see political advocacy or CSR as a strategic function and are more likely to view it as a strategic hindrance, serving only to add cost and complexity. Therefore, the function and structure here will be driven mainly by the CEO or top management team instead of a mid-level department.

High Political Orientation and Low Social Responsiveness

The *dealmaker* occupies the final quadrant of Figure 6.3. These are firms that are politically engaged but do not participate much, if at all, in social initiatives. These are often state-owned or state-influenced enterprises, in which government activities and political events are integral to the strategic management options and decisions of the enterprise. Actions can only occur through negotiation and bargaining with external political actors. In most contexts, dealmakers compete with each other for political access and influence. As we will discuss in the next section, this type of external configuration is commonly found in many emerging and transitional economies but also in developed economies with firms that are heavily dependent on public procurement contracts.

Nonmarket Architecture Globally: Historical Considerations for Moving Forward

To move forward in developing external affairs functions, one must first look to the past. While firms are actively developing external affairs departments to deal with political and social issues, these functions have evolved differently in various parts of the world because of either colonial effects or variations in sociopolitical and cultural systems. Moreover, structures within the external affairs function have also varied from country to country because of different market-led principles and business-like structures and standards.

For instance, as we see in the public policy literature, the U.S. political system operates in the context of a federal structure and a written constitution, in which firms legitimately interact with social, political, and legal actors and institutions to create value in the market and nonmarket.[62] Therefore, within the U.S. context, the nonmarket system has been adjusting and changing with time, economic change, and social pressures,[63] affecting the design and structure of corporate external affairs. However, there is a disparity between the functioning of the U.S. political and social system from the 1960s—as a state model of inputs and outputs—and the current political and social system, which is more dominated by interests.[64]

The situation in the EU is very different from that in the U.S. Each EU nation has created different approaches to the role of the state in society and the economy, in some cases dating back more than a thousand years.[65] What we know from history is that each European state has been exposed to high uncertainty during the 20th century, ranging from fascism to communism, occupation, civil war, and empire breakdown.[66] From the early 1990s on, following the fall of the Berlin Wall, the reunification of eastern and western Europe, and increased globalization, we witnessed the development and legitimization of the external affairs function in most large corporations across Europe.[67] To influence individual and collective political systems, firms have needed a sense of history and cultural empathy. In addition, they have had to develop a nonmarket function that applies to both political and social spheres. We argue that firms in Europe and the U.S. started developing specific structures to deal with nonmarket forces, usually from within public affairs practice. Indeed, good public affairs practice at an EU level has required sensitivity to national, regional, and local identities, since sensitivity to ethnic identity is built into the national structure of each state. Perhaps the differences within Europe are underlined by the fact that the EU operates with more than twenty official languages.[68] Both the U.S. and the EU highlight the variation required by a firm when structuring external affairs functions to deal with different institutional environments. The complexity increases when we consider other parts of the world such as Southeast Asia and sub-Saharan Africa.[69]

For most Asian and African external affairs functional structures, we can discern three distinct periods of nonmarket evolution. If we use Haque's study as a basis, these are the *colonial,* the *postcolonial,* and the current *new nonmarket* stages.[70] However, considerable gaps between these ideal periods have shaped the actual administrative practices and structures of external affairs in Asia and Africa.[71] The evolution has developed variations among countries in these regions in terms of the extent to which they conform to the original models because of their differences in colonial backgrounds and national contexts. For instance, Thailand has developed a very different nonmarket context from that of many of its Southeast Asian neighbors because it was the only country in the region not to be colonized by a European power.

A history of colonization deeply affects the nature of nonmarket legal systems, administration, and business and industry norms and behaviors.[72] Countries as diverse as Malaysia, Nigeria, Kenya, Tanzania, Nigeria, Gambia, Uganda, and Singapore share the common legacy of the British Empire. Indonesia and South Africa experienced Dutch influence. The Philippines came under both Spanish and American control at different times in its history. Cambodia, Vietnam, Algeria, Tunisia, and Morocco were all ruled by the French and share some commonalities as a consequence.[73]

Building on the idea of external affairs functions dealing with variations in the political and social environment globally, we note that, in a well-established and consistent environment, these functions can operate with obvious benefits to integrating market strategies with nonmarket strategies.[74] However, multinational firms must consider how their external affairs departments adapt to regulatory quality and political instability in the new territories, especially when they have foreign-owned business units in different countries.

Conclusions and Managerial Implications

This chapter explored the ideas of nonmarket architecture and external affairs functions. We find that companies are increasingly facing concurrent and coordinated pressures from governmental and civil society stakeholders. Therefore, the traditional separation between legal or regulatory affairs functions and corporate activities focused on a broader set of stakeholders is not appropriate. Many large organizations have developed dedicated external affairs departments to deal with political and social aspects of the nonmarket environment.

We adopt an organizational design perspective to better understand the external affairs function and consider structural issues in understanding task specialization, centralization, size, and reputation to create influence in the nonmarket. We argue that most firms would be well served to recognize the interdependencies between the political and social environments and the executives engaged within them to unify these functions. We also acknowledge that these external affairs functions will vary across the world as a result of institutional voids, colonial legacy, and market dynamics. In summary, there are several key learning points in this chapter for strategic managers and business leaders:

- Nonmarket architecture consists of task specialization, centralization, and size, which, if managed appropriately, can help to develop a reputation that leads to influence in the nonmarket.

- External affairs functions that have a policy specialization and a communications specialization are likely to have greater influence in policy attainment and/or social engagement. While having dual specializations increases costs, it may lead to greater benefits.

- External affairs functions that have greater centralization in decision-making are likely to react more quickly to political and social issues.

- Managers should be aware that how they approach and structure their external affairs functions and activities is likely to be contingent on their basis of competition (differentiator versus low cost, built-in as opposed to bolt-on responsibility) and on the nature of ownership of the company.

In the next chapter we will introduce a comprehensive and robust political and social strategy framework for incubating interest: the *creating, controlling, coordinating, and changing* (4C) framework. This framework offers a specific approach to alignment that unifies a range of disparate elements. We introduce concepts and mechanisms for interests as a way to describe how firms can deal with the complex market and nonmarket conditions in their environment and leverage the information they obtain to create the conditions for a more receptive and responsive set of governmental and non-governmental stakeholders. Moreover, we discuss the nature and purpose of interest representation and survey the management and policy literatures to introduce key concepts and consider the roots of modern corporate interest mobilization within the political and social spheres.

Notes

* Portions of this chapter have been adapted from Lawton, McGuire, and Rajwani 2013 and Doh, J.P., Howton, S.D., Howton, S.W., and Siegel, D.S. (2010). Does the market respond to an endorsement of social responsibility? The role of institutions, information, and legitimacy. *Journal of Management,* 36(6): 1461–1485.

1. Walker, R. (2003). *The Guts of a New Machine.* <http://www.nytimes.com/2003/11/30/magazine/the-guts-of-a-new-achine.html> (accessed November 20, 2012).

2. Drug Watch (2012). *The influence of Big Pharma in America.* <http://www.drugwatch.com/2012/01/19/influence-of-big-pharma/> (accessed November 28, 2012).

3. Tumulty, K and Scherer, M. (2009). How drug-industry lobbyists won on health-care. *Time Magazine.* <http://www.time.com/time/magazine/article/0,9171,1931729,00.html> (accessed November 5, 2012).

4. See also Lawton, T.C. (2012b). Why your company needs a second CEO. *U.S. News & World Report.* November 2. <http://www.usnews.com/opinion/blogs/economic-intelligence/2012/11/02/why-your-company-needs-a-second-ceo> (accessed June 4, 2013).

5. Coen, D. and Willman, P. (1998). The evolution of the firm's regulatory affairs office. *Business Strategy Review,* 9(4): 31–36; Hillman et al. 2004.

6. Galbraith, J.R. (1973). *Designing complex organizations.* Reading, MA: Addison-Wesley; Hillman et al. 2004.

7. Galbraith, J.R. (1977). *Organizational design.* Reading, MA: Addison-Wesley.

8. Galbraith 1973.

9. Pedler, R. (ed.) (2002). *European Union lobbying: changes in the arena,* Basingstoke: Palgrave Macmillan; Coen et al. 2010.

10. Grunig, J.E. (2006). Furnishing the edifice: ongoing research on public relations as a strategic management function. *Journal of Public Relations Research,* 18: 151–176.

11. Pinkham, D.G. (1998). Corporate public affairs: running faster, jumping higher. *Public Relations Quarterly,* 43(2): 33–37.

12. Grunig 2006.

13. Richardson and Jordan 1979.

14. Chandler 1962.

15. Wasserman, N. (2008). Revisiting the strategy, structure, and performance paradigm: the case of venture capital, *Organization Science,* 19(2): 241–259.

16. Wasserman 2008.

17. Miles, R.E., Snow C.C., Meyer A.D., and Coleman H.J. (1978). Organizational strategy, structure, and process. *Academy of Management Review,* 3(3): 546–562.

18. Wasserman 2008.

19. Mitzberg, H. (1979). *The structuring of organizations: a synthesis of the research.* Englewood Cliffs, NJ: Prentice Hall. See also Miller, D. (1996). Configurations revisited. *Strategic Management Journal,* 17: 505–512.

20. Blau, P.M. and Schoenherr, P.A. (1971). *The structure of organizations.* New York: Basic Books.

21. Hillman et al. 1999.
22. Lawton and Rajwani 2011.
23. DiMaggio, P.J., (1988). Interest and agency in institutional theory. In L.G. Zucker (ed.). *Institutional patterns and organizations: culture and environment*. Cambridge, MA: Ballinger Publishing: 3–21.
24. Porter, M.E. (1991). Towards a dynamic theory of strategy. *Strategic Management Journal*, 12 (S2): 95–117.
25. Lawton and Rajwani 2011.
26. Mata and Portugal 1994.
27. Lawton, Rajwani, and Doh 2013.
28. Archibugi, D., Rinaldo, E., and Simonetti, R. (1995). Concentration, firm size and innovation: evidence from innovation costs. *Technovation*, 15(3): 153–163.
29. Lawton, Rajwani, and Doh 2013.
30. Galbraith 1977.
31. Lawton, Rajwani, and Doh 2013.
32. Lenox, M.J and Nash, J. (2003). Industry self-regulation and adverse selection: a comparison across four trade association programs. *Journal of Business Strategy and the Environment*, 12: 1–14.
33. Lawrence, P.R. and Lorsch, J.W. (1967). *Organization and environment: managing differentiation and integration*. Unpublished manuscript, Harvard University.
34. Scott, W.R. and Davis, G.F. (2006). *Organizations and organizing: rational, natural, and open systems perspectives*. Upper Saddle River, NJ: Pearson Prentice Hall.
35. Fredrickson, G. (1980). The lineage of new public administration. In C.J. Bellone (ed.). *Organization theory and the new public administration*. Boston, MA: Allyn & Bacon.
36. Mintzberg, H. (1973). *The nature of managerial work*. New York: Harper & Row Publishers.
37. Willman, P., Coen, D., Currie, D., and Siner, M. (2003). The evolution of regulatory relationships; regulatory institutions and firm behavior in privatized industries, *Industrial and Corporate Change*, 12(1): 69–89.
38. Miller, D. (1987). Strategy making and structure: analysis and implications for performance. *Academy of Management Journal*, 1: 7–32; Van de Ven, A.H., Delbecq, A.L., and Koening, R. (1976). Determinants of coordination modes within organizations. *American Sociological Review*, 41: 322–338.
39. Cloudman, R. and Hallahan, K. (2006). Crisis communications preparedness among U.S. organizations: activities and assessments by public relations practitioners. *Public Relations Review*, 32(4): 367–376.
40. Knoke, D. (1990). *Organizing for collective action: the political economics for associations*. New York: Aldine de Gruyter.
41. Berens, G. and van Riel, C.B.M. (2004). Corporate associations in the academic literature: three main streams of thought in the reputation measurement literature. *Corporate Reputation Review*, 7(2): 161–178.
42. Roberts, P.W. and Dowling G.R. (2002). Corporate reputation and sustained superior financial performance. *Strategic Management Journal*, 23: 1077–1093.
43. Rindova, V.P., Williamson, I.O., Petkova, A.P., and Sever, J.M. (2005). Being good or being known: an empirical examination of the dimensions, antecedents, and

consequences of organizational reputation. *Academy of Management Journal*, 48: 1033–1049.

44. Bromley D.B. (2001). Relationships between personal and corporate reputations. *European Journal of Marketing*, 35: 316–334.

45. King, B.G. and Whetten, D.A. (2008). A social identity formulation of organizational reputation and legitimacy. *Corporate Reputation Review*, 11: 192–207.

46. Deephouse, D.L. and Carter, S.M. (2005). An examination of differences between organizational legitimacy and organizational reputation. *Journal of Management Studies*, 42: 329–360.

47. Fombrun, C.J. (1996). *Reputation: realizing value from the corporate image.* Cambridge, MA: Harvard Business School Press.

48. BBC (2012a). *Barclays: Cameron says bank faces serious questions.* <http://www.bbc.co.uk/news/business-18622264> (accessed November 28, 2012).

49. Who is lobbying? (2012) *Barclays Group.* <http://whoslobbying.com/uk/barclays_group> (accessed November 28, 2012).

50. Rogers, D. (2012). *Barclays corporate affairs chief Howell James steps down.* <http://www.brandrepublic.com/news/1155351/> (accessed November 28, 2012).

51. Jenkins, P. (2010). Poll finds solid support for tougher action. *Financial Times*, January 24: a report of the results of a Financial Times/Harris poll in which 80 percent of respondents thought there should be a cap on bankers' salaries and bonuses. <http://www.ft.com/cms/s/0/22a05e66-0952-11df-ba88-00144feabdc0.html#axzz2eiPfcqm9> (accessed on May 20, 2013). For further details, see Black, J. (2010). *Managing the financial crisis: the constitutional dimension.* London: LSE Law, Society and Economy Working Papers.

52. Jepperson, R.L. (1991). Institutions, institutional effects, and institutionalism. In W.W. Powell and P.J. DiMaggio (eds.). *The new institutionalism in organizational analysis.* Chicago, IL: University of Chicago Press: 143–163.

53. Also for other high visibility industries as we will discuss further in Chapter 9.

54. The framework is used here to explore and speculate, in order to go beyond simplistic explanations and see a range of structures to influence political and social actors.

55. Lawton, Rajwani, and Doh 2013.

56. Taylor, A. and Helfat, C.E. (2009). Organizational linkages for surviving technological change: complementary assets, middle management, and ambidexterity. *Organization Science*, 20(4): 718–740.

57. Van Deusen, C.A. and Mueller, C.B. (1999). Learning in acquisitions: understanding the relationship between exploration, exploitation and performance, *The Learning Organization*, 6(3-4): 186–193.

58. Cao, Q., Gedajlovic, E., and Hongping, Z. (2009). Unpacking organizational ambidexterity: dimensions, contingencies, and synergistic effects. *Organization Science*, 20(4): 781–797.

59. Deshmukh, R. and Adhikari, A. (2009). *TATA Power: corporate social responsibility and sustainability.* Oikos Case Writing Competition, 2nd prize in sustainability category. St. Gallen, Switzerland: Oikos International.

60. Deshmukh and Adhikari 2009.

61. McWilliams, A. and Siegel, D. (2011). Creating and capturing value: strategic corporate social responsibility, resource-based theory and sustainable competitive advantage. *Journal of Management,* 37(5): 1480–1495.

62. Przeworski, A. (2000). *Democracy and development: political institutions and well-being in the world, 1950–1990.* New York: Cambridge University Press.

63. Spencer, T. (2013). The external environment of public affairs in the European Union: public policy, processes and institutions. <http://www.tomspencer.info/articles/PublicAffairsHandbook.pdf> (accessed March 22, 2013).

64. Spencer 2013.

65. Spencer 2013.

66. Spencer 2013.

67. Pedler 2002.

68. Spencer 2013.

69. Pedler 2002.

70. Haque, M.S. (1996). The contextless nature of public administration in Third World countries. *International Review of Administrative Sciences,* 62(3): 315–329.

71. Painter, M. (2004). *Public sector challenges and government reforms in South East Asia: Report 2001.* Research Institute for Asia and the Pacific, University of Sydney, Australia.

72. Hughes, O. (2003), *Public management and administration: an introduction.* 3rd ed. Basingstoke: Palgrave Macmillan.

73. Hughes 2003.

74. Garton Ash, T. (2000). *History of the present: essays, sketches, and dispatches from Europe in the 1990s.* New York: Random House.

Section III
Creating Aligned Strategy

7

Sensing to Incubate Interest*

A wise ruler ought never to keep faith
when by doing so it would be against his interests.[1]

Niccolò Machiavelli

In the aftermath of colossal financial losses in 2008 and 2009 and a subsequent historic bailout, the U.S. banking sector attracted intense regulatory scrutiny. In late 2009, the U.S. House of Representatives passed the Wall Street Reform and Consumer Protection Act. The key provisions mandated greater oversight and transparency of transactions and established resolution authority to allow financial firms to be unwound in an orderly fashion after failure. In this context, those with an interest in political and social action included corporate clients, trade unions, the U.S. Chamber of Commerce, the American Bankers Association, the International Financial Management Association (IFMA), and other interest groups.[2] Financial institutions with a vested interest in the nature and extent of new legislation and regulatory oversight included JP Morgan, Goldman Sachs, and Morgan Stanley. Together, these companies spent around $400 million during 2010 alone in attempts to influence the direction of U.S. financial reform.[3] Countervailing interests came in the form of the newly established Consumer Finance Protection Bureau (CPFB) and housing and labor groups, which lobbied hard for greater government control over banking and finance. The outcome was a reworked 2,300-page bill, now known as the Dodd-Frank Wall Street Reform and Consumer Protection Act, signed into law in the summer of 2010. Billed as an effort to prevent a repeat of the financial crisis, the Dodd-Frank Act was a victory for those favoring greater oversight of U.S. banking and financial services. Senior management at large financial institutions did not publicly oppose the new legislation for fear of a popular and political backlash. Instead, they lobbied discreetly behind the scenes for preferential carve-outs to offset what they called the costly and often contradictory demands of the act.[4]

In 2009, Suzlon, a large Indian-based wind turbine producer and a global player in the renewable-energy sector, deployed extensive resources to inform citizens and policymakers about the advantages of wind energy.[5] The company faced the challenge of getting legislation in place to nurture the development of renewable power, particularly in the U.S., but also elsewhere around the world.[6] Through the efforts of its top management team, Suzlon helped influence the discussion on sustainability and renewable power through organizations such as the European Commission, the World Economic Forum, and the United Nations, as well as through an active outreach program to the media.[7] It offset counter-interests from the nuclear and oil industries and developed its own market and nonmarket strategies to ensure that its interests were heard. Suzlon's chairman and managing director, Tulsi R. Tanti, commented, "We are looking at the global economy and society and how we can promote affordable sustainability...It's the whole piece working towards sustainability."[8]

These examples illustrate how company interests interplay with counter-interests and how companies can mobilize to influence the political or social aspects of the nonmarket to protect or promote their market positions. In Section II of the book we focused on managing uncertainty, considering the pathways and mechanisms by which firms can influence the political and social arena and how these activities lead to aligned market and nonmarket strategies. We also discussed the alignment strategies used by some firms to realize their potential for rapid and profitable growth.

In Section III, we introduce a comprehensive and robust political and social strategy framework that we refer to as *sensing, shaping, and aligning* (SSA). This sequential framework offers a specific approach to alignment that ties together a range of disparate elements. In this chapter, we introduce the concept of *sensing* interests as a metaphor to describe how firms can alert themselves to the complex conditions in their nonmarket environment and leverage interests to obtain and create the conditions for a more receptive and responsive set of governmental and nongovernmental stakeholders.[9] Moreover, we provide background insights into interest representation, review relevant management and policy literatures, introduce key concepts, and consider the roots of modern corporate interest mobilization within the political and social spheres and in the context of nonmarket strategy.

Exploring the Notion of Special Interest

Most top management teams have a visual representation of where they want to take their organizations.[10] However, this picture tends to be framed by the market, rather than the nonmarket, context. For most executives, organizational special interests in the political and social domains are vague and ambiguous. Managers often lack the understanding and capability to forge a nonmarket strategy through effectively identifying critical developments, issues, and actors in their nonmarket environment. Research indicates that for many firms the understanding of interest structure and positioning is hazy and uncertain,[11] which results in a failure to make their interests sufficiently inclusive, far-reaching, and tangible.[12] In this chapter, we demonstrate how the often fuzzy concept of *interest* can be made real and dynamic, and in so doing further elucidate and advance the process of creating nonmarket strategies. We propose a technique for developing organizational interests that relies on critical reflection and analysis that can generate a multidimensional interest representation for dealing with sociopolitical issues.

Research shows that interests are ubiquitous in most economies and in the political and social systems of nation-states.[13] In some countries, interests are closely aligned with political parties and exercise influence through those parties.[14] Thus, drawing on Grossman and Helpman, we define *interests* here as *an individual, firm, or group of firms who are concerned with some particular part of the economy and who try to influence legislators, society, or bureaucrats to act in their favor*.[15] In Chapter 9 we will broaden this set of actors to include a wider range of stakeholders with which firms interact and an additional set of strategic options through which companies leverage these relationships to develop legitimacy.

In most countries (there are notable exceptions) firms do not represent their interests individually or collectively by aligning with a specific political party. For example, in EU member states, interest groups, for the most part, are not identified with parties.[16] But as might be expected, individual interests do favor the party or parties in power. In the U.K., despite the Conservative Party being perceived by most as the natural party of business, many executives and entrepreneurs supported the Labour Party under the premierships of Tony Blair and Gordon Brown. In the U.S., business interest groups typically are not identified with specific parties and in many instances provide financial support to both major parties. Therefore, we believe that interests can follow a dual process by influencing parties in the nonmarket arena via individual or advocacy coalition pathways. In this vein, both Etzioni and Spiller suggest that individual or group interests help or influence social-political power concentrations and the polity.[17] In other words, in the democratic electoral process, the egalitarian one person–one vote system can be important in giving firms some indirect influence in elections.[18] If we bear that in mind, firm interests in the nonmarket allow the political process to be more broadly responsive and accurate, and not simply society- or NGO-focused. Although business lobbying and corporate interest representation have been tainted by instances of illicit influence and money buying access, firms both large and small do have legitimate interests. In an inclusive, fully functioning democracy, these interests are as legitimate as those of a trade union or an environmental action group. It is only through corporate engagement in the legislative process that we can ensure public policy is balanced and reflects both societal and industry needs.

The underlying assumption is that if all interests, whether individual or group, are involved in the formation of public policy, there will be winners and losers. In many cases this can be relative, as a consensual approach often emerges. An example is the manner in which periodic renewals to U.S. agricultural legislation—so-called farm bills—are developed and assembled, balancing and integrating the competing and complementary positions of numerous constituencies and interests. Hence, for most firms, the way non-market interest is built and conveyed is fundamental to sustaining profits.[19] But how can commercial organizations mobilize their current and emerging interests over time? The next section will explore corporate interest mobilization.

Mobilizing Interests: Levels, Organizations, Relationships, and Targets

Interests can be understood as the mobilization of attention in response to particular aspects of the political or social order, or the (expected) results of particular policies.[20] This interest is often based on existing or emerging firm objections to specific political or social policies.[21] However, objections alone are not enough to explain the emergence of interest mobilization. For interest to form, the mobilized targets need to be aligned with the interest. As a result, a series of individual or collective action strategies needs to be developed.[22]

Using CPA and CSR research, our framework of interest mobilization addresses these issues by focusing on factors that make firms engage in political and social activities.[23] We build on previous research that suggests looking at interest mobilization in several ways—levels, organization, relationships, and targets.[24] Through this delineation, we first draw on Kubler's argument that interest mobilization should be structured by solidary incentives—that is, the interpersonal rewards that attach to ongoing participation in specific issues at different levels.[25] Secondly, these interest movements also provide enhanced relationships that are crucial to the translation of the group's complaints or difficulties into action. Thirdly, these movements favor targets and resultant organizational structures that can lead to political and social effectiveness. In general, this approach rests on the argument that individual

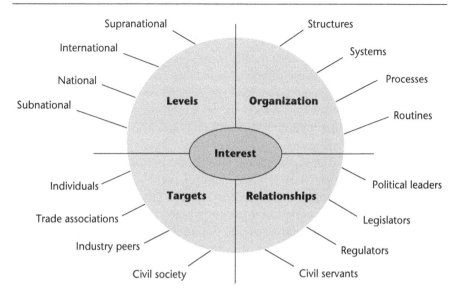

Figure 7.1 Mobilizing interest

Source: Although conceptually distinct, this figure is a visual adaptation of Figure 5.1, The Vision Wheel, in Finkelstein, S., Harvey, C., and Lawton, T. (2007). *Breakout Strategy: meeting the challenge of double-digit growth*. London and New York: McGraw-Hill.

firms are embedded within political and social networks, and more or less formal political and social structures, all of which are likely to influence decisions to engage in collective action (voluntary associations, professional associations, and so on), peer action, or individual action. Moreover, attempts to understand how firms can mobilize their interests to generate influence can help firms sustain a competitive advantage.[26] In the next section, we attempt to elaborate the mobilization elements that are significant facilitators for triggering influence, as we show in Figure 7.1.

Understanding Different Levels in Mobilizing Interest

Most governments work closely with industry and societal stakeholders. As a result, firms develop their interests to positively influence the process of making public policy. There is a general recognition that governance institutions benefit from being open to outside input and ideas and that consultation procedures legitimately form part of the overall legislative process.[27] Therefore, when firms develop their interests in a specific political or social issue, the different levels in the political and social strata must be considered.

Interests in political or social issues can be shared at supranational, international, national, or subnational levels—all of which may regulate or otherwise affect the economic and social activity of private enterprises.[28] No consensus has yet emerged from the academic literature as to how this works or can best be labeled. According to Lehman, the following terms have been used most frequently to describe these interests: *individual firm interests, interest groups, pressure groups, lobby groups, promotion groups,* and *advocacy coalition groups.*[29] These words refer to specific aspects of interest representation. The next sections will look at the different levels at which political and social interests can be positioned and addressed.

First, we consider the *supranational* level. Supranational authority is above and beyond the nation-state. A good example is the EU, specifically institutions such as the European Commission and the European Court of Justice. Lucas suggests that supranational interests place the nation-state and firm interests beyond the "insularity of purely national-domestic frames of reference and activity."[30] The concept of supranationality reveals the interaction of nongovernmental actors with legal authorities that transcend national borders.[31] Political or social interests at the supranational level play an ever-increasing role in global policymaking and global policy arenas. Witness how in the EU, for instance, environmental protection and business sustainability debates and initiatives are increasingly shifting from the national level to a European level. The distinction between national-, international-, and supranational-level interests becomes less transparent around the global legal and political commitments pertaining to human rights, environmental protection, health, crime, trade, labor practices, intellectual property, and scientific research.[32] However, all firms need to understand that supranational organizations such as the EU, IMF, UN, WTO, and World Bank can either help or hinder their competitive advantage. For example, Lawton and McGuire highlighted how the strategic choices of European firms within the chemicals and textiles industries were restricted by WTO rulings.[33] The responses of firms varied significantly and even displayed some industry variance. Many textiles firms sought to sustain their competitive advantage through value chain disaggregation and product and locational adjustment strategies. In contrast, firms in the more nationally based and structurally embedded chemicals sector attempted to defend their intellectual property-based competitive advantage by lobbying their national governments to seek rule harmonization within the WTO.[34]

Secondly, we can speak of interest at the *international* level. International authority reflects the creation of agreements and institutions derived from cooperation and mutual consent between nation-states. Unlike supranational authority, it does not involve the shift of power away from national governments, but rather the encouragement of consensus between countries. An example is the International Organization for Migration (IOM), which serves to promote cooperation and coordination between its 149 member states on the humane and orderly management of migration.[35] At both levels, however, the senior management of companies and interest groups need to understand where decision-making authority resides and how to optimally influence legal rulings and policy outcomes. Interest at an international level is about gaining access to networks and opportunities. The international system is composed of interlocking networks, resources, and interests, particularly between host countries and firms.[36] Not all aspects of this system are well understood. For instance, the impact and influence of foreign lobbying on domestic political parties has been largely neglected as a subject of management and economic research.[37] Hamada investigated political contributions from one domestic interest group to a political party with the purpose of shielding against imports into the home market, while a foreign lobby simultaneously donated to the same party to exert pressure for more open market access.[38] Like Hamada, we believe firms need to consider the effect on their business strategies of two-way lobbying within and across national borders.

Third is interest at the *national* level. While there are significant cross-sectoral differences in terms of policy impact, it is not hard to find a range of illustrative examples to show that, irrespective of size, more nationally focused firms must develop their own interests and/or join (or form) wider national lobbying groups.[39] As with political or social activities at the national level, group activity is concerned with technical issues that are of high or low political or social salience. It is, therefore, necessary to distinguish between what Wilson describes as high- and low-interest politics, a distinction that we could also extend to social activities.[40] The greater the impact of national policy on firm profits, the more firms should develop high-interest tactics in targeting national-level political and social actors. For instance, the former Dutch national airline, KLM, used interest-led tactics to have its voice heard before the 1997 deregulation of the European airline industry. Inspired by the need for growth and restricted by its small home geography, KLM shared its interests in more landing rights and slot allocations with the International Air Transport Association (IATA), the European Parliament, and the European Commission. Ultimately, the firm was successful in having its individual views heard and also in collective advocacy, particularly through the Association of European Airlines (AEA), ensuring that the case for European air transport deregulation was advanced despite the opposition of several powerful European governments and airlines.[41]

Finally, we consider interest at the *subnational* level. This is most relevant in countries with federal structures such as Australia, Brazil, Germany, India, and the U.S.[42] In these instances, the legislative and regulatory authority of subnational entities such as the *Freistaat* of Bavaria or the state of Texas can be significant for firms. In a federal structure, policies that connect the different regions may be contingent on the extent and the nature of local firms.[43] Local firms that have a multi-regional focus can more successfully internalize inter-jurisdictional externalities than the firms with interests in a single region.[44] Consider the national- and EU-level lobbying effectiveness of luxury car manufacturer BMW, a Bavarian-based company with global market appeal and multi-regional reach. In 2012 it was accused of using subnational and international lobbying tactics to simultaneously defend against European plans to improve the fuel efficiency of cars while simultaneously promoting its green credentials and environmental strategies.[45] BMW lobbied extensively at all levels of governance, particularly in 2007 and 2008, against a 2015 target of $120g/CO_2$ per kilometer for average emissions.[46] Ultimately, it would appear that their multilevel lobbying efforts and activist political and social strategies helped secure a weaker target of $130g/CO_2$.[47]

Organizational Structures in Mobilizing Interest

Building on Lehmann's ideas and the concepts of different levels in the nonmarket field,[48] we can usefully organize the activities of lobbyists and their interests into four categories: *routines*, the establishment of certain practices for firms, such as the gathering of information; *processes*, attempts that are not routinized, but which can influence decision-making processes from inside or outside the firm and are more sporadic in the nonmarket (for example, meeting European Commission officials or participating in public hearings); *systems*, the set of processes that work together as a part of a mechanism or interconnected network to influence the nonmarket (for instance, by direct participation in the decision-making process of expert committees selecting research proposals with other firms); and *structures*, the various structural configurations required to participate in policy development or internally assimilate nonmarket information. An example, as we discussed in Chapter 6, is the functions and structures for scanning and analyzing the nonmarket environment.[49] The next section will expand on these four organizational attributes to mobilize interest.

Routines. Organizational routines are very important in the nonmarket. According to Pavitt, these are defined as "the regular and predictable behavioral patterns within firms that are coping with a world of complexity and continuous change."[50] Drawing on Pavitt and Miner, we define these nonmarket routines as a repetitive and coordinated set of nonmarket actions—for instance, organizing an annual conference or seasonal cocktail parties.[51] Many firms show striking differences in these nonmarket routines. They may have particular preferences, forms of management, or lobbying styles.[52] These differences are influenced by geographical factors, cultural differences, history, size of the organization, and the context.[53] In both academic and practically oriented lobbying literature, lobbying organizations influence policymakers and society through routines. Nonmarket routines can include everything from giving gifts to sending regular emails, handwritten letters, or telephoning; getting an article published; issuing a white paper; meeting with congressional or parliamentary aides; meeting with a legislator; and hosting events or parties.[54] Nonmarket routines are essentially characterized by direct and indirect information exchanges between firms and governmental officials. These can also include testifying before congressional or parliamentary committees and magistrates. Other nonmarket routines, more common in countries like the U.S. than elsewhere, include giving money to political campaigns, producing research papers to generate debate, publishing voting records, and running public relations campaigns.[55] All these nonmarket routines are seen to be building blocks of learning and knowledge management for the nonmarket. These routines may affect governmental policy by influencing elections or shifting public opinion. Consequently, they can be controversial within wider society.

Processes. Many studies on organizational processes tend to share a common perspective, that certain companies control unbalanced amounts of the managerial processes that influence political and social actors.[56] These processes are sometimes not routinized despite having established procedures and protocols. Therefore, they can be reactive and more informal responses by managers in practice—before they become routines. Some research has investigated interest-led processes by market and nonmarket managers to influence national accounting standards.[57] According to Watts and Zimmerman, these managerial decision-making processes affected the development of the Financial Accounting Standards Board (FASB).[58] When looking at corporate document submissions to the FASB regarding policies on price level adjustments, the authors found that large firms expecting reduced earnings were lobbying intensely and had established robust processes to do so.

Systems. The growth of nonmarket systems has created the need for knowledge to deal with opportunities and threats outside and inside the firm's boundaries. Firms must understand how these complex nonmarket systems—made up of cumulative processes or sets of processes—bundle between and across different levels so as to optimize their interests in securing policy attainment or responding quickly to social issues that might affect their bottom line. The firm-level systems have played an important role in encouraging civic interests for many years in democratic countries, especially in overriding national regulations that protected certain individual and corporate interests at the expense of consumers.[59] We argue that these nonmarket systems act as a set of organizational processes that work together as part of a mechanism or interconnected network to influence the nonmarket.

Structures. Most firms' political and social interests are composed of different structures. Some industries dominated by small companies tend to be represented by national trade associations, while highly regulated sectors tend to be represented by direct nonmarket structures.[60] The large structures can include departments dedicated to sharing interests with political or social actors.[61] The structural configurations tend to be centralized or decentralized in functionality with the government affairs and/or corporate responsibility departments having authority to influence the rules of the game. In Chapter 6 we discussed in more detail how these nonmarket structures can help to formulate interests to reduce costs and/or increase benefits.

Targets in Mobilizing Interest

Not all legislation or social concerns influence whole industries and might instead relate to specific segments, groups of companies, or individual firms. Consequently, the more targeted a particular lobbying effort, the greater the probability that the interest will be genuinely considered.[62] We believe that mobilizing political or social interests requires firms to target key *individuals*, *trade associations*, and *other interest groups or peer groups*. Building on the CPA and CSR literature on target setting in lobbying, we will look at the different targets in more detail.

Individuals. Targeting individual actors or agents that are influential is important in positioning political and social interests.[63] On the whole, U.S. firms mobilize their interests in a way similar to that of their European counterparts.[64] Both in the U.S. and Europe, lobbyists define their targets and then approach them with information customized to shape the rules of the game and legislative systems.[65] Primary lobbying targets are the various components of legislative decision-making: civil servants, legislators, executive branch officials, regulators, and key political staff aides. Additionally, they may pursue indirect lobbying channels, such as political constituents and other individual contacts that can help convey the lobbying interests to those officials contacted.[66]

Trade associations. Firms also need to consider trade associations when mobilizing interests. As we have seen in Chapter 5, collective action is vital to ensure that firms maintain their competitive advantage and convey their interests. These associations are usually composed of member companies, or national industries in the case of international associations. They can also be nonprofit or nongovernmental. Examples include the Christian Music Trade Association and the Southeast Asian Council for Food Security and Fair Trade. The benefits of joining a trade association include increased social capital through membership networks; access to knowledge, advice, and expertise;

expanded societal engagement and citizenship; insight into regulatory trends and developments; and the potential ability to influence policy outcomes.[67]

Other interest groups or peer groups. Firms also need to consider other types of meta-organizations or nongovernmental organizations (NGOs) when developing and disseminating their interests. For instance, NGOs like Friends of the Earth and Oxfam can be cultivated as partners to align interests in support of or against specific policies or governmental positions. Chapter 9 delves more deeply into details and examples of these other interest groups. Firms can align their interests with other coalition actors to generate even more influence in the nonmarket, as we have seen in the pharmaceutical industry, in which large pharmaceutical firms ally with both doctor and patient groups to lobby governments on drug-related laws.

Relationships in Mobilizing Interest

Relationships are crucial in mobilizing interest, as we will see further in Chapter 9. With a variety of interpretations,[68] social capital has become a ubiquitous metaphor in the study of organizations. The compelling idea embodied in the notion of social capital is implicitly or explicitly present in various research streams that focus on how social relationships or ties enhance an actor's ability to attain its goals.[69] Some research has identified how networks can enhance firm performance.[70] In particular, political and social networks can facilitate access to information, resources, and opportunities.[71] On both sides of the Atlantic and elsewhere in the world, in-house lobbyists within the external affairs departments of firms typically develop extensive networks.[72] Thus, actors with networks rich in social capital have privileged access to resources and information to influence policy outcomes. This should, in turn, better enable them to lead, organize, and mobilize other actors toward collective goals. Relationships aimed at shaping political and social policies can be with regulators, legislators, government ministers, and civil servants.

Regulators. In a narrow sense, regulation is a set of authoritative rules supplemented by public agency and intended to evaluate compliance. In a wider sense, it is an all-encompassing concept of governance. Much of the formal literature on lobbying is concerned with influencing a single decision-maker—a regulator.[73] According to this literature, a regulation refers to a precise requirement to which a firm must adhere. These regulations are the primary mechanism by which legislation is imposed on firms, and they create efficiency in terms of optimal behavior. Firms must consider the regulators when mobilizing their interests, as regulators can create constraints for organizations, especially when firms enter host markets. For instance, in 2010, Saudi

Arabia's communications and information technology regulator blocked the messenger function on Blackberry smartphone devices when it discovered that the Canadian parent company, Research in Motion (RIM), was encrypting personal data.[74] RIM defended its interests by lobbying the Canadian and U.S. governments to broker conversations with the Saudi government and regulators to lift the ban. The ban was subsequently lifted.

Legislators. Despite the commonalities between regulation and legislation, legislation refers to the rule of law placed by a government or legislating body on either an industry (or sector thereof), a section of a community, or an entire population.[75] It must be closely followed to remain within the legal parameters of that particular state or industry. In the work of Groseclose and Snyder,[76] lobbyists in the U.S. and similar legislative systems attempt to influence legislators through political action committees or political campaign contributions. With this in mind, the legislation literature in political science examines the influence of legislators and suggests that firms must acknowledge the difference between developed and developing countries when forging relationships with these actors.[77] Firms clearly need to consider legislators when mobilizing their interests in both the political and social arenas.

Political actors. There is some overlap in definition with civil servants, but political actors can also include public relations specialists, universities and faculty members, journalists, lawyers, accountants, and even doctors and engineers. These actors can be found in the world of lobbying, as they can help to mobilize interest representation. Most have professional bodies that represent them and are bound by specific interests and codes of conduct. However, firms that wish to mobilize their interests need to consider these wider political forces in building relationships to win in the nonmarket. For instance, the airline industry has been actively using a variety of political actors to create influence and protect itself from emergent policies. It did so in the aftermath of the 9/11 attacks, when European long-haul airlines were prevented from flying into U.S. airspace and subsequent security policies required enhanced security measures such as new cockpit doors on planes.[78] In these scenarios, European airlines engaged various political actors through sharing interests with the International Air Transport Association (IATA) and journalists, as well as using research papers produced by academics, to show the negative effects of these measures on the air transport industry.

Civil Servants. Civil servants—or what some people call public servants—work in the public sector, usually as active employees in government divisions or agencies. Civil servants can include state employees at national, regional, or substate levels, including municipal government, although this differs from country to country. For instance, in the U.K., only Crown personnel (those employed directly by central government) are referred to as civil servants, while employees from local or city government are not.[79]

Civil servants in many countries play important roles in the policy-making process. In some democratic countries, such as Brazil and Canada, the federal public services comprise departments, agencies, commissions, boards, councils, and crown corporations, and some provincial governments also have regional public servants.[80] Therefore, in the mobilizations of interest, firms may want to engage with civil servants in public administration when transmitting and positioning their interests in a responsible manner. These civil servants can influence the policy-making process and can protect or promote business interests. It is important to note that civil servants have codes of practice regarding how organizations, particularly companies, can engage with them. Therefore, firms are often best advised to engage civil servants primarily through information exchange, especially when dealing with national issues.[81]

Building and Maintaining an Interest

Building strong interests can allow firms to enhance performance.[82] For Exxon to prosper in the 1990s and beyond, it invested heavily in incubating its interest for the future, especially with regards to energy policy around deep-water drilling and climate change.[83] The pharmaceutical industry attained a major legislative win with the 2003 Medicare Modernization Act in the U.S., which added a prescription drug benefit to Medicare (without requiring the government to negotiate pricing).[84] According to Friedman, this specific legislation made an extra income of $242 billion for the pharmaceutical industry over a ten-year period.[85] These examples highlight the importance of interest design. Firms in these industries all had interests to sustain their nonmarket positions.

As we can see in Figure 7.2, our interest process model, built on different strands within CPA literature[86] and CSR research,[87] defines organizational interest in terms of four domains of response and choice in growing interest: *creating, controlling, coordinating,* and *changing (4C)*. Ensuring equilibrium among these factors is the basis for successful interest building. Interest-based views emanate from the equilibrium achieved between an organization's internal and external stakeholders. Successful interest is generated through responding to the internal organization and the external dimensions of the political and social environment.[88] We will next explore each dimension in more detail.

Creating. The policy literature reminds us that it is vital to be well briefed before embarking on political or social influencing.[89] Research shows that developing a deep understanding—and genuine appreciation and identification—of specific interests is an obvious and critical starting point

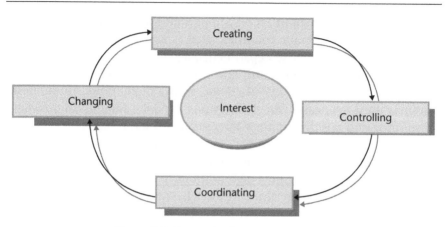

Figure 7.2 Categories for growing interest

for effectively engaging that interest and its close partners.[90] Moreover, being aware of the content and focus of interest, as well as the background of the particular individual targets for that interest, is the starting point when creating interests.[91] It is important that the firm understands precisely the nature of the politics surrounding an issue when scanning the environment.

Controlling. After creating the interest, firms must consider their interests relative to those of opponents and proponents of an issue. The resource-based view of the firm reminds us that many firms are able to locate and control access paths to advance their interests.[92] But some firms may also commit all of their available resources to the promotion of a single interest, while others may distribute theirs among a wide array of issues. These political resources are characterized and defined as having organizational (an in-house, permanent, industry/government affairs office or person), relational (formal or information relationships with political actors), public image (perception of stakeholders), reputation (individual and firm responsibility), and financial (direct finance, such as political campaign contributions, and indirect finance, such as funding events and conferences) resources.[93] For example, changing public policy on oil pricing controls generated an estimated $831 billion of extra revenue for oil companies between 1980 and 1990. Hence, dedicating even as much as a billion dollars in financial resources and events—an absurdly high figure—might well be a rational approach for the oil lobby.

Coordinating. After controlling political resources and underpinning them with interests, some scholars have defined the coordination of interests as ensuring a locus of ongoing, proactive, planned lobbying activities to build effective communication with political and social actors.[94] The extent to which organizations influence the formation of public policy using their interests depends, in part, on how well they coordinate that activity. As we have seen in previous chapters, the external affairs department or an interest group representing the firms' interests is crucial in coordinating political and social action. Politicians have many competing demands for their attention and often have little actual time to devote to the detailed process of legislative development.[95] Therefore, the channels by which firms approach the coordination of interest structures, relationships, targets, and timing are crucial to creating impact in the political and social spheres.

Changing. We can see from the points above that coordination factors are important, and political science research shows that firms that coordinate and change their interest can create advantages.[96] If organizations have not yet developed strong interests to protect their market positions, they are likely to have less influence in the political and social landscape. Therefore, organizations need to proactively look for an opportunity to incrementally advance their interest and must consider changing aspects of their approach and position depending on the target. For instance, in the airline industry, firms frequently change their interest (particularly on taxes or environmental issues) over a period of time, in response to shifting stakeholder positions, new technologies, and political developments. This renewal enables firms to remain in touch with, and in command of, new political and social trends. In summary, the interplay of politics and social obligation is art and science, and sensing and seizing the moment for a specific interest ensures success. We believe these advances in influence often build up over months or even years, rather than occurring rapidly or instantaneously. Accordingly, the best approach to exercising influence may be long-term and gradual in nature.

Conclusions and Managerial Implications

In sensing the nonmarket, how firms mobilize their interests is a critical variable in engaging effectively with political and social actors and in aligning market and nonmarket strategies. In this chapter, we developed and highlighted the importance of the broader corporate political and social interests in the success of firms in nonmarket contexts. The concept of interests has informed social movement research by revealing that the timing and fortune of social movements are mainly contingent on the micro institutional structures and the sociopolitical environments.[97] Because of its focus on institutionalized politics, the concept of mobilizing interest has fueled research on institutional and sociopolitical factors that illuminate the development and the impact of firms across nonmarket contexts.[98] We demonstrated how interest can be used as a practical tool within the strategic management process by specifying a set of political and social goals from now to the future. This imbues the interest tool with a dynamic and forward-looking quality. In summary, there are several key learning points in this chapter for strategic managers and business leaders:

- Interest mobilization has several factors that determine influence in the nonmarket—*levels, organization, relationships,* and *targets.*
- Firms must respond by growing their interest in the nonmarket using a *creating, controlling, coordinating,* and *changing (4C)* approach. Ensuring equilibrium among these factors is the basis for successful interest building.
- Interest-based views emanate from the equilibrium achieved between an organization's internal and external stakeholders.

In the next chapter we will explore the fundamental challenge for any company that wants to develop an aligned strategy through compiling high-quality information on specific political and social issues. We will explore the influence of information as a key determinant by which companies win—or lose—in the nonmarket environment. We suggest the practical steps that executives can use in developing an *information package* to create value. Typically, the most basic sense of shaping the policy-making process requires using high-quality information to share individual interests. The lobbying activity must ultimately harness this information to persuade legislators or societal actors of the firms' nonmarket position.

Notes

* Portions of this chapter have been adapted from Lawton, Rajwani, and Doh 2013; and Lawton, McGuire, and Rajwani 2013.
1. Machiavelli, N. (2003). *The Prince.* Translated with an introduction by G. Bull. London: Penguin.
2. Interview with Nuno Brito e Cunha, Equity Sales Analyst at Espirito Santo Investment Bank, London, June 11, 2013.
3. Financial Crisis Inquiry Commission (2011). *The financial crisis inquiry report:* xviii. <http://c0182732.cdnl.cloudfiles.rackspacecloud.com/fcic_final_report_full.pdf.> (accessed December 10, 2012).
4. *The Economist.* (2012). Unhappy birthday to you. July 28th. <http://www.economist.com/node/21559657> (accessed December 10, 2012).
5. World Economic Forum and Boston Consulting Group (BCG) Report (2011), *Redefining the future of growth: the new sustainability champions.* <http://www3.weforum.org/docs/WEF_GGC_SustainabilityChampions_Report_2011.pdf> (accessed December 10, 2012).

6. World Economic Forum and Boston Consulting Group (BCG) Report 2011: 40.

7. World Economic Forum and Boston Consulting Group (BCG) Report 2011: 40.

8. World Economic Forum and Boston Consulting Group (BCG) Report 2011: 40.

9. Chapters 8 (Shaping), 9 (Aligning), and 10 (Balance) will be closely linked to Chapter 7 (Sensing), as we will show the steps in formulating, aligning, and implementing political and social nonmarket strategies. To ensure consistency, there are some purposefully designed overlaps between Chapter 7 on the antecedents in mobilizing interests and key stakeholders discussed in Chapter 9. The key differences between Chapters 7 and 9 are in how you position firm interest and stakeholder engagement.

10. Weick, K.E. (1979). *The social psychology of organizing.* 2nd ed. New York: McGraw-Hill.

11. Hansen and Mitchell 2000.

12. Getz 1997; Vining, A.R., Shapiro, D.M., and Borges, B. (2005). Building the firm's political (lobbying) strategy. *Journal of Public Affairs*, 5: 150–175.

13. Grossman, G.M and Helpman, E. (2001) *Special interest politics*. Cambridge, MA: MIT Press.

14. Grossman and Helpman 2001.

15. Grossman and Helpman 2001.

16. There are some exceptions. For example, in the U.K. there are 15 trade unions officially affiliated with, and providing funding to, the Labour Party,

17. Etzioni, A. (1985), Special interest groups versus constituency representation: research in social movements. *Conflicts and Change*, 8: 171–195; Spiller 1990.

18. Etzioni 1985.

19. Kim, J. (2008). Corporate lobbying revisited. *Business and Politics*, 10: 1–23.

20. Kübler, D. (2001). Understanding policy change with the advocacy coalition framework: an application to Swiss drug policy. *Journal of European Public Policy*, 8: 623–641.

21. Grier, Munger, and Roberts 1994.

22. Hillman and Hitt 1999.

23. Doh, Lawton, and Rajwani 2012; Lawton and Rajwani 2011.

24. McAdam, D., McCarthy, J.D., and Zald, M.N. (1988). Social movements. In N.J. Smelsered (ed.). *Handbook of Sociology*. Newbury Park, CA: Sage.

25. Kübler 2001; Duffy, G. and Lindstrom, N. (2002). Conflicting identities: solidary incentives in the Serbo-Croatian war. *Journal of Peace Research*, 39(1): 69–90.

26. Kim 2008.

27. Lawton, T. (1996). Industrial policy partners: explaining the European level firm–Commission interplay for electronics. *Policy and Politics*, 24(4): 425–436.

28. Lawton, T. (1999). Governing the skies: conditions for the Europeanization of airline policy. *Journal of Public Policy*, 19: 91–112.

29. Lehman, W. (2003). Lobbying in the European Union: current rules and practices, AFCO 104 EN. <http://www.uni-mannheim.de/edz/pdf/dg4/AFCO104_EN.pdf> (accessed March 26, 2013).

30. Lucas, M. (1999). Nationalism, sovereignty, and supranational organization: 7. <http://www.ifsh.de/pdf/publikationen/hb/hb114.pdf> (accessed March 26, 2013).

31. Lucas 1999: 7.

32. Lucas 1999: 12

33. Lawton, T.C. and McGuire, S.M. (2005). Adjusting to liberalization: tracing the impact of the WTO on the European textiles and chemicals industries. *Business and Politics*, 7(2): 1–23.

34. Lawton and McGuire 2005.

35. For further details, see the IOM website <http://www.iom.int/cms/en/sites/iom/home.html> (accessed June 10, 2013).

36. Wöll, C. (2007). Leading the dance? Power and political resources of business lobbyists. *Journal of Public Policy*, 27: 57–78.

37. Endoh, M. (2005). Cross-border political donations and pareto-efficient tariffs. Working paper. <http://www.econ.yale.edu/growth_pdf/cdp915.pdf> (accessed March 26, 2013).

38. Hamada, K. (1993). International negotiations and domestic conflicts: a case for counter lobbying. In L.R. Klein (ed.). *A quest for a more stable world economic system: restructuring at a time of cyclical adjustment.* Boston: Kluwer Academic Publishers.

39. Lux, S., Crook, T.R., and Woehr, D.J. (2011). Mixing business with politics: a meta-analysis of the antecedents and outcomes of corporate political activity. *Journal of Management*, 37: 223–247.

40. Wilson, J.Q. (1995). *Politics organizations.* Princeton, NJ: Princeton University Press.

41. Lawton, Rajwani, and Doh 2013.

42. Bardhan, P.K. and Mookherjee, D. (2000). Capture and governance at local and national levels. *American Economic Review*, 90(2): 135–139.

43. Guriev, S., Yakovlev, E., and Zhuravskyaya, E. (2007). *Inter-regional trade and lobbying.* Working paper from Centre for Economic and Financial Research: 1–34.

44. Guriev et al. 2007.

45. Vaughan, A. (2012). BMW accused of hypocrisy over opposition to European car targets. *The Guardian.* <http://www.guardian.co.uk/environment/2012/jul/09/bmw-hypocrisy-european-car-targets> (accessed March 26, 2013).

46. Vaughan 2012.

47. Vaughan 2012.

48. Lehman 2003.

49. Lawton, Rajwani, and Doh J 2013.

50. Pavitt, K. (2002). Innovating routines in the business firm: What corporate tasks should they be accomplishing? *Industrial and Corporate Change*, 11(1): 117–123 (117).

51. Miner, A.S. (1990). Structural evolution through idiosyncratic jobs: the potential for unplanned learning. *Organization Science*, 1: 195–210.

52. Meznar and Nigh 1995.

53. Stinchcombe, A.L. (1965). Social structure and organizations. In J.G. March (ed.). *Handbook of organizations.* New York: Rand McNally: 142–193.

54. De Figueiredo and Tiller 2001.

55. De Figueiredo and Tiller 2001.

56. Kirsch, R. and Day, R. (2001). Lobbying and the International Accounting Standards Committee. Working paper. Poole, U.K. <http://eprints.bournemouth.ac.uk/3080/> (accessed March 26, 2013).

57. Watts, R.L. and Zimmerman, J.L. (1978). Towards a positive theory of the determination of accounting standards. *Accounting Review* 53(1): 112–134.

58. Watts and Zimmerman 1978.

59. Lehman 2003.

60. Lehman 2003.

61. See Chapter 6 for more detail.

62. Lehman 2003.

63. Coen, D. (2002). Business interests and European integration. In R. Balme, D. Chabanet, and V. Wright (eds.). *L'action collective en Europe*. Paris: Sciences Po Press: 255–292.

64. See Clamen, M. (2000). *Le lobbying et ses secrets*. 3rd ed., Paris: Dunod; Mack, C.S. (1997). *Business, politics, and the practice of government relations*. Westport, CT: Quorum Books; and Gardner, J.N. (1991). *Effective lobbying in the European Community*. Deventer: Kluwer.

65. Greenwood, J. (2002). *Inside the EU business associations*. Basingstoke, U.K.: Macmillan.

66. Mack 1997.

67. This is a paraphrasing of the top five reasons to join a trade association, as advanced by the Great Plains International Trade Association, a Midwestern U.S., nongovernmental organization that offers companies in that region advice and assistance in developing domestic and international trade. Available at <http://www.factsfiguressolutions.com/post/top-5-reasons-to-join-a-trade-association/> (accessed on March 26, 2013).

68. Granovetter, M.S. (1973). The strength of weak ties. *American Journal of Sociology*, 78(6): 1360–1380; Coleman, J.S. (1990). *Foundation of social theory*. Cambridge, MA: Harvard University Press; Nahapiet, J. and Ghoshal, S. (1998). Social capital, intellectual capital, and the organizational advantage. *Academy of Management Review*, 23(2): 242–266.

69. Sun, P., Mellahi, K., and Wright, M. (2012). The contingent value of corporate political ties. *Academy of Management Perspectives*, 26: 52–67.

70. Lazer, D. and Friedman, A. (2007). The network structure of exploration and exploitation. *Administrative Science Quarterly*, 52(4): 667–694.

71. Campbell, K., Marsden P., and Hurlber J.S. (1986). Social resources and social economic status. *Social Network*, 8: 97–117; Podolny, J. (2001). Networks as the pipes and prisms of the market. *American Journal of Sociology*, 107(1): 33–60.

72. Mack 1997.

73. Vining, Shapiro, and Borges 2005.

74. BBC (2010). Saudi Arabia begins Blackberry ban, users say. <http://www.bbc.co.uk/news/world-middle-east-10888954> (accessed August 6, 2010).

75. DifferenceBetween.Net (2013). Difference between legislation and regulation. <http://www.differencebetween.net/miscellaneous/difference-between-legislation-and-regulation/> (accessed March 26, 2013).

76. Groseclose, T. and Snyder, J. (1996). Buying supermajorities. *American Political Science Review*, 90(2): 303–315.

77. White, G. (2010). Legal system contingencies and dynamic capability determinants of wholly owned foreign subsidiary relational ties. Academy of Management Conference, Montreal, Canada.

78. Lawton and Rajwani 2011.

79. Page, E. and Jenkins, B. (2006). *Policy bureaucracy: government with a cast of thousands*. New York: Oxford University Press.

80. Ministry of Federal Administration and State Reform (1995). *Plano Diretor da Reforma do Aparelho do Estado*. Brasília: Presidency of the Republic, Imprensa Nacional.

81. Page and Jenkins 2006.

82. Kim 2008.

83. Plater, Z. (2011). The Exxon Valdez resurfaces in the Gulf of Mexico and the hazards of megasystem centripetal di-polarity. *Boston College Environmental Law Review*, 38(2): 1–27.

84. Drutman, L. (2010). The business of America is lobbying: explaining the growth of corporate political activity in Washington, DC. <http://www.leedrutman.com/uploads/2/3/0/1/2301208/the_business_of_america_is_lobbying.pdf> (accessed March 27, 2013).

85. Friedman, J. (2009). The incidence of the Medicare prescription drug benefit: using asset prices to assess its impact on drug makers. Working paper. <http://www.hks.harvard.edu/fs/jfriedm/partd.pdf.> (accessed March 27, 2013).

86. Epstein, E.M. (1980). Business political activity: research approaches and analytical issues. *Research in corporate social performance and policy*, 2: 1–55.

87. Scherer, A.G. and Palazzo, G. (2011). The new political role of business in a globalized world: a review of a new perspective on CSR and its implications for the firm, governance, and democracy. *Journal of Management Studies*, 48(4): 899–931.

88. Schuler, D. and Rehbein, K. (1997). The filtering role of the firm in corporate political environment. *Business and Society*, 36(2): 116–139.

89. Wöll 2007.

90. Mueller, D. (2003). *Public choice III*. Cambridge, U.K.: Cambridge University Press.

91. Werner, T. and Wilson, G. (2010). Business representation in Washington D.C. In D. Coen, W. Grant, and G.Wilson (eds.). *The Oxford Handbook of Business and Government*. Oxford: Oxford University Press: 261–284.

92. Dahan 2005a.

93. Dahan 2005a.

94. Mueller 2003.

95. Hojnacki, M. and Kimball, D. (1999). The who and how of organizations' lobbying strategies in committee. *Journal of Politics*, 61(4): 999–1024.

96. Caldeira, G.A., Jojnacki, M., and Wright, J.R. (2000). The lobbying activities of organized interests in federal judicial nominations. *Journal of Politics*, 62(1): 51–69.

97. Hensmans, M. (2003). Social movement organizations: a metaphor for strategic actors in institutional fields. *Organization Studies*, 24(3): 355–381.

98. Kübler 2001.

8

Shaping Information Value

> It is a very sad thing that nowadays there is so little useless information.[1]
>
> *Oscar Wilde*

In the mid-1990s the Walt Disney Company faced a nonmarket challenge that threatened its very foundation. The copyright on Mickey Mouse was scheduled to expire in 2003, on Pluto in 2005, on Goofy in 2007, and on Donald Duck in 2009. In response, the company developed an information-sharing strategy to target the U.S. Republican Party leadership (particularly the then Senate majority leader Trent Lott and House majority leader Newt Gingrich) to move copyright extension legislation forward.[2] Simultaneously, the key message was to maintain Disney's market position in Europe and avoid talking about profits. The interest was built around being allied with key members of Congress. This meant that Disney had to use an *information package* for its lobbying campaign, combined with campaign contributions. Of the thirteen initial sponsors of the House bill, ten received campaign contributions from Disney's political action committee. These included Rep. Howard Berman (D-Calif.), a senior member of the Judiciary Committee.[3] However, the American Libraries Association urged its 54,000 individual members to call their local lawmakers and encourage them to reject the change. With this in mind, Disney engaged all interests by gathering information on their positions, which resulted in libraries and consumer groups winning some concessions. The libraries, schools, and archives were given wider use of copyright materials without having to get the permission of the copyright owner. In the end, the copyright period for a cultural work was extended for an additional twenty years, which gave Disney global protection of its copyright on Mickey Mouse for a total of ninety-five years.[4]

From this example, we can see how nonmarket strategy information can help shape the political and social arenas. A fundamental challenge for any company that wishes to develop an aligned strategy is to put together detailed and reliable information on specific issues in the political and social contexts.[5] This chapter explores the power of information as a key determinant of which companies win—or lose—in the nonmarket environment.[6] Typically, the essence of influencing nonmarket actors requires using high-quality information for and from different stakeholders.[7] We advance the practical steps that managers can use in developing an information package to create value in the nonmarket. The nonmarket activity must ultimately harness this information to persuade legislators or citizens to align with the firm's nonmarket position.[8] The next section will explore the definition of nonmarket information and consider how to develop an information package to target key stakeholders.

What is Information?

Information is a key resource for all corporations in the market and nonmarket environment, especially in the coordination of activities to sustain competitive advantage.[9] Despite the difficulty of distinguishing between information and knowledge, at the conceptual level, "information can be understood as the flow of signals and knowledge can be viewed as the interpretations of those signals. In the broadest sense, information is the substance to create knowledge,"[10] and we will therefore focus on the *flow* of signals rather than on the interpretation. Some scholars have referred to information flow as being *data exchanges*.[11]

The significance of information exchanges has been acknowledged in the nonmarket field and, as Bhatt notes, is a concern that is attracting attention among both academics and executives.[12] Depending on the nonmarket issue, information flow can be used for different exchanges in coordinating interests to either defend or create advantageous positions in the nonmarket. If organizations have difficulties exchanging information with political and social agents and institutions, they will be less likely to establish competitive positions in nonmarket arenas. Accordingly, most firms not only take advantage of simple information exchanges with nonmarket actors, but also work to share information with key stakeholders about harmful legislation or risky social developments. As we discussed in Chapter 6, by generating and processing useful nonmarket information through nonmarket structures and learning, many business organizations have strengthened their competitive positions. In essence, firms that freely exchange information with nonmarket actors such as legislators or social activists often sustain advantage for longer.[13]

From a corporate perspective, a thorough analysis of nonmarket information (data) related to specific issues becomes an important task.[14] If an organization insulates itself from the nonmarket, it is likely to limit its exposure to nonmarket information and thus create a situation in which its reactive non-market activities could be inherently deficient. Therefore, firms should make efforts to proactively monitor, gather, and collect information from the non-market about forthcoming legislation or emergent social issues. If the needs of nonmarket actors are ambiguous or there is no understanding on the issue, the firm should generate information by making use of futuristic scenarios to visualize the potential threats and future opportunities in engaging with nonmarket actors. Take the examples of JP Morgan and Microsoft: both invest heavily in nonmarket activities and have government affairs and corporate responsibility functions to exert influence in their nonmarket environments. During the 1990s, Microsoft was embroiled in court cases that stemmed from its alleged monopoly position in many software markets. With its market vulnerabilities exposed, the corporation subsequently organized its nonmarket information to engage with stakeholders to bolster its market positions and succeeded in receiving only minor penalties in the U.S. On the other hand, JP Morgan has long anticipated the need to proactively deploy different types of information to highlight its positions and interests. Its information exchanges have consistently helped to minimize the regulatory constraints on institutions, markets, and its products.[15]

As the Microsoft and JP Morgan examples indicate, in uncertain nonmarket environments, business organizations are advised to continually generate, process, and distribute information about their nonmarket interests.[16] Similar ideas are evident in Bonardi et al.'s study of nonmarket participation.[17] Using the case of U.S. electric utilities, they looked at the determinants of firms' nonmarket strategy using information and financial resources to influence nonmarket actors. Lawton, et al., in their systematic review of CPA research, found that firms with a sophisticated approach to the nonmarket generated, processed, and distributed more information about their interests than their less proactive peers.[18] More importantly, research shows that political and social actors in the nonmarket require information from firms to optimize their own positions and choices.[19] However, what are the different types of information in the nonmarket? The next section will discuss each aspect of nonmarket information, beginning with how companies convey an amount of information to key stakeholders that does not necessarily equate with quality information.

Nonmarket Information and Knowledge Codification

To define and measure information quality and quantity for the nonmarket context, we must first consider the characteristics of research-based and non-research-based information exchanges. Building on previous work, we believe that research-based information exchanges—those grounded in facts and figures—can allow executives to create impact in the nonmarket.[20] Moreover, firms must consider information as the main basis of political and social action, especially in relation to rivals' moves in the nonmarket.[21] There is evidence to suggest that the quality of information exchanged using research analysis may actually help persuade nonmarket actors on specific pieces of legislation.[22] Conversely, non-research-based information exchanges—mainly conversations minus data, facts, and figures—might have less influence in the nonmarket context. Bringing together information and research abilities highlights the importance of knowledge codification and experience articulation.[23]

To understand the conditions of information exchange, scholars have looked at the interaction effects between information and knowledge. It is important to understand the difference between the two knowledge types, *explicit* and *implicit*, in relation to information. Explicit knowledge is simple to capture, define, and transfer in different formats, whereas implicit knowledge is hard to codify and transfer because of its being deeply rooted in the minds of individuals who often cannot easily articulate their premises and knowledge bases.[24] This is evident in external affairs functions that have developed these two knowledge types through experience accumulation and knowledge codification.[25] This knowledge codification, which refers to conversions of knowledge into messages that can then be processed as information,[26] allows executives to recognize reputable and high-status actors, to know how to develop personal interactions with key nonmarket actors, and to understand how to develop expertise in the policymaking process and social arenas. More importantly, it can help organizations select the correct information package for specific nonmarket scenarios and contexts.

All of these examples show how knowledge is interrelated with nonmarket information, where information oriented around research may be used in different formats. In other words, it is the codified knowledge that firms can leverage to share strategic information on social or political issues via face-to-face meetings, communication networks, electronic document exchange, and telephone conversations to convey explicit knowledge into different combinations. In the previous chapters, we suggested that the application of information results in increased accuracy, coordination, and efficiency.[27] The next section will explore how firms can deliver information using codified knowledge on *targeting*, *quality*, *frequency*, *resources*, and *relationships* in the nonmarket.

How to Deliver Nonmarket Information

To more thoroughly explore the concept of nonmarket information, we have developed a framework related to studies of the nonmarket,[28] drawing mainly

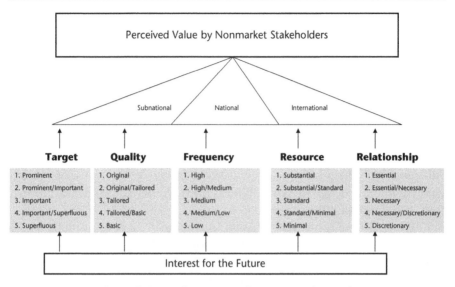

Figure 8.1 Developing an information value pack

on strategic information transmission[29] and reputation building literatures.[30] What matters is not only who in the field is "best" in terms of codifying their interest, but also who can put together the most compelling and consistent information offering to government and civil society. We argue that, to effectively orchestrate nonmarket strategies, companies need to look at their nonmarket information—or what we call their information value package—used to influence target interest groups at subnational, national, international (or regional), and supranational levels.[31] With that in mind, to further elaborate on our information delivery process approach, we have developed a framework in Figure 8.1 indicating to managers the key factors to consider when formulating their nonmarket strategy.

Research suggests that many CPA and CSR managers are often unsure how to configure an information value package[32]—that is, the way in which governments or other stakeholders preferentially perceive a firm's nonmarket information. We argue that a simple information value package consisting of five distinct but interrelated practices—*targeting, quality, frequency, resources, and relationships*[33]—creates tangible and intangible nonmarket benefits for the firm. Once the interest position is defined, as shown in Figure 8.1, the firm distinguishes itself from the competition through its unique configuration of these systemic elements. The 1–5 Likert-type scaling of each variable denotes the relative emphasis placed by a firm. Firms can identify their relative strategic weakness on specific issues by gauging which of these elements requires more focus and attention. Interest representation is the optimal approach for firms to influence policy and affect key stakeholders in the nonmarket.[34]

The information delivery process can be divided into several practical stages when creating perceived value[35] for political and social actors. According to De Fouloy,[36] the first step in building information value for nonmarket activities at any level of governance, regardless of country context, is to assemble an information network with institutions, associations, and partners that can provide an indispensable alarm system and a means of accessing and distributing vital information. Secondly, the earlier the firm intervenes in the legislative process, the more effective it is in achieving its goals. As we can see in Figure 8.1, adapting and conveying the right message to key institutions will potentially help influence key decision-makers.[37] We next look at each element in more detail, drawing on ideas from nonmarket, strategic information, and reputation literatures.

Targeting. To build on what we said in Chapter 7, it is important, before engaging in political or social arenas, to understand the agendas and interests of specific actors and institutions. For instance, a corporation like General Electric (GE) or Air France (AF), that wants to influence the EU emissions trading system (so-called "cap and trade") is most likely first to contact the European Commission's Directorate General (DG)[38] for Climate Action—or DGs more closely aligned with their industry interests, such as the Directorate General for Mobility and Transport or for Energy. Adapting nonmarket information packages to the interests of these specific DGs will help a GE or an AF gain attention and influence the policy process.[39] Since officials and experts at the European Commission are the wellspring of most EU legislation and regulation, this is often the optimal starting point for any firm. However, managers need to evaluate the order in which they target institutions and actors at national and supranational levels according to the issue and area in question. For instance, the EU has ultimate authority for European trade negotiations. Companies attempting to influence trade policy are, therefore, advised to prioritize the European Commission's DG for Trade. In contrast, when it comes to visa and immigration issues for its workers, companies need to target national central government departments and can largely ignore EU-level institutions.

Quality. The quality and reliability of information is crucial to having an input and impact. The quality of information is commonly thought of as a multidimensional concept with varying attributed characteristics, depending on a person's viewpoint.[40] Most commonly, information quality refers to data that are fit for use.[41] This implies a degree of relativity, as data considered appropriate for one use may not possess sufficient attributes for another use.[42] Therefore, the best way to capture any official's interest and also indirectly influence decision-makers is to provide quality, original information.[43] Since information quality varies from basic and unverified data to original and tested data, and stakeholders seek to be persuaded with hard, robust data, quality data needs to be statistically rigorous and trustworthy. Strong, robust research makes for a more compelling message and increases the likelihood that nonmarket actors will be receptive.

Frequency. The frequency of information delivery is also important, according to some scholars.[44] The quantity and timing of interventions in the political or social spheres can determine your performance outcomes.[45] As we have argued, corporations must build connections with nonmarket actors, but the success of these relations is based both on the frequency of interaction and the intensity of the relationship.[46] Inevitably, this can stray beyond the limits of propriety and result in inappropriate relationships between companies and nonmarket actors such as politicians. In late 2012, for example, a British government-commissioned investigation into the relationship of the press with the public, police, and politicians (the so-called Leveson Inquiry[47]) reported that senior politicians—including the current and previous two prime ministers—developed "too close a relationship with the press in a way which has not been in the public interest."[48]

Despite the irresponsible aspects of information exchange that can occur, regular and responsible exchanges are intended to ensure that firms can legitimately interact with political and regulatory agents and voice their opinions, preferences, and grievances. The frequency will usually increase once the relationship develops and transparency ensues. Lindhahl points out that frequencies in communication are likely to complement other lobbying tactics.[49] However, Fogarty, Hussein, and Ketz state that the frequency of political and social information exchanges carried out to date still requires more research.[50]

Resources. As we have noted elsewhere in this book, there is increased discussion about the use of social capital within a political context and also some references to political capital in management literature.[51] However, there is little consensus on how social and political capital operate together within the nonmarket sphere, and there are no consistent definitions of these forms of capital as constructs.[52] Because the construct has multiple applications at the individual, organizational, and societal levels of analysis,[53] the operationalization of nonmarket capital poses significant challenges. At the individual level, much of the focus has been on evaluating the political capital of elected government officials.[54] At the societal level, research has centered on how civil society activity prompts participation in political and social arenas and leads to democratic reform.[55] We concentrate on nonmarket capital at the organizational (firm) level.

Some scholars suggest that nonmarket capital is a specialized form of social or reputational capital. Building on Nahapiet and Ghoshal's conceptualization of social capital,[56] Shaffer and Hillman state that nonmarket capital entails resources "embedded within, available through, and derived from the network of relationships possessed by a social unit."[57] In other words, nonmarket capital is a firm's investment in the capability to develop access to deliver specific information to decision-makers.[58] Few studies equate non-market capital closely with the benefits derived from political and social relationships, such as information provision with policymakers and increased knowledge accumulation about public policy arenas.[59] Drawing on Shaffer and Hillman, we define nonmarket capital as the ability to influence government policy and societal perceptions, using specific and valuable information.[60] We offer a more generalized definition of nonmarket capital, drawing directly from resourced-based and nonmarket literatures.[61] The antecedents of nonmarket capital are a firm's unique resources and skills plus the market and political networks it occupies.[62] There are two primary inputs into the strength of ties and network benefits that result from them. First, a company has a set of resources and skills from its business position and its market activities that may combine to produce political and social capital under certain conditions. Secondly, a company's political and social ties and network benefits are the result of its connections to other markets and actors. The firm's position within these networks (for instance, does it occupy a central position?) is an important factor in explaining the variance of nonmarket capital. The characteristics of a firm's market and nonmarket networks— as well as its own position within those networks—are likely to affect the strength of its ties to public officials and the benefits that flow from those relationships. These benefits may include information about pending policies, invitations to important meetings, and appointments to key policy advisory groups.

Our conceptualization of nonmarket capital provides a firm-specific measure of political and social performance that embodies both tangible and intangible benefits. Previous studies, which have focused primarily on the relationship between industry political action and legislative outcomes, have come up short in terms of predictive power.[63] Our definition suggests that firms receive other important benefits from nonmarket capital, including special access to privileged information through participation in committees and other policy or regulatory forums.

We further argue that the type of nonmarket resources and capital that are developed between firms and public officials and the eventual activation of these resources or capital is contingent upon a firm's unique and valuable capabilities, network density, and structural and positional embeddedness. The next section will delve more deeply into relationships to better understand how firms can use relationships to exchange information. We will draw on previous research in the social capital literature to show how a firm's structural and positional embeddedness affects its decisions to form new ties within existing networks.[64]

Relationships: While relationships certainly overlap with resources, they require more attention in the delivery of information. It is very rare that a single relationship can make a strong enough case to protect firm profits. Building relationships with related groups (for instance, European trade associations and specific European Commission directorates or units) is indispensable to delivering corporate political and social information packages.[65] In some cases, firms set up ad hoc coalitions to present a united front on a particular issue.[66] Relationships also have cross-cultural variances. Building a rapport with U.S. officials requires a very different approach and style from that required to establish relations with Chinese or Indian officials.

As we have already indicated, the initial step for companies when developing nonmarket resources is to form network ties with elected and/or administrative officials or other important stakeholders. A tie is characterized by the intensity of interaction between partners and their resource commitment.[67] Firms must decide whether it is strategically advantageous to form a weak or a strong tie. Weak ties involve a lower resource commitment, are less frequent, and constitute more of an arm's-length transaction. Economic examples include marketing agreements and licensing and patent agreements between companies.[68] Strong ties involve greater resource commitments and more frequent interactions. Partners have to invest significantly in these relationships before they yield any benefits.

The decision whether to form a weak or a strong relationship with public officials may be based on an analysis of the different roles that ties play and the diverse political circumstances that exist. Corporations have a finite amount of time and energy to invest in relationships, so they have to decide which approach will be most beneficial.[69] An advantage of weak ties is that they are cheaper to form and still convey elements of the company's message. Formation occurs through fairly ordinary activities such as providing a legal campaign contribution or meeting at a social event. Weak ties are also easier to maintain than strong ties because they involve less contact. Another advantage of weak ties is that firms can still gain access to some unique information. A weak tie may also serve as a bridging function, enabling a firm to make the connection between two networks.[70] If a firm is operating in an uncertain environment, weak ties may be helpful in understanding environmental trends.[71] The downside of weak ties is that the firm is unlikely to get specific or detailed information about an issue or agenda because it lacks intimacy with the informant. This may limit the firm's ability to receive and give the full offering of nonmarket benefits that a political agent can provide or receive.

The formation of strong ties obviously involves greater resource and time commitments to convey information. However, a strong tie with officials also yields strategic benefits. A firm will receive an increased volume of information as well as a deeper knowledge of specific topics.[72] Strong ties also enhance trust, mutual gain, reciprocity, and a long-term perspective.[73] In the political arena, this may imply that a firm will gain an in-depth understanding of pending political and policy activities. In addition, a firm with strong ties may develop goodwill and a history of reciprocity with elected officials that yield other benefits such as political sponsorship and access to congressional or parliamentary hearings and advisory committees. However, with strong ties, the firm has considerable time and effort invested in a particular politician or other official. The firm may be vulnerable if that official leaves office, loses his or her position of power (such as when the government changes), or is involved in a scandal. The next section explores how companies can monitor their information delivery in a consistent way.

Information Exchanges in Practice

A large portion of the nonmarket literature is devoted to giving advice to managers and firms wishing to establish a successful temporary or long-term advantage.[74] In most cases, saying that firms should demonstrate intelligent and prudent behavior can summarize these how-to templates. We show that, for every specific political or social arena, firms have to observe and consider the issues at stake, the stakeholders involved, the time dimension, and the arena boundaries, as well as their best practices. Pedler and Van Schendelen summarize this by calling for a lot of "preparatory homework" and "fine-tuned fieldwork" for information delivery.[75] The so-called *best practices* are never permanently fixed but are dependent on new insights and are thus constantly in development. From the approach introduced earlier in Figure 8.1, we identify how to stretch information across the nonmarket to create influence. But how can firms monitor their information packages consistently?

Directors of nonmarket strategy functions (government affairs, corporate responsibility, and so on) frequently mention monitoring the political and social landscape as a key element of their work, although this function tends to be neglected in the strategy literature.[76] Monitoring means going through agendas and finding what needs to be copied to which nonmarket actors.[77] Monitoring is often recommended at a more sophisticated level than simply trawling through transcripts of legislative proceedings and press releases. It can involve many forms of useful political intelligence.[78] Airline companies such as Lufthansa and Air France-KLM constantly monitor their information packages and information from the nonmarket in relation to targeting, quality, frequency, resources, and relationships in the nonmarket.[79] Subsequently, these companies use sophisticated information technologies to monitor and codify those five factors.

The purpose of detailed monitoring and researching is essentially to enable the corporation or client to develop messages related to public policy issues and to identify the most appropriate or effective ways of communicating information (or key messages) to relevant politicians and officials.[80] There are numerous options or routes available. A tried-and-tested approach is to contact legislators and policymakers on the basis of issues: a lobbyist usually seeks to demonstrate awareness that the target has a known interest in the relevant policy area. Politicians and officials generally accept that lobbyists often have a better understanding of the issues than they do. The information exchange events hence act as a bridge across which messages can flow in order to ensure that policy decisions are better informed. This tactic can best be summarized in the words of one director of government affairs: "It's not that you have a huge academic background or skills. . . . what will impress these people are the intensity of the relationship and the rigor in the information delivery."[81]

In summary, nonmarket studies have tended to focus on firms, noting the size and type of firms involved in the process,[82] but have often neglected to explore the importance of information delivery.[83] According to Mazey and Richardson, many multinationals from highly regulated industries are deeply involved in providing information.[84] These firms craft nonmarket strategies and organize their information packages (campaigns) using external lobbyists on occasion, but it is mainly the firm's own executives who carry messages to politicians and officials.[85] Firms that are serious about the development and delivery of information packages are able to create real impact in the nonmarket environment.

Conclusions and Managerial Implications

In this chapter we argue that information is of critical importance when developing a nonmarket strategy. However, nonmarket strategy can appear unstructured, even when leveraging accurate information. Therefore, we advance five elements that firms must consider when shaping and delivering their information package: targeting, quality, frequency, resources, and relationships. Firms distinguish themselves from the competition and create the foundations of nonmarket advantage through their unique configuration of these systemic variables in the nonmarket. Ultimately, firms must try to develop unique information packages that increase their legitimacy and reputation in given nonmarket environments. Consequently, there are several key learning points in this chapter for strategic managers and business leaders:

- Information packages need to be defined and delivered in relation to specific issues.

- Managers need to plan their information exchanges with sufficient attention to targeting, quality, frequency, resources, and relationships.

- Managers who proactively configure their information delivery process enhance their chances of getting their messages across to key nonmarket stakeholders.

In the next chapter, we broaden our focus to include the range of stakeholders with whom the firm interacts—or is affected by—and the various modes and mechanisms firms use to engage these stakeholders. The firm and its external stakeholders in the political and social arenas have a symbiotic and complementary relationship. Chapter 9 reviews various strands in contemporary research on stakeholder management and then sets out practical techniques—stakeholder mapping and valuation, and the sample stakeholder assessment exercise—to help managers explore how their organizations can create alignment with external stakeholders.

Notes

1. Wilde, O. (1894). A few maxims for the instruction of the over-educated. First published anonymously in the *Saturday Review*, 17 November.
2. <www.opensecrets.org> (accessed January 20, 2012).
3. <http://www.public.asu.edu/~dkarjala/commentary/ChiTrib10-17-98.html> (accessed January 20, 2012).
4. <http://waccglobal.org/en/20044-communication-today-old-challenges-and-new-realities/489-Contemporary-denial-of-access-Knowledge-IPR-and-the-public-good.html> (accessed January 20, 2012).
5. Wöll 2007. See also Yoffie 1988 and Yoffie and Bergenstein 1985.
6. Policymakers literally are unsure about what kind of interest is represented by the lobbying firms with which they are interacting. We find this possibility plausible, given the very large number of lobbyists who inhabit Washington, DC, Brussels, and other political centers of the world (as we remarked in the introductory chapter). The other interpretation is that the policymaker does know which group the lobbyist represents but is unsure about that group's position on the policy in question.
7. Lagerlöf, J. (1997). Lobbying, information, and private and social welfare. *European Journal of Political Economy*, 13: 615–637.
8. Aggarwal, V.K. (2001). Corporate market and nonmarket strategies in Asia: a conceptual framework. *Business and Politics*, 3(2): 89–108.

9. Wood, D. (1990). *Business and society: instructor's manual*. London: Longman Higher Education; Baron 1995a.

10. Bhatt, G.D. (2000). Information dynamics, learning and knowledge creation in organizations. *The Learning Organization*, 7(2): 89–99 (90); Nonaka, I. and Takeuchi, H. (1995). *The knowledge creating company: how Japanese companies create the dynamics of innovation*. Oxford: Oxford University Press.

11. Kirby, A. (1988). Trade associations as information exchange mechanisms. *The RAND Journal of Economics*, 19: 138–146; Mirman, L.J., Samuelson, L., and Schlee, E.E. (1994). Strategic information manipulation in duopolies. *Journal of Economic Theory*, 62: 363–384.

12. Bhatt 2000; Baron 1995a.

13. Yoffie and Bergenstein 1985.

14. Bhatt 2000.

15. Financial Crisis Inquiry Commission (2011). *The financial crisis inquiry report*: xviii. <http://c0182732.cdnl.cloudfiles.rackspacedcloud.com/fcic_final_report_full.pdf. (accessed March 21, 2012).

16. Frynas et al. 2006.

17. Bonardi et al. 2006.

18. Lawton, McGuire, and Rajwani 2013.

19. Baye, M., Kovenock, D., and de Vries, C. (1996). The all-pay auction with complete information. *Economic Theory*, 8: 291–305.

20. Milgrom, P. and John, R. (1986). Relying on the information of interested parties. *Rand Journal of Economics*, 17(1): 18–32.

21. Austen-Smith, D. (1995). Campaign contributions and access. *American Political Science Review*, 89: 566–581.

22. Baron 1995a.

23. Cowan, R., David, P.A., and Foray, D. (2000). The explicit economics of knowledge codification and tacitness. *Industrial and Corporate Change*, 9(2): 211–253.

24. Kogut, B. and Zander, U. (1992). Knowledge of the firm and the replication of technology. *Organization Science*, 3: 383–397.

25. Lawton and Rajwani 2011.

26. Cowan, R. and Foray, D. (1997). The economics of codification and the diffusion of knowledge. *Industrial and Corporate Change*, 6(3): 595–622.

27. Lawton and Rajwani 2011.

28. Baron 1995a.

29. Crawford, V.P. and Sobel, J. (1982). Strategic information transmission. *Econometrica*, 50(6): 1431–1451.

30. Carter, S. (2006). The interaction of top management group, stakeholder, and situational factors on certain corporate reputation management activities. *Journal of Management Studies*, 43(5): 1145–1176.

31. Lawton and Rajwani 2011.

32. Lawton and Rajwani 2011. Op cit. See also Scherer and Palazzo 2011.

33. Lawton and Rajwani 2011; Baron 1995a.

34. Greenwood 2002.

35. Perceived value is defined here as the stakeholder or beneficiary receiving added value information. In other words, it is important information that helps the

social or political actor to better understand the firm's position, which in turn helps and supports the policymaking process.

36. De Fouloy, C.D. (2001). *The professional lobbyist's desk reference*. Brussels: Gateway.
37. Persson, T. and Helpman, E. (1998). Lobbying and legislative bargaining. *NBER Working Paper No. 6589*.
38. A European Commission Directorate General is the administrative and policymaking equivalent of a national government department. For instance, the Directorate General for Mobility and Transport is essentially the EU's version of the United States Department of Transportation or the Ministry of Transport of the Russian Federation.
39. Barrett, S.A. (1990). Deregulating European aviation: a case study. *Transportation*, 16: 311–327.
40. Klein, B.D. (2001). User perceptions of data quality: Internet and traditional text sources. *Journal of Computer Information Systems*, 41(4): 9–18.
41. Wang, R.Y. and Strong, D.M. (1996). Beyond accuracy: what data quality means to data consumers. *Journal of Management Information Systems*, 12(4): 5–33.
42. Knight, S. and Burn, J. (2005). Developing a framework for assessing information quality on the World Wide Web. *Informing Science Journal*, 8: 160–172.
43. Caulkin, S. and Collins, J. (2003). *The private life of public affairs*. London: Green Alliance.
44. Coen, D. (1999). The impact of U.S. lobbying practice on the European business–government relationship. *California Management Review*, 41: 27–44. See also De Figueiredo J.M. and Silverman, B.S. (2006). Academic earmarks and the returns to lobbying. *Journal of Law and Economics*, 49: 597–626.
45. Lawton and Rajwani 2011.
46. Bouwen, P. (2002). Corporate lobbying in the EU: the logic of access. *Journal of European Public Policy*, 9(3): 365–390.
47. For further details, see <http://www.levesoninquiry.org.uk/> (accessed June 12, 2013).
48. Winnett, R. (2012). Leveson Report: David Cameron became too close to newspaper executives. *The Telegraph*. 29 November. <http://www.telegraph.co.uk/news/uknews/leveson-inquiry/9712801/Leveson-Report-David-Cameron-became-too-close-to-newspaper-executives.html> (accessed June 12, 2013).
49. Lindahl, F.W. (1987). Accounting standards and Olson's Theory of Collective Action. *Journal of Accounting and Public Policy*, 6: 59–72.
50. Fogarty, T.J., Hussein, M.E.A., and Ketz, J.E. (1994). Political aspects of financial accounting standard setting in the USA. *Accounting, Auditing & Accountability Journal*, 7: 24–46.
51. Shaffer and Hillman 2000.
52. Lawton, McGuire, and Rajwani 2013.
53. Blumentritt, T. and Rehbein, K. (2008). The political capital of foreign subsidiaries: an exploratory model. *Business & Society*, 47(2): 242–263.
54. Lawton, McGuire, and Rajwani 2013.
55. Booth, J.A., and Richard, P.B. (1998). Civil society, political capital, and democratization in Central America. *Journal of Politics*, 60: 780–800.

56. Nahapiet and Ghoshal 1998.

57. Shaffer and Hillman 2000: 180.

58. Oberman, W. (2004). A framework for the ethical analysis of corporate political activity. *Business & Society Review*, 109: 245–263.

59. Mahon, J. and McGowan, R. (1996). *Industry as a player in the political and social arena: defining the competitive environment.* Westport, CT: Quorum.

60. Shaffer and Hillman 2000.

61. Adler, P.S. and Kwon, S.W. (2002). Social capital: prospects for a new concept. *Academy of Management Review*, 27: 17–40; Wasserman, S. and Faust, K. (1994). *Social network analysis: methods and applications.* Cambridge, MA: Cambridge University Press; Lawton, McGuire, and Rajwani 2013.

62. Lawton, McGuire, and Rajwani 2013.

63. Wright, J.R. (1985). PACs, contributions, and roll calls: an organizational perspective. *American Political Science Review*, 79: 400–414; Hall, R.L. and Wayman, F.W. (1990). Buying time: moneyed interests and the mobilization of bias in congressional committees. *American Political Science Review*, 84: 797–820.

64. Gulati, R. and Gargiulo, M. (1999). Where do interorganizational networks come from? *Journal of Sociology*, 104: 1439–1494.

65. Barrett 1990.

66. Getz 1997.

67. Rowley, T.J. (1997). Moving beyond dyadic ties: a network theory of stakeholders' influences. *Academy of Management Review*, 22: 887–910.

68. Rowley 1997.

69. Seibert, S.E., Kraimer, M.L., and Liden, R.C. (2001). A social capital theory of career success. *Academy of Management Journal*, 44: 219–237.

70. Seibert et al. 2001.

71. Rowley 1997.

72. Uzzi, B. (1997). Social structure and competition in interfirm networks: the paradox of embeddedness. *Administrative Science Quarterly*, 42: 35–67.

73. Larson, A. (1992). Network dyads in entrepreneurial settings: a study of the governance of exchange relationships. *Administrative Science Quarterly*, 37: 76–105.

74. De Figueiredo and Tiller 2001.

75. Pedler, R.H. and Van Schendelen, M.P.C.M. (eds.) (1994). *Lobbying the European Union.* Aldershot, U.K.: Dartmouth.

76. Interview with Malcolm Lane, Director of Government Affairs, Tata Group. London, January 6, 2012.

77. Interview with Malcolm Lane, Director of Government Affairs, Tata Group. London, January 6, 2012.

78. Nugent, N. (2004). *The government and politics of the European Union.* Durham, NC: Duke University Press.

79. Lawton and Rajwani 2011.

80. Mack, C. (1990). *The executive's handbook of trade and business associations: how they work—and how to make them work effectively for you.* Westport, CT: Greenwood Publishing.

81. Interview with Malcolm Lane, Director of Government Affairs, Tata Group. London, January 6, 2012.

82. Hillman et al. 2004.
83. Nobes, C.W. (1992). A political history of goodwill in the UK: an illustration of cyclical standard setting. *Abacus*, 28(2): 142–161.
84. Mazey and Richardson 1993.
85. Beresford, D.R. (1995). How should the FASB be judged? *Accounting Horizons*, 9(2): 56–61.

9

Aligning with Stakeholders*

The job of management is to maintain an equitable and working balance among the claims of the various directly affected interest groups.[1]

Frank W. Abrams

In 2009, after several years of preparation, Oxfam America, a part of the international development organization, and Swiss Re, the global reinsurer, along with other partners, piloted Horn of Africa Risk Transfer for Adaptation (HARITA). This was an innovative model designed to help propel some of the poorest farmers in Ethiopia out of poverty by helping them to cope with climate-related risk. Oxfam's goal for HARITA was to successfully develop a scalable model that could be replicated in developing countries across the globe. It was aimed at farmers to help them deal with the effects of drought and other weather-related challenges associated with climate change. Swiss Re served initially as a funder and technical adviser for HARITA but sought to use the project to better understand insurance markets in developing countries[2]—a perfect example of strategy alignment in practice.

Similarly, in 2010, Kenya's Equity Bank adopted a strategy of engaging various stakeholders as it sought to establish strong ties within the broader social and political environment. The bank's objective was, in part, to foster prosperity for Kenyan citizens by generating wealth for different communities. The bank developed a number of cross-sectoral partnerships that ranged from collaboration with agrochemical manufacturers such as Agmark and trade organizations such as the Eastern Africa Grain Council to not-for-profit organizations such as Millennium Promise and aid agencies such as the German government's GTZ and the United Nations World Food Program.[3] Equity Bank also developed strategic partnerships with organizations such as the Alliance for a Green Revolution in Africa and The International Fund for

Agricultural Development, a United Nations agency that provides cash guarantees that reduce the bank's risk when lending to smallholder farmers who have little or no collateral.

These two examples highlight the importance of engaging different stakeholders when developing a nonmarket strategy. Indeed, the firm and its external stakeholders in the political and social arenas have a symbiotic and complementary relationship. In Chapter 7, we focused on how firms can cultivate and respond to various types of interests. In this chapter, we broaden that focus to include the range of stakeholders with whom the firm interacts—or is affected by—and the various modes and mechanisms firms use to evaluate those stakeholders. This chapter reviews numerous strands in contemporary research on stakeholder management and then sets out practical techniques—stakeholder mapping and valuation, and the sample stakeholder assessment exercise—that can help managers create better alignment with their stakeholders.

Before looking at those tools and techniques, let us further explore the term *stakeholder management.*

Untangling Stakeholder Management

Stakeholder management has gained considerable attention as a unifying framework for understanding the complex interactions between firms and their internal and external constituencies. The terms *stake* and *stakeholder* need to be defined for our discussion of the theory in relation to the nonmarket. A "stake" in an organization rests on "legal, moral, or presumed" claims or on the capacity to influence an organization's "behavior, direction, process, or outcomes."[4] Similarly, Reed suggests that "stakes are understood to impose normative obligations...it's an interest for which a valid normative claim can be advanced."[5]

Practicing managers and management scholars recognize the fundamental interdependencies that exist between firms and their stakes in the political and social arenas. Chester Barnard described the business of firms as a "cooperative" organization based on rational thinking.[6] This characterization of stakeholders has continued to fascinate scholars in the decades since Barnard's seminal work. Building on those ideas, we can trace the concept of stakeholders through various studies, beginning in the 1960s.[7] As we noted in Chapter 1, according to Schwartz and Carroll[8] and Jones and Wicks,[9] stakeholder theory presumes that the corporation possesses connections with, and linkages to, many constituent groups ("stakeholders") that affect and are affected by its decisions.[10] Furthermore, the theory is especially concerned with the nature of these relationships in terms of both processes and outcomes for the firm and its stakeholders. In addition, there is a normative element that presumes that the interests of all (legitimate) stakeholders have intrinsic value, and no set of interests is assumed to dominate the others.[11] Finally, the theory is a practical one in that it focuses on managerial decision-making.[12]

Although the stakeholder concept has developed in various ways,[13] it has been expressed most often in the moral prescription embodied in the Frank W. Abrams quote at the beginning of this chapter—that managers should, to some degree, respect the interests of all stakeholders as they make decisions. Speaking in the 1940s, the chairman of Standard Oil of New Jersey (now ExxonMobil) defined these "stakeholders" (not his term) as stockholders, employees, customers, and the public at large.[14] The list of stakeholders that most modern corporations have can be extensive. It includes governments, employees, investors (shareholders and lenders), customers, unions, regulatory authorities, joint venture and other alliance partners, private organizations (NGOs and occasionally the media), and local communities and citizens.[15] Increasingly, it also concerns both downstream and upstream partners in the supply chain. Post et al. develop a useful stakeholder view of the corporation in which stakeholders are positioned in three concentric circles around the company[16] that correspond to the strategic settings of the firm: the *resource-based view* includes customers/users, employees, and shareholders; *industry structure* embraces supply chain associates, regulatory authorities, unions, and joint venture partners and alliances; and the *social and political arena* contains government, private organizations (mainly NGOs), and local communities and citizens. This approach emphasizes that the focus of this book is on the third strategic setting of the firm—the social and political arenas.

Corporate governance scholars have, in the past, tended to emphasize one particular class of stakeholders, namely shareowners.[17] This view—often called stockholder management—retains support in many circles but is generally regarded by proponents of stakeholder management as morally unjustified.[18] In Chapter 2, we engaged with contrasting views on the role of business in society and attempted to move beyond ideology and toward a more pragmatic perspective. In keeping with this approach, we contend that to focus attention on only one of the core stakeholders is to ignore important peripheral stakeholders such as citizens, community activists, and NGOs whose interests also ought to be considered, if not captured, in business strategies to ensure nonmarket success.

As we already noted, a particular variant of corporate social responsibility often called "strategic" CSR[19] and corporate political activity[20] constitute two key conceptual pillars in the nonmarket field. Together, they suggest that a company's social and political practices are—and should be—integrated into its business and corporate-level strategies. Baron[21] has argued that companies compete for socially responsible customers by explicitly linking their social contribution to product sales or by engaging with political stakeholders to defend their market position. Some scholars have sought to isolate normative and instrumental underpinnings of the stakeholder approach.[22] In addition, they have attempted to develop highly actionable frameworks of stakeholder theory that allow managers to classify and stratify stakeholders according to their relative salience.[23] Stakeholder engagement tools have evolved even further to be viewed as strategic or instrumental tools for the firm. This view has come increasingly to enhance the nonmarket literature, with important implications for collective understanding about the role of nonmarket stakeholders in society. The next section will consider how firms can assess, value, and leverage their external stakeholders to garner advantages in their nonmarket environments.

Stakeholder Assessment and Valuation

Mitchell, Agle, and Wood proposed a model of stakeholder salience, based on the relative *power*, *urgency*, and *legitimacy* of stakeholder claims, that can be used to better understand nonmarket stakeholders. According to the authors, power is often achieved by obtaining valued resources needed by the focal firm; this creates disparities between stakeholders.[24] In their model, *power* represents a measure of how freely those who possess it can exercise their influence and will ultimately represent how the firm interacts with these individuals.[25] *Urgency*, defined in terms of the "degree to which stakeholder claims call for immediate attention,"[26] depends on how time-sensitive or critically important the issue under consideration is.[27] *Legitimacy*, derived from firm behaviors that are proper, trustworthy, expected, and accepted among society, represents the final element of the stakeholder saliency model.[28]

All three elements have been empirically tested, and while there is some evidence that these three variables are not fully independent, our Table 9.1 provides a framework for managers to determine which stakeholders pose threats and/or opportunities and which may have less relevance or importance for the firm. This simple illustration shows how stakeholders can be rated across these three attributes, with the sum of those rankings yielding a net assessment of the relative salience of that particular stakeholder. While this is hardly an exact science, bringing some semblance of rigor to this process—instead of reacting and responding on the basis of impression, intuition, or other emotional assessment—can be a useful starting point in evaluating which stakeholders really count.

Table 9.1 Sample stakeholder assessment exercise: rating current and future stakeholder salience

Salience Measure 1-most; 4-least Current/Future Potential	Power	Urgency	Legitimacy	Total
Stakeholder 1	2/4	3/4	4/4	9/12
Stakeholder 2	3/4	3/4	1/4	7/12
Stakeholder 3	2/4	3/4	3/4	8/12

Extending Stakeholder Assessment to the "A" Framework

Moving beyond the assessment and valuation approach shown in Table 9.1, Cummings and Doh[29] suggest that the Mitchell, Agle, and Wood model can be connected to another framework to help managers identify and map key value creators and destroyers on the basis of their impact upon value creation in their economic, political, social, and technological environments. As we can see in Figure 9.1, this framework provides a basis and sequence from which managers can pursue a comprehensive stakeholder valuation analysis.

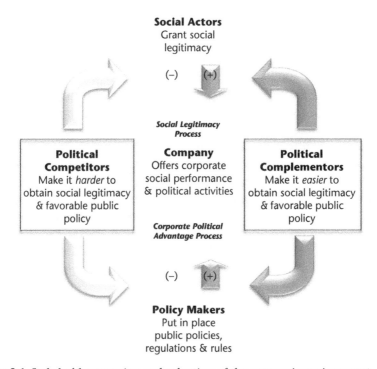

Figure 9.1 Stakeholder mapping and valuation of the economic environment

The first step in the framework is mapping out which stakeholders are important and how they can exert their power. As we have mentioned, the strategies pursued in each environment will be different, as will the targeted stakeholders.[30] When looking into the economic sphere first, it is important to recognize that there can be economic competitors and complementors present, by which we mean stakeholders who serve to work against the firm's interest and those who work to support those interests. In addition, the main goal of this realm is to successfully generate economic value by strategically using inputs to create meaningful products and services.[31] Therefore, by separating those who compete or impede the achievement of strategic goals from those who facilitate the end goal and working with the latter group, the firm will be able to better manage and anticipate changes in both the market and nonmarket environments. Figure 9.1 maps out this economic value-creation process by clearly showing how each stakeholder has an impact on the firm.

In addition to the economic environment, managers also must be cognizant of political, social, technological, and environmental aspects,[32] as these serve to enhance strategic forward thinking and planning to create firm value and preparedness. In light of the nonmarket environment in particular, firms are often forced to take on social activities in addition to those intended to pursue economic benefits. Consequently, company resources are frequently used to enhance or repair social legitimacy with different stakeholders.[33]

According to Cummings and Doh, within the nonmarket environment, firms employ economic resources to shape public policy using core stakeholders, as in the telecommunications example of MCI's efforts in the 1970s to break up AT&T.[34] In other words, the purpose of using the nonmarket environment is to employ resources to gain a public policy advantage and to then seek legitimacy through political or social activities. In doing so, the firm is able to use power and influence strategies to gain a competitive advantage in the marketplace. It is also not uncommon for firms to pursue both strategies at the same time: gaining political advantage and social legitimacy.[35]

Creating a political advantage can be accomplished in various ways, but it most often needs involvement from policymakers or social actors. These are stakeholders involved in public policy decisions or individuals who provide information on social issues that constrain or release firm value.[36] In addition, as in the economic environment, the political environment also contains individuals who serve to help or harm the cause, often referred to as political competitors and political complementors.[37] Paying close attention to those stakeholders in each category is essential when pursuing social legitimacy to gain a corporate political advantage.

The third nonmarket environment that firms should be aware of is the technological, in which the goal is to persuade stakeholders to adopt a specific technology or business model.[38] This concept is very different from the economic environment because it does not directly pertain to the exchange of resources, but rather to relationships with stakeholders and their influence on the subsequent adoption or diffusion of technology. The diffusion method allows a product to become so widespread that a business model acceptance results.[39]

One way to accomplish this task is through a "Trojan horse" or "entrenchment strategy," in which a technology is given away for free or at extremely low prices to ensure adoption and create a desire for future products under the same model.[40] This is a forceful method, given that acceptance often leads to staying power if the technology is unique and requires some base of knowledge that users do not want to abandon. However, managers must also be aware that technology is ever-changing; to maintain a competitive advantage they must also pay careful attention to competitor offerings. It is not uncommon for a superior product to lose out because a competitor had a larger product offering, as in the case of Betamax versus VHS in the now dated clash over the global standard for video recordings. Firms must not only diffuse technology across a large customer base, but also offer complementary products that will further enhance the model.[41]

Given that technology is never stagnant, it is essential for companies to learn how to move with the nonmarket environment. Firms must constantly be aware of what the competition is working on and what consumers are looking for in their products, must continually learn and seek creative combinations of market and nonmarket strategies to gain a competitive advantage,[42] and must identify those who serve to affect the strategy. Key adopters and end-user stakeholders are important to the process, given that key adopters choose to forgo their own ideas and processes for those of the focal organization and that end users are those who adopt a technology for its use.[43]

However, as in the economic and political environment, firms must also be aware of competitors and complementors in the highly competitive and fast-moving technological environment. For instance, every additional customer gained significantly increases the value for all adopters as well as the focal company's hope of staying power.[44]

Knowledge of all the stakeholders within each environment and how they serve to help or deter the focal company and business model will pay huge dividends when formulating competitive strategies. Firms need to consider creating alignment with their stakeholders in the nonmarket. However, how can this alignment process work with different stakeholders?

Aligning with Stakeholders

In keeping with the theme of this book, we consider aligning with stakeholders to be part of the broader concept of aligning market and nonmarket strategy.[45] In this context, we argue that alignment considers *collaboration* with key stakeholders (to seek mutually beneficial outcomes where feasible), *trust* (to conduct engagement in a manner that fosters integrity, transparency, and mutual respect), and *inclusiveness* (understanding and involving stakeholders).[46] Alignment, which suggests the identification of interests— that is, where the concerns and priorities of the focal company and the stakeholders overlap or are mutually beneficial[47]—may take several forms and be advanced through a range of activities, both between the company and relevant stakeholders and, more broadly, as part of coalitions and other collaborative initiatives.

Collaboration with Stakeholders

The first step in aligning with stakeholders is to consider the concept of collaboration. Corporations are increasingly engaging with nonprofit partners as they develop, refine, and adapt business models to reach underserved communities around the world,[48] and as a result, collaboration between corporations and NGOs is on the rise.[49] Sometimes termed *social partnerships*, *collaborative social initiatives*, or *social alliances*, relationships between NGOs and corporations comprise an exchange of complementary resources, not unlike those that occur in alliances among private-sector firms.[50] However, cross-sector partnerships are unique in that they can provide both NGOs and corporations with access to skills, competences, and capabilities different from those that are available within their own organization or that might result from alliances among same-sector organizations. According to Rondinelli and London, collaborative relationships among NGOs and corporations can offer corporations the opportunity to achieve the legitimacy and develop the capabilities needed to respond to the increasing pressures from stakeholders to address environmental and other social issues.[51] For example, Doctors Without Borders/Médecins Sans Frontières (DWB) provides a reliable, efficient, and trustworthy partner for pharmaceutical companies to distribute medications in developing countries, conveying potential reputation benefits (or costs) that are unique to DWB's status as a nonfirm, nongovernmental stakeholder. NGOs may also provide unique, on-the-ground knowledge and resources that support the success of CSR efforts. It has been argued that "nongovernmental organizations are uniquely positioned to develop some of the most innovative and successful business models in the developing world."[52] For NGOs themselves, cross-sector partnerships with corporations yield valuable strategies and resources from the business world, including financial and technical expertise, human resources, and reputational benefits.

While the logic behind cross-sector collaborations may be strong, participation in such partnerships presents challenges for corporate and nonprofit partners alike. Corporations and NGOs have fundamentally different structures and values,[53] and relations between corporations and NGOs have sometimes been characterized by hostility and mistrust. Cross-sector partnerships also face additional challenges when it comes to organizational learning. Organizational learning generally requires a level of common experience—a condition that is often weak or missing in alliances between for-profit and nonprofit organizations.[54] This lack of common experience, trust, and communication can result in misunderstandings and internal conflict, even when partnerships that appear to signal shared values and commitments are proposed. Because of these differences, cross-sector partnerships require ongoing maintenance, attention, and commitment through which their members "continually negotiate a workable set of cultural practices among themselves."[55] An example is the case of Grupo Balbo.

Grupo Balbo, a family-owned sugar company based in Brazil, sells domestically and to major Western food and beverage companies. It crushes approximately six million tons of cane annually, generating 293,000 tons of sugar along with 318 million liters of ethanol. Grupo Balbo was interested in transitioning the entire sugar industry into a fully organic sector.[56] In order to jump-start this process, the company began to collaborate on the creation of Brazil's first national organic certification system. It also engaged in discussions with Brazilian and German environmental politicians[57] to promote tax incentives and other policies favoring organic production. The company partnered and collaborated with a governmental environmental research department to conduct hundreds of biodiversity field studies and initiated discussions with a variety of organizations and NGOs to increase knowledge of the impact of organic sugar cane production. Finally, they published data both online and offline, including a sustainability report. This was done not only to increase transparency and establish confidence among stakeholders, including cross-sector partners from the retail and confectionery industries, but also to spread knowledge and understanding of organic cultivation of sugar cane.[58] This example highlights how a firm enables the group to distinguish itself from *greenwashers*,[59] particularly given the current lack of organic certification standards.

Drawing on the Grupo Balbo example, it is important to recognize that challenges are magnified when cross-sector partners begin to consider scaling or moving beyond small, localized demonstration projects to broader, more comprehensive, sustainable initiatives to build trust. As partnerships expand to include additional participants and resources and larger geographic coverage, new risks can manifest themselves in terms of low trust. So how do companies force a trust alignment with their stakeholders in the nonmarket environment?

Developing Trust with Stakeholders

Building trust is another fundamental element of any stakeholder management process within the nonmarket. Appropriate and diligent planning and preparation by any firm will go a long way to assisting in building trust and in ensuring that the initial stakeholder engagement is more likely to be successful.[60] With this in mind, various factors need to be carefully managed to prevent a lack of trust, including imbalance of the relationship, cultural barriers, and ways of working with different stakeholders.[61] Therefore, to understand trust-related challenges in stakeholder management, we need to better understand trust in the management literature.

Trust has been defined as "the willingness of a party to be vulnerable to the actions of another party."[62] Lewicki et al. define trust as "confident positive expectations regarding another's conduct."[63] From both those definitions, there exists a truster and a trustee in any given trust relationship who are willing to be open to each other's actions.[64] Thus, the trustee's beliefs and values may affect that relationship in either a positive or a negative way.[65] Drawing on those views, we argue that trust is vital to any stakeholder engagement in the nonmarket, as different stakeholders may have different perspectives on, and conditions for, trust.[66] There are several reasons why a community or civil society stakeholder may trust a firm more. The building of trust is a crucial part of meaningful engagement resulting in information being shared both ways between firms and sociopolitical actors, with trust becoming an enabler or a barrier.[67] Consequently, significant willingness from both parties to understand the other's viewpoints can improve the ability to find commonalities to enhance mutual value.[68]

Ability, predictability, and reliability can be important elements of trust.[69] Offering reliable information to optimize policies is important, and the potential effects of trust on satisfaction and policy uncertainty reduction are equally important.[70] However, what has been missing from existing studies is a better understanding of reliability to ensure trust in engaging with nonmarket actors. Research suggests that firms viewed as reliable or credible in delivering information can build trust with their stakeholders over the long term, which ultimately helps them to maintain their competitive advantage.[71]

To illustrate the points above in relation to operationalizing trust, consider this example. A leading retailer invests significant time and resources in developing relations with a range of nonmarket stakeholders. The intent and approach is focused on starting open communication and building a transparent relationship that the company can draw upon in future.[72] To achieve this objective, the firm dedicated significant head office and local staff time, as well as engaging the external affairs services of consultants and other outside partners, over a twelve-month period. But what happens if they then allow an eighteen-month time lapse during which no follow-up or further exchanges take place with the nonmarket stakeholders? Research by Jeffery suggests that increased negative publicity surrounding the actions of the business organization in its market environment would potentially lead to negative outcomes in its nonmarket environment.[73] Therefore, in this given scenario, corporations that re-establish contact with stakeholders and request that they reject specific legislation might face resistance. Moreover, this would raise concerns on the part of stakeholders, principally because of the long "period of silence" on the part of the business organization.[74] Not only would the stakeholders potentially decline to help, but the perceived poor corporate communications with stakeholders might lead to significant deterioration of trust between organization and stakeholders—not least because expectations raised in the introductory process were not fulfilled. Though this example is hypothetical, it does raise important questions for firms regarding proactive stakeholder engagement and the maintenance of trust. As with most relationships, they do not survive over the long term if the initial courtship is not translated into regular and consistent displays of affection and appreciation.

That illustration suggests that trust implies the informal exchange of information, as we discussed in Chapter 8. This tends to occur under conditions of asymmetric information—market or nonmarket situations in which firm responses cannot be directly observed. Therefore, the trust propensity of stakeholders is to cooperate to produce economically, politically, or socially efficient outcomes.[75] As we can see from Knack and Keefer's study, in higher-trust environments agents tend to spend less time protecting themselves from being expropriated.[76] This raises an important point again that trust is at the core of stakeholder management, and managers who actively embed it into their nonmarket strategy will not only succeed but will reduce potential risks emanating from the nonmarket context. However, trust raises the issue of integrity in the stakeholder engagement process.

Trust increases when the stakeholder perceives the organization as being reliable, but what about integrity?[77] Trust is context-specific and depends on the situation. There are several potential attributes that might serve as antecedents of trust. Mayer and Davis identify attributions of ability and integrity as primary antecedents of trust.[78] Integrity is based on perceptions of the organization and its key decision-makers as honest and forthcoming, such that they will uphold their commitments and not act improperly or unfairly.[79] Mishra and Spreitzer highlight that firms need to show a strong record of ethical and responsible behavior with their stakeholders.[80] Once firms engage in a manner that fosters mutual respect and trust, they can achieve nonmarket legitimacy.[81] More importantly, ideal stakeholder engagement creates integrity-based trust, indicative of activities managed as part of the firm's compliance with social values and expectations.[82]

Past challenges aside, Swiss food group Nestlé emphasizes integrity and trust with stakeholders. For instance, the corporation puts considerable resources into ensuring sustainable management of their cocoa supply chain. Notwithstanding some challenges in engaging all stakeholders, in November 2011, Nestlé commissioned a team of twenty local and international experts to conduct an assessment of its cocoa supply chain in the Ivory Coast.[83] The assessment team included representatives from the Centre de Recherche et d'Action pour la Paix, Abidjan; Afrique Secours et Assistance; Human Resources Without Borders; and the Sustainable Livelihoods Foundation.[84] The goals of the assessment were to identify stakeholders in Nestlé's cocoa supply chain, map the supply chain in the Ivory Coast, and assess the associated labor risks in the supply chain.[85] Data were taken through individual and group interviews; on-site observations using buying centers, farms, villages, and camps; and documentation review of suppliers and farms. More than 500 interviews were conducted with different market and nonmarket stakeholders. The outcomes were mainly in the form of recommendations, particularly on child labor monitoring and rehabilitation systems and on regulatory gaps with respect to labor standards in the agriculture sector.[86] This specific example shows how Nestlé uses stakeholder engagement processes to build trust and integrity.

As we noted above, integrity is vital in stakeholder management, but despite progress in the theorization of the different trust processes in relation to nonmarket[87] studies, we find this area still emerging.[88] However, many of the previous studies match both concepts without looking into their internal characteristics and interrelations, especially in relation to which forms of CPA and CSR lead to which type of trust or integrity in the stakeholder engagement process.[89]

Another element that needs attention here is inclusiveness. Different stakeholders need to be included and involved in developing nonmarket strategies. The Nestlé example shows us the way to engage with different stakeholders, but we require other examples, especially from the public sector. So how do firms involve and include different stakeholders?

Developing Inclusiveness with Stakeholders

We find from extant management research that involving certain (or even key) stakeholders from the political and social arenas can be challenging,[90] but the process of involvement can allow transparent communication and open feedback, which leads to such mutual benefits as the optimization of regulations and the protection of profits from harmful social issues. Therefore, firms that plan any new nonmarket activity must review these principles using consultation opportunities to align with stakeholders. There are many examples of creating inclusivity with stakeholders, but the following Australian case illustrates how it can lead to mutual benefits in practice.

The Maritime Crew Visa (MCV) was revealed by the Australian government in 2005 as a $100 million border security program.[91] Looking at this through the public-sector lens, the immigration department recognized a number of potential risks for the shipping industry in dealing with the new visa regulation. To help manage such risks, it was essential for the Department of Immigration and Citizenship to engage closely with key stakeholders from the shipping industry, particularly its main industry body, Shipping Australia Ltd.[92] The objective was to ensure that the visa product was developed with a sound understanding of how the industry operated and would access the visa.[93] It was also important to share information effectively with the shipping operators, agents, and crews themselves.[94] To this end, the Department of Immigration and Citizenship and Shipping Australia Ltd agreed to establish an industry working group that would meet approximately every three months.[95] Including only a few crucial industry stakeholders, the director of Seaport Policy Section and the First Assistant Secretary Border Security Division, the working group acted as a sounding board for the MCV's policy and legislative development and provided critical assessment and advice in relation to the MCV's communication strategy.[96] This stakeholder engagement was a significant factor in the success of the MCV. Like most relationships, it relied on honesty, openness, compromise, and a commitment to achieving mutual benefits.[97] To otherwise engage in a consultation process without such elements would have critically damaged both the outcomes of the initiative and the longer-term relationship with a valued client.

Stakeholder Management and Industry Dynamics

In accordance with the idea of aligning with stakeholders, nonmarket activities vary depending on the industry characteristics. Industry structures influence choices on the appropriate CSR or CPA projects and tactics. This is in part due to the industry characteristics determining the expectations of stakeholder behaviors.[98] Castelló and Galang suggest that industry familiarity and visibility are the two major components affecting the local acceptability of companies' nonmarket initiatives.[99] They explain that "familiarity" is about companies trading in industries that are less familiar to the local stakeholders that face greater institutional distance.[100] Here, local stakeholders are more likely to misinterpret the company's products and production processes.[101] Conversely, they explain that unfamiliar products and services that put at risk local cultural norms may increase the liability of firms from industries with little penetration in those markets. Examples include pharmaceutical and extractive industries, which can send mixed signals to different stakeholders. Consequently, they are likely to face more hostility over time.[102] In industries with greater public familiarity, such as air transport, manufacturing, and consumer products, elevated stakeholder engagement leads to significant legitimation efforts by corporations. Therefore, we believe that unfamiliar industries require higher levels of stakeholder engagement with communities and governments than familiar industries do, as the expectations are greater for communication and dialogue. However, despite this proposition needing to be tested across different industries and contexts, we believe it sheds light on the importance of stakeholder engagement and management.

We can see the importance of familiarity, but what about the visibility of industries? Castelló and Galang claim that firms that operate in industries with higher visibility to the general public face greater institutional and stakeholder burdens than those in less visible industries.[103] They explain that industry visibility comes from binary industry characteristics:[104] the degree of risk that the firm's operations require[105] and whether those operations create benefits for the local economy.[106] Examples of these visible industries include extractive, tobacco, air transport, defense, alcohol, banking, and pharmaceutical industries, as they all share those characteristics.[107] Firms in these industries are often expected to compensate the local community for whatever environmental risk they generate by promoting the value of the company's existence beyond the profit motive. We, therefore, propose that stakeholder engagement strategies depend on industry visibility and will be salient in more visible industries.[108]

Perhaps one of the most dramatic illustrations of stakeholder management in visible industries is Royal Dutch Shell's experience in the 1990s. According to Post, Preston, and Sachs, in incidents that have been debated in the media, Shell had to engage with two major nonmarket issues: its confrontation with Greenpeace over its plan to dispose of the Brent Spar oil storage terminal by submerging it in the North Sea and its poor relationships with the national government and regional communities in Nigeria.[109] The Brent Spar issue led to challenges from environmental stakeholders (particularly Greenpeace) and political stakeholders (especially the German government and EU politicians).[110] Conversely, the attack on Shell's involvement in Nigeria—particularly in the oil-rich Niger Delta region—came from human rights stakeholders and even *The Economist* magazine.[111]

These two specific issues caused Shell's top management team to acknowledge the strategic significance of nonmarket challenges. The outcome was an attempt to make internal changes to organizational structures and replace the old culture with a new culture of stakeholder fit.[112] Shell created new ways to assess their social and political arenas using stakeholder management tools similar to those discussed above to engage with the nonmarket and market actors. It is important to acknowledge that in Shell's next foreign venture, in Peru, they were organized differently around various stakeholders, using a formal plan for stakeholder involvement with local communities and interests as well as international stakeholders (human rights organizations and environmentalists). Despite ultimately being discarded, this Peruvian project (Camisea Venture) was a model for future Shell projects in Canada (Athabasca) and the Philippines (Malampaya).[113] Shell understood how visible its industry is and, therefore, responded and embedded new principles and practices into its business and culture. This level of commitment to stakeholders and integration of community and NGO relations into business strategy process is crucial to maintaining a competitive advantage.

Conclusions and Managerial Implications

We believe the techniques discussed in this chapter are powerful, not only because of the analytical insight they provide, but also because their application helps executives to develop a belief in the strategic importance of nonmarket stakeholder alignment. Equipped with a clear and widely shared understanding of the desired stakeholders, day-to-day decisions can be made with more confidence in aligning for advantage.

As we have seen from strategic responses by Kenya's Equity Bank and Shell, companies should consider the following when seeking to align market and nonmarket strategies as they incorporate stakeholder interests and relationships:

- External stakeholders can both facilitate and constrain corporate market and nonmarket strategies and the alignment between the two. In some instances, the same stakeholder can have both facilitative and limiting effects on those strategies.

- A simple inventory and assessment of the relative importance of stakeholders and their current and potential influence on the company is also a useful starting point in calibrating the impact of various stakeholders and developing productive non-adversarial relationships with stakeholders.

- Understanding the dynamic interactions between and among stakeholders and the evolutionary nature of their positions and influence can help to clarify their current relevance and future trajectory and preempt potentially negative and damaging events.

In the next chapter we provide a map for linking political and social strategies to business objectives and market positions. We advance the business case for investing in political and social strategies that follow a sequence and process within an organization. We start from the premise that every organization is a community dedicated to the maintenance and development of a value-creating system. To implement a political and a social strategy to deliver value to different stakeholders, the individual elements of implementation must be built, maintained, and reinforced by keeping a balance between the various determinants of organizational performance.

Notes

* Portions of this chapter have been adapted from Cummings and Doh 2000; and Oetzel, J. and Doh, J.P. (2009). MNEs and development: a review and reconceptualization. *Journal of World Business*, 44(2): 108–120.

1. The Chairman of Standard Oil of New Jersey, as quoted in Smith, H. (2012a). *Who stole the American dream?* New York: Random House: 37.

2. Doh, J.P., London, T., and Kilibarda, V. (2012). *Building and scaling a cross-sector partnership: Oxfam America and Swiss Re empower farmers in Ethiopia*. Ann Arbor, MI: William Davidson Institute Global Lens Case 1: 429–185.

3. Boston Consulting Group and World Economic Forum 2011.

4. Mitchell, Agle, and Wood 1997: 858.

5. Reed, D. (1999). Stakeholder management theory: a critical theory perspective. *Business Ethics Quarterly*, 9(3): 467.

6. Barnard, C. (1962), *The functions of the executive*. Cambridge, MA: Harvard University Press.

7. Post, J., Preston, L., and Sachs, S. (2002). Managing the extended enterprise: the new stakeholder view. *California Management Review*, 45(1): 6–28.

8. Schwartz and Carroll 2008: 148–186.

9. Jones and Wicks 1999.

10. Freeman 1984.

11. Clarkson 1995; Donaldson, T. and Preston, L.E. (1995). The stakeholder theory of the corporation: concepts, evidence, and implications. *Academy of Management Review*, 20(1); 65–91.

12. Donaldson and Preston 1995.

13. Jones and Wicks 1999.

14. Smith, H. (2012b). When capitalists cared. *The New York Times*. September 2: A19. <http://www.nytimes.com/2012/09/03/opinion/henry-ford-when-capitalists-cared.html?_r=0> (accessed April 5, 2013).

15. Post, Preston, and Sachs 2002.

16. Post, Preston, and Sachs 2002.
17. Bowie, N.E. (2004). *Management ethics*. Malden, MA: Blackwell Publishers.
18. Boatright, J.R. (2006). What's wrong—and what's right—with stakeholder management. *Journal of Private Enterprise*, 2: 106–130.
19. McWilliams, Siegel, and Wright 2006.
20. Lawton, McGuire, and Rajwani, 2013.
21. Baron 2001.
22. Jones, and Wicks 1999.
23. Mitchell, Agle, and Wood 1997.
24. Mitchell, Agle, and Wood 1997.
25. Mitchell, Agle, and Wood 1997.
26. Mitchell, Agle, and Wood 1997: 864.
27. Mitchell, Agle, and Wood 1997.
28. Suchman, M. (1995). Managing legitimacy: strategic and institutional approaches. *Academy of Management Review*, 20(3): 571–610.
29. Cummings and Doh 2000.
30. Cummings and Doh 2000.
31. Cummings and Doh 2000.
32. Baron 1995a.
33. Legitimacy here is viewed in terms of being in compliance with the law. See Cummings and Doh 2000: 6.
34. Cummings and Doh 2000.
35. Cummings and Doh 2000: 8.
36. Cummings and Doh 2000: 9.
37. Cummings and Doh 2000.
38. Cummings and Doh 2000.
39. Cummings and Doh 2000: 13.
40. Cummings and Doh 2000: 13.
41. Cummings and Doh 2000: 15.
42. Cummings and Doh 2000: 16.
43. Cummings and Doh 2000: 16.
44. Cummings and Doh 2000: 18.
45. Baron 1995a.
46. Cummings and Doh 2000.
47. Baron 1995a.
48. Dahan, N., Doh, J.P., Oetzel, J., and Yaziji, M. (2010). Corporate-NGO collaboration: creating new business models for developing markets. *Long Range Planning*, 43(2): 326–342.
49. Doh, J.P. and Teegen, H. (2003). (eds.). *Globalization and NGOs: transforming business, government, and society*. Westport, CT: Praeger Publishers; Hess, D., Rogovsky, N., and Dunfee, T.W. (2002). The next wave of corporate community involvement. *California Management Review*, 44(2): 110–125; Rondinelli, D. and London, T. (2003). How corporations and environmental groups collaborate: assessing cross-sector collaborations and alliances. *Academy of Management Executive*, 17(1): 61–76; Chesbrough, H., Ahern, S., Finn, M., and Guerraz, S. (2006). Business

models for technology in the developing world: the role of non-governmental organizations. *California Management Review*, 48(3): 48–76; Pearce and Doh 2005; Selsky, J.W. and Parker, B. (2005). Cross-sector partnerships to address social issues: challenges to theories and practice. *Journal of Management*, 31(6): 849–873.

50. Eisenhardt, K.M. and Schoonhoven, C.B. (1996). Resource-based view of strategic alliance formation: strategic and social effects in entrepreneurial firms. *Organization Science*, 7(2): 136–150.
51. Rondinelli and London 2003. See also Waddock, S.A. (1988). Building successful social partnerships. *Sloan Management Review*, 29(4): 17–23; Westley, F. and Vredenburg, H. (1991). Strategic bridging: the collaboration between environmentalists and business in the marketing of green products. *Journal of Applied Behavioral Science,* 27(1): 65–90.
52. Chesbrough et al. 2006: 48.
53. Rondinelli and London 2003.
54. Rondinelli and London 2003.
55. Parker, B. and Selsky, J.W. (2004). Interface dynamics in cause-based partnerships: an exploration of emergent culture. *Nonprofit and Voluntary Sector Quarterly*, 33: 458–488 (458).
56. Boston Consulting Group and World Economic Forum 2011.
57. They primarily focused on elected officials from mainstream green parties, particularly the *Partido Verde* in Brazil and the *Bündnis 90/Die Grünen* in Germany.
58. Boston Consulting Group and World Economic Forum 2011.
59. Greenwashers are those companies that create PR spin around green, environmental initiatives that in practice often have little substance or organizational impact.
60. Mayer, R.C., Davis, J.H., and Schoorman, F.D. (1995). An integrative model of organizational trust. *Academy of Management Review*, 20: 709–734.
61. Jeffery, N. (2009). *Stakeholder engagement: a road map to meaningful engagement.* Cranfield School of Management, U.K.: Doughty Centre for Corporate Responsibility: 1–46.
62. Mayer, Davis, and Schoorman 1995: 712.
63. Lewicki, R.J., McAllister, D.J., and Bies, R.J. (1998). Trust and distrust: new relationships and realities. *Academy of Management Review*, 23 (3): 439.
64. Mayer, Davis, and Schoorman 1995.
65. McKnight, D.H., Cummings, L.L., and Chervany, N.L. (1998). Initial trust formation in new organizational relationships. *Academy of Management Review*, 23: 473–490; Shankar, V., Urban, G.L., and Sultan, F (2002). Online trust: a stakeholder perspective, concepts, implications, and future directions. *Journal of Strategic Information Systems*, 11: 325–344.
66. Shankar, Urban, and Sultan 2002: 328
67. Jeffery 2009: 21
68. Jeffery 2009: 21
69. Mishra, A.K. (1996). Organizational responses to crisis: the centrality of trust. In R. Tyler (ed.). *Trust in organizations: frontiers of theory and research.* Thousand Oaks, CA: Sage: 261–287.

70. Shankar, Urban, and Sultan 2002: 328
71. Sultan, F., Urban, G.L., Shankar, V., and Bart, I. (2002). *Determinants and conse-quences of trust in e-business*. Working paper 02142. Cambridge, MA: Sloan School of Management.
72. Jeffery 2009: 21
73. Jeffery 2009: 21
74. Jeffery 2009: 21
75. La Porta, R., López-de-Silanes, F., Shleifer, A., and Vishny, R.W. (1997). Trust in large organizations. *American Economic Review*, 87(2): 333–338.
76. Knack, S. and Keefer, P. (1997). Does social capital have an economic payoff? A cross-country investigation. *Quarterly Journal of Economics*, 112(4): 1251–1288.
77. Mayer, R.C. and Davis, J.H. (1999). The effect of the performance appraisal system on trust in management: a field quasi-experiment. *Journal of Applied Psychology*, 84(1): 123–136.
78. Mayer and Davis 1999.
79. Pirson, M. and Malhotra, D. (2007). *What matters to whom? Managing trust across multiple stakeholder groups*. The Hauser Centre for nonprofit organizations, Harvard University. Working paper no. 39: 1–37.
80. Mishra, A.K. and Spreitzer, G.M. (1998). Explaining how survivors respond to downsizing: the roles of trust, empowerment, justice, and work redesign. *Academy of Management Review*, 23(3): 567–588.
81. Suchman 1995.
82. Castelló, I. and Galang, R.M.N. (2012). Looking for new forms of legitimacy in Asia. *Business & Society*. First published online: December 21: 1–39; Oliver, C. (1996). The institutional embeddedness of economic activity. *Advances in Strategic Management*, 13: 163–186; Pavlou, P.A. (2002). Institution-based trust in interorganizational exchange relationships: the role of online B2B marketplaces on trust formation. *Journal of Strategic Information Systems*, 11: 215–243.
83. Fair Labor Association Report (2012). *Sustainable management of Nestlé's cocoa supply chain in the Ivory Coast: focus of labor standards*. <http://www.fairla-bor.org/report/assessment-nestle-cocoa-supply-chain-ivory-coast> (accessed December 12, 2012).
84. Fair Labor Association Report 2012.
85. Fair Labor Association Report 2012.
86. Fair Labor Association Report 2012.
87. Palazzo, G. and Scherer, A. (2006). Corporate legitimacy as deliberation: a com-municative framework. *Journal of Business Ethics*, 66: 71–88.
88. Castelló and Galang 2012.
89. Castelló and Galang 2012.
90. Palazzo and Scherer 2006.
91. Australian Government, Department of Immigration and Citizenship (2008). *Stakeholder engagement: practitioner handbook*. <http://www.immi.gov.au/about/stakeholder-engagement/_pdf/stakeholder-engagement-practitioner-handbook.pdf> (accessed December 12, 2012).
92. Australian Government, Department of Immigration and Citizenship 2008.

93. Australian Government, Department of Immigration and Citizenship 2008.
94. Australian Government, Department of Immigration and Citizenship 2008: 8.
95. Australian Government, Department of Immigration and Citizenship 2008: 8.
96. Australian Government, Department of Immigration and Citizenship 2008: 8.
97. Australian Government, Department of Immigration and Citizenship 2008: 8.
98. Gardberg, N. and Fombrun, C. (2006). Corporate citizenship: creating intangible assets across institutional environments. *Academy of Management Review*, 31(2): 329–346.
99. Castelló and Galang 2012.
100. Castelló and Galang 2012.
101. Gardberg and Fombrun 2006.
102. Castelló and Galang 2012: 18.
103. Castelló and Galang 2012: 19.
104. Castelló and Galang 2012: 19.
105. Gardberg and Fombrun 2006; Castelló and Galang 2012: 19.
106. Rosenzweig, P.M., and Singh, J.V. (1991). Organizational environments and the multinational enterprise. *Academy of Management Review*, 16(2): 340–361.
107. Castelló and Galang 2012.
108. Castelló and Galang 2012.
109. Post, Preston, and Sachs 2002: 19.
110. Post, Preston, and Sachs 2002: 20.
111. *The Economist.* (1995). Multinationals and their morals. December 2: 18.
112. Post, Preston, and Sachs 2002: 20.
113. See Shell's website for the white paper on *Doing business that's socially responsible*, as cited in Post, Preston, and Sachs 2002: 20.

Section IV
Delivering with Impact

10

Ensuring Balance

Balance your thoughts with action.[1]

Bruce Lee

In 1978, having completed a correspondence course in ice cream making, two old friends, Ben Cohen and Jerry Greenfield, opened an ice cream shop in a renovated gas station in Burlington, Vermont. Within two years they were packing their innovative ice cream in pints and selling it to a fast-growing and enthusiastic consumer base. Despite efforts from established competitors such as Häagen-Dazs, Ben & Jerry's continued to grow, both across the U.S. and internationally. From the early days, the company became as well known for its social and environmental activism as it did for its products. In essence, it was a values-led company from the outset, concerned as much with the environmental impact of product packaging as with sales volume. Many fans of this aligned approach were concerned when Cohen and Greenfield sold the company in 2000 to Anglo-Dutch consumer goods giant Unilever. They need not have worried, since Unilever, then run by Irishman Niall Fitzgerald, did not interfere with Ben & Jerry's social mission. If anything, Unilever absorbed some of these ethics and approaches into its own corporate culture. The activism continued, ranging from opposition to oil exploration in the Arctic National Wildlife Refuge to the company's more controversial support for the Occupy Wall Street movement. As Ben & Jerry's Unilever-appointed CEO, Jostein Solheim, says, being a values-led company means that you do what you believe in.[2] You do things that you have deep convictions about, not necessarily things that the consumer wants or that the market dictates. "It's authentic, it's real; it's not done by a third-party agency, advertising agencies, or lobbyists," Solheim notes. "It is done by us because we really believe in it."[3]

Solheim, a twenty-year Unilever employee before joining Ben & Jerry's, observes that the main difference between Ben & Jerry's and every other business unit or individual company he has worked in lies in putting heart first. At Ben & Jerry's, managers ask "Is this the right thing to do?" and then work out how to do it in a way that makes sense by focusing on the company's social, product, and economic objectives. Every initiative echoes this three-part mission statement, and every decision the CEO makes has to be viewed through that lens. This exemplifies the philosophical difference between Ben & Jerry's and a more explicitly market-driven organization, which will typically say, "If we don't have a stable society, we won't have a very good marketplace for our product." These types of companies might also contribute to sustainability for reputational purposes (to help them sell their product) and for economic reasons (because going green helps to save money by removing unnecessary costs). These are all legitimate reasons, and it can reasonably be argued that it does not really matter what the reasons are—these companies will do good for society through creating stable markets and will do good for the environment because they are going to remove carbon or reduce garbage output. However, Ben & Jerry's is more purposeful and balanced in its approach. The company objective is to create what it calls *linked prosperity networks* by making the world's best product with the least possible environmental impact, earning an above-industry-average return for shareholders, and fostering a positive social impact.

From the outset, the Ben & Jerry's stance was to balance societal needs with market and nonmarket objectives and to embed this within the company's mission, culture, and decision-making process. It is this balanced approach to strategy formulation and execution that differentiates the Vermont ice cream manufacturer from other companies that adopt social causes or adapt to more sustainable business practices.

Another example of balance in principle and practice is the Social Initiatives Group (SIG) of India's ICICI Bank, which had a mission to build the capacities of the poorest of the poor to participate in the larger economy.[4] The group identified and supported initiatives designed to break the intergenerational cycle of poor health and nutrition to ensure essential early childhood education and schooling as well as access to basic financial services.[5] Thus, by promoting early child health, catalyzing universal elementary education, and maximizing access to micro financial services, ICICI Bank believed that it could balance the capacities of India's poor to participate in larger socio-economic processes and thereby help the overall development of the country and their own firm performance.

ICICI started by understanding and balancing the systems of service delivery in the market environment with the nonmarket environment. In respect to the nonmarket, they approached key elements in formulating their political and social strategies—developing access to political and social actors, gathering and analyzing data, defining objectives, allocating budgets, leveraging networks, and identifying critical knowledge and practice gaps in their function. In this way, they developed a nonmarket implementation plan tracked against non-market goals, actions around projects, and scalable initiatives to deal with gaps identified. This was undertaken in collaboration with research agencies, NGOs, companies, government departments, local stakeholders, and international organizations.[6] The outcome of this approach *might* lead to increased revenues through the multiplier effects in the longer term, but it *would* provide better education for communities to create healthier families in the short term and eventually lead to more prosperous communities down the line.[7]

From these examples, we can see how nonmarket strategy implementation can help shape the political and social spheres. In this chapter, we provide a route map for linking political and social strategies to business objectives and market positions. We advance the business case for investing in political and social strategies within a commercial organization. We start from the premise that every organization is a community dedicated to the maintenance and development of a value-creating system in the market and nonmarket. To implement nonmarket strategies, firms must assess and evaluate the political and social benefits and costs of delivering value to different stakeholders. We suggest that individual elements of the nonmarket strategy must be built, maintained, and reinforced by keeping balance across various steps that determine business performance.[8]

Nonmarket Strategy Implementation Process

Management is about balancing the market and nonmarket spheres. However, it also requires executives and scholars to consider new approaches to solving emerging issues from the political and social arenas. In this book, we have identified a process model for bringing together the key components for the management of nonmarket strategy. At this point, we define our nonmarket strategy implementation model as the system to deliver nonmarket information to key stakeholders and thus synchronize political and social perception with corporate reality.[9]

In accordance with previous chapters, each aspect of the model is a function of a set of corporate political and social activities, as we show in Figure 10.1. Phases 1 to 5 are required to implement a nonmarket strategy that runs in parallel with market-based business strategies. As the Ben & Jerry's example illustrates, the nonmarket strategy implementation process is ideally built on a firm's values and vision and delivered through its organizational culture.

To illustrate our model, reflect on Royal Dutch Shell's 1990s nonmarket challenges as we discussed in Chapter 9. In learning the lessons of the Brent Spar debacle and the public fallout from its activities in Nigeria, Shell's top

Figure 10.1 Implementing nonmarket strategies

management team recognized the need to be proactive and strategic in approaching nonmarket contexts and challenges. This resulted in the development of its "New Shell" organizational structure.[10] In this novel design, the managers established new internal reporting procedures that allowed them to monitor and analyze the company's political and social environments. Moreover, they followed a nonmarket strategy process similar to our model, called *triple bottom line*, to analyze different environments, develop specific nonmarket objectives, identify implementation tactics, and monitor performance with financial, social, and political measures.[11]

It was Shell's planning and external affairs department that started this new program by conducting stakeholder engagement round tables at various locations around the world. This resulted in 1997 in the emergence of a new purpose: "helping people build a better world."[12] It also led to the creation of an internal publication called *Interchange* to better manage public affairs. With that example in mind and drawing on previous chapters, the next section explores each phase of Figure 10.1, using our nonmarket strategy implementation model to better understand the ideal steps in the execution of successful nonmarket strategy.

Political and Social Positioning Analysis

In the first phase of delivering a nonmarket strategy, it is essential for firms to undertake a *nonmarket positioning analysis* to situate themselves in the global and regional economies and to simultaneously plan their interactions with government and related agencies to obtain favorable policy outcomes while being seen by society as creating positive externalities.[13]

As we discussed in Chapter 4, the geographic context of a firm's operations is critical in this initial stage. Therefore, firms must evaluate the market and nonmarket characteristics of their home and host countries or of countries they plan to enter. This multidomestic focus suggests that a firm must be sensitive to the individual characteristics of different target countries.[14] With regards to a country's home market, this requires a consideration of existing and potential competitors, suppliers, and so on. An assessment of a country's nonmarket environment focuses on a general evaluation of the institutional framework and political system, combined with a specific assessment of existing or emergent policies and legislation on inward investment, joint venture requirements, exporting, labor law, local content rules, intellectual property rights, and technology transfer agreements, among other considerations.[15]

As we discussed earlier in the book, corporate political and social analysis is a vital first step in determining the path toward meaningful nonmarket implementation. Usually, managers focus exclusively on the market environment and on organizing a firm's response to, and positioning in, competitive industry arenas. Traditional market analysis focuses on issues such as entry barriers, the threat of new entrants, and the scale and reach of incumbents. By comparison, the often neglected nonmarket analysis emphasizes positioning for interest representation and the competitive impact of social activism. Building on De Fouloy,[16] we argue that the first step in implementing nonmarket strategy is to conduct political and social analysis at all levels (supranational, international, national, and subnational, as we discussed in Chapter 7). Each level requires separate managerial attention to address the needs and expectations of stakeholders.

This first phase allows managers to identify key issues, important interests, types of information, and key stakeholders.[17] In all of these factors, executives need to capture and balance between political and social aspects of the nonmarket strategy and relate these to how firms compete nationally and internationally in their market environment. We suggest that once the analysis is complete, the firm can start to create prioritized nonmarket objectives. As with market strategies, managers should develop a maximum of five strategic objectives—having too many nonmarket objectives can spread resources and capabilities too thinly.[18]

Political and Social Objectives

At this point, it is vital that organizations extract key objectives and boundaries that track closely with emerging issues from Phase 1. Organizations also need to recognize that these *nonmarket objectives* help to reduce threats and exploit opportunities.[19] These chosen objectives need to address the key stakeholders that the firm prioritizes, depending on the nature of the organization, its business model, its market objectives, and the industry sector.

Building on Mitchell, Agle, and Wood,[20] we suggest that nonmarket objectives are usually predetermined by *interest* (the degree to which stakeholders are motivated by, and mobilized around, an issue), *influence* (the ability of stakeholders to galvanize public interest and the receptivity of citizens or political actors to an issue), and *salience* (the extent to which business organizations perceive that an issue, together with a stakeholder's stance on an issue, is of importance or relevance). However, as stakeholders are heterogeneous, taking this phase further depends on the important information regarding an organization's wants and needs.[21] Once the firm defines them, its management can establish the path forward in terms of actions and accountability.

For instance, let us take a nonmarket scenario in which a consumer boycott has a multilayered impact on a firm. Beyond the direct impact on revenues and reputation, there may be greater impacts on its relationship with stakeholders. These effects may profoundly and even irreversibly change the rapport between a firm and its stakeholders in the market and nonmarket environments. They may also lead or contribute to the decline of the firm's market and brand value. All of these dynamics were present during the boycott that targeted Danone SA, the French multinational food and beverage firm in 2001.[22] The French corporation is a leading global food and beverage company, positioned just behind Nestlé and Unilever in size and market reach. In 2001, Danone was accused by the French media of cutting 3,000 jobs in Europe,[23] and this quickly led to massive product boycotts.[24] The Communist and Socialist mayors of big towns across France ordered their hospitals, schools, and public-sector cafeterias to stop purchasing Danone products. Support for the boycott grew swiftly and spread to supermarket chains and postal workers' and bank unions. The French Green Party joined in, followed by France's leading antiglobalization association, Attac, and then about a hundred deputies in the National Assembly, representing all the parties of the left.[25] According to Hunter, Le Menestrel, and De Bettignies, this nonmarket crisis caused Danone to lose colossal market value.[26] The corporation's top management team swiftly evaluated the situation and developed market and nonmarket objectives to end the threat by addressing the concerns through social and political measures, including legal action against newspapers and speaking to regulators and financial analysts.[27] Moreover, they controlled transparency and developed objectives to deal with threats from the media and citizens action groups. The managers' robust implementation of this nonmarket strategy was integral to Danone's successful response to the boycott. So how do firms actually translate the nonmarket objectives into tactics and initiatives?

Political and Social Initiatives

This phase in the implementation process recognizes that the greatest levels of success depend on choosing correct *nonmarket programs and initiatives* to align stakeholders with nonmarket objectives. As we discussed in the last chapter, to successfully achieve each nonmarket strategic objective, firms must recognize their stakeholder management as a core competence.[28] As Jeffery notes, the recognition and embedding of this competence in the corporate culture is an important step that can lead to success in execution, as the interests and objectives of organizations and stakeholders can be aligned during these initiatives. This is not to assume that organization and stakeholders will necessarily want identical outcomes, but if a common interest can be identified, it may act as a critical means to leverage a solution to an issue and thereby satisfy both parties.[29] Figure 10.2 captures the key elements needed to successfully implement initiatives and projects associated with each nonmarket objective in Phase 2.

As we have shown in Figure 10.2, challenges and problems are likely for those firms that do not embed stakeholder management in their corporate cultures, as this can lead to a failure in aligning market strategies with their nonmarket initiatives. When firms are more reactive than proactive in the planning process, these tactical initiatives, or what we call projects, are sometimes misaligned with the setting of the nonmarket objectives.

Research has emphasized the importance of enhanced alignment between the interests of stakeholders and managers in a firm's external affairs department and also, interestingly, between stakeholders and other business units within the same firm.[30] However, is important to note that various business units may have different needs, which creates misalignment as to how or why to undertake a project or activity.[31] To add to this problem, a lack of

Figure 10.2 Aligning and translating nonmarket objectives into action

support from upper-echelon management teams can also result in a lack of required resources or capabilities to undertake the nonmarket strategy over the long term.

Therefore, as with Lufthansa (mentioned in Chapter 6), we find that establishing an external affairs department to take on a central nonmarket strategy management role and support business units on pertinent issues helps to create a more coordinated approach in delivering nonmarket strategy.[32] However, we argue that organizations must slowly develop a culture of alignment to guide sociopolitical initiatives and projects.[33] This nonmarket view needs to be integrated across all business units to ensure a shared understanding of values and vision,[34] and a common approach to implementation. As we have seen from the Ben & Jerry's example in this chapter, these values should inform all the nonmarket objectives and associated projects. The embedding of nonmarket competence in a firm's culture will help to make the external affairs function, top management teams, and assorted business units more responsive to new stakeholder groups, concerns, and issues in the nonmarket.

In engaging with new and old stakeholders, we argue that current or newly created external affairs functions should be used to develop various programs and initiatives to establish alignment through better use of firm resources and capabilities. These functions must develop resources and capabilities to learn, listen, and relate better to their stakeholders so as to maintain their advantage and reduce negative externalities in the environment.[35] In the case of Tata Steel, the Indian manufacturer, its external affairs function used a centenary healthcare project to include child education, immunization and childcare, plantation activities, AIDS awareness, and other healthcare projects to help create stronger societies and, therefore, to generate more business prosperity in the future. Hence, creating a multiplier effect through good behavior ultimately contributes to the company's bottom line.[36] For Tata Steel it was important to underpin its healthcare projects and programs with its giving culture and specific resources—physical, financial, human, intellectual, social, and political capabilities.[37] Ultimately, the company involved various stakeholders in defining its nonmarket objectives to complement its market strategies and laid the groundwork for a long-term business development.

Political and Social Performance Measurement

In this phase, which overlaps with the previous one, the external affairs function and/or top management teams assign responsibility for specific stakeholders associated with each nonmarket objective. Developing clear and defined targets is critical to accountability in nonmarket implementation and performance. Building on previous studies of strategic implementation,[38] we argue that organizations should develop several measurable goals associated with each nonmarket objective. These need to be *focused* (simple and clearly defined), *realistic* (attainable), *quantifiable* (measurable with tangible evidence), and *time-bound* (linked to boundaries and frames). Looking at two examples, Lexmark and Heinz, we find that both companies developed nonmarket measurement frameworks similar to ours that generated clarity and showed outcomes in practice.

Lexmark, the global print management firm, made a commitment to reduce the consumption of natural resources at all its leased and owned manufacturing facilities, research and development facilities, and office spaces worldwide. Lexmark wanted to track greenhouse gas emissions as well as usage of natural gas, fuel oil, diesel, gasoline, and electricity using the Greenhouse Gas Protocol methodology.[39] As a result, it established the following two long-term nonmarket goals and measures to guide its energy-conservation nonmarket objective: "to reduce greenhouse gas emissions by 20 percent (2005–2017) and achieve a 20 percent reduction in electricity consumption for headquarters, manufacturing and development (2005–2017)."[40] While there is still much work to do, with reductions of up to 16 percent by 2011, the company has made significant progress toward achieving its nonmarket goals.

In 2007 the global food conglomerate H.J. Heinz Company developed a commitment to CSR and CPA embedded in an updated culture of "integrity, ethics, transparency, and community engagement."[41] Between 2007 and 2010 the company developed market and nonmarket objectives around increasing knowledge and awareness of health issues for consumers and political and social actors.[42] Given that one of its main products, ketchup, is a source of lycopene, an antioxidant naturally occurring in tomatoes that has been found to potentially reduce incidence of prostate and other cancers,[43] Heinz was selected to partner with the Prostate Cancer Research Foundation of America to further the goal of preventing cancer through nutrition education and research. Measures used here were "time spent on media platforms" and "attendance at conferences and meetings."[44] Heinz also developed other nonmarket projects, including accessing U.S. political actors to influence emergent food nutritional policies. Measures here mostly centered around political campaign contributions for access to key government actors. Finally, the corporation developed several environmental projects to reduce metal waste by 10 percent and water waste by 12 percent and mitigate other environmental risks to meet emerging policies on climate change.[45]

The Lexmark and Heinz examples both illustrate the importance of measurement in the nonmarket strategy implementation process and emphasize issues of monitoring and accountability.

Political and Social Performance Monitoring

The final phase considers progress in implementation monitoring. In assessing the overall direction of projects and programs, we urge managers and scholars to consider risks. Research shows that there are many risks associated with corporate political and social projects that need to be monitored. An insightful report from U.S. nonprofit organization The Conference Board indicates that large companies have begun to combine risk management and strategy in organization-wide structures, leveraging their mandatory internal control and compliance procedures to establish a comprehensive risk management (RM) infrastructure.[46]

Some studies have found that RM is a top-down initiative that is fully supported by the corporate board and includes a preventive, control-based aspect and a forward-looking and entrepreneurial aspect.[47] The oversight of RM is part of the fiduciary responsibilities of all directors, and companies might consider whether the risks posed by political spending or collaborative social activities with NGOs should be considered during the company's risk assessment process.[48] We argue that an RM framework can be used to *monitor*, *assess*, and *respond* to nonmarket risks for each project or program to help clearly communicate a company's long-term business strategy.

Building on our discussion of risk identification and mitigation in Chapter 4, we contend that RM oversight monitoring procedures add to corporate governance practices to reduce nonmarket uncertainty. We believe that details on nonmarket risks and benefits acquired through RM can help senior managers and board members execute their political and social responsibilities appropriately. However, just as there are many ways to set up sociopolitical spending and oversight teams, there is no one-size-fits-all RM process. But we find that a number of firms like Dell and Intel provide a common base of practical knowledge of how monitoring and a code of conduct properly work.[49]

Adopting a code of conduct for political or social *spending* by a firm is the crucial method of ensuring that a company's employees are aware of, and acting in accordance with, company policy. The code sets a compliance standard for employees. Companies including Tata Consultancy Services, Dell, Intel, and Merck have developed codes of political and social conduct and have posted them on their websites. Typical elements of these codes include company policies on public disclosure of expenditures of corporate funds on political and social activities; disclosure of levies and other subscription payments made to trade associations and other tax-exempt organizations that the company anticipates will be used for sociopolitical expenditures; and the establishment of boards' of directors policies on monitoring of political and social spending.[50]

For instance, as DeNicola et al. noted, in 2004, Merck contributed more than $10,000 to support Samac Richardson's bid to become a Mississippi Supreme Court judge.[51] The applicant was a strong supporter of tort reform, a stance endorsed by many companies. However, Richardson's position on certain social issues raised problems for Merck's reputation. What was a relatively modest contribution from the company resulted in Merck being listed in *Time* magazine as "one of 18 companies that gave money to judicial candidates whose conservative views clashed with the corporations' progressive policies."[52] DeNicola et al. observed that:

> Merck has since adopted internal policies designed to minimize any future risks related to political and social spending. In 2005, they began disclosing their political contributions and also reported on their social initiatives, taking an important step toward protecting themselves against imprudent political and social spending decisions on various projects and programs. In 2009, Merck announced it would expand its ban on giving political donations to lower-court judicial campaigns and to state Supreme Court candidates.[53]

The firm now publicly endeavors to be open and transparent about its political and social activities.

As seen from the Merck example, firms can face problems in the nonmarket if they fail to follow a process. The next section will explore nonmarket implementation problems in more detail.

Nonmarket Strategy Implementation Problems

The nonmarket strategy implementation process requires tactics, sequence, and order. Moreover, it requires organizations to develop a culture of performance with integrity. Such a culture is created by incentives and transparency as much as by penalties to force organizations to use guiding principles and policy standards. Before the financial crisis of 2007–2008, few sizable banks and financial services companies were publicly known for espousing high levels of ethics and integrity in their business practices. In a sense, these were, at best, irrelevant during the good times that preceded the collapse of Lehman Brothers. But when the market context changed as a result of the onset of a global financial crisis, the nonmarket context also rapidly altered. Now government and civil society began to scrutinize the ethical standards of the banks left standing. The value—both market and nonmarket—of many financial services organizations tumbled as they were shown to have performance cultures motivated more by avarice than by integrity.

For example, the U.S. Federal Home Loan Mortgage Corporation (Freddie Mac) was prohibited by law from making contributions to any election campaigns. Federal Election Commission (FEC) regulations also "prohibited a corporation (including its officers, directors, or agents) from facilitating or acting as a conduit for contributions."[54] However, in 2006, the FEC fined Freddie Mac $3.8 million—one of the largest fines in U.S. history— for violating campaign finance law.[55] This action was prompted by Freddie Mac's engaging in prohibited political activities, particularly donations to the Republican Governors Association and the underwriting of fundraising events for Congressional members. These attempts at political risk management were intended to raise Freddie Mac's profile in state capitals and on Capitol Hill. But it is illegal to use corporate funds to do so, as the law only allows for PACs, which collect personal donations from company employees. The fine caused a lot of senior executives to rethink how they were conducting their campaign-finance activities.[56]

As the Freddie Mac example illustrates, the responsibility for implementing political spending policies is distinct from the responsibility to oversee political budgets. Corporate governance research shows that in developing firms' political spending policies, management and the board may find it helpful to first decide whether to limit the company's political spending to funds voluntarily contributed to a company-maintained PAC or whether to permit corporate treasury funds to be used for such spending.[57] After making that decision, the executives involved should identify the types of individuals and organizations that are appropriate recipients of the company's resources. These are individual candidates, committees, political parties, other political groups, issue advocacy groups, trade associations, or charities. Thereafter, those individuals or groups responsible for making spending decisions determine approval procedures and decide what type of reporting needs to be completed.[58] As a matter of general practice, board members do not need to regularly approve political or social spending decisions, but they should be comfortable with questioning the guidelines for the company's political or social giving program.[59] Astute board members should ensure that there are robust governance and monitoring processes in place to instill confidence in the overall political and social engagement of the corporation with different stakeholders.[60]

Conclusions and Managerial Implications

Business strategy considers how firms structure to compete in light of their overall environment and choice of market and nonmarket strategies, and particularly how firms balance their implementation considerations. At the level of nonmarket strategy, firms must engage in calculations about possible supporters and opponents on critical issues on both the demand side (what benefits will different stakeholders receive from success on an issue) and on the supply side (who will be able to generate political or social action). These considerations will often influence a firm's decision on market strategy and also its approach to nonmarket implementation.

In terms of tactics, firms must assess their capacity for executing market and nonmarket strategies; build capabilities if needed, particularly in nonmarket strategy; and foster a culture of stakeholder management in both arenas. Market tactics are instinctive to most managers. By these we mean a firm's competitive decisions and actions regarding, for example, new product development, branding, and customer service. Nonmarket tactics include lobbying, grassroots activity, coalition building, testimony, political entrepreneurship, electoral support, communication and public advocacy, and judicial engagement.[61] Organizational tactics are how a firm's management structures, operational systems, and processes are configured and reconfigured to deliver market—and nonmarket—success. In the Freddie Mac case, the company adapted to pressures and constraints and used its experience to address a broader set of concerns regarding its political programs. In contrast, the earlier Lexmark and Ben & Jerry's examples show how firms can develop open and transparent nonmarket objectives to implement nonmarket strategy.

This chapter suggests several broad managerial implications for the alignment of market and nonmarket strategies:

- Managers need to acknowledge the five phases of the nonmarket strategy implementation process: analysis, objectives, initiatives, performance management, and monitoring.

- Nonmarket analysis is the first step toward understanding the external environment using tools mentioned in this book. Tools such as stakeholder analysis, interest analysis, information delivery analysis, and real options analysis are vital to staying ahead of the game. Most managers need to scan their environment to defend against emerging threats and exploit opportunities arising from the political and social arenas.

- Nonmarket objectives need to be developed from the analysis to provide pathways for business organizations to get to specific destinations.

- Nonmarket initiatives and programs are ways in which companies can deliver on those key nonmarket objectives.

- Nonmarket performance management is the fourth phase that firms must use to measure their implementation performance in the sociopolitical sphere. They must develop goals associated with the projects to track performance.

- Nonmarket monitoring is the final step in successful nonmarket implementation, requiring companies to foster a culture of integrity and ethics and thereby reduce risks associated with engaging with market and non-market stakeholders.

When adopted and integrated, all of these steps will enhance the chances of success and competitive advantage for any firm planning to take non-market strategy seriously. In the next chapter, we show how institutional voids between home and host countries pose challenges for firms seeking to understand existing and emerging nonmarket environments, particularly in a multipolar world economy. We note that developed economies tend to function under a system of public ordering in which laws and regulations are used to protect private property and enforce contracts and intellectual property. In some country or regional environments, these institutions are missing or deficient, for example in many developing and emerging economies. Consequently, we draw from international management literature, which has explored new institutionalism, comparative capitalism, and institutional economics views, to explore the frontiers of research in this growing area.

Notes

1. Little, J. (ed.) (2000). *Striking thoughts: Bruce Lee's wisdom for daily living*. Boston, MA: Tuttle Publishing: 43.
2. Interview conducted by Thomas Lawton with Jostein Solheim, Ben & Jerry's CEO, Burlington, Vermont, January 13, 2012.
3. Interview conducted by Thomas Lawton with Jostein Solheim, Ben & Jerry's CEO, Burlington, Vermont, January 13, 2012.
4. Boston Consulting Group and World Economic Forum 2011.
5. Boston Consulting Group and World Economic Forum 2011.
6. Boston Consulting Group and World Economic Forum 2011.
7. See the ICICI website and Boston Consulting Group and World Economic Forum 2011.
8. Boddewyn and Brewer 1994.
9. De Figueiredo J.M. (2009). Integrated political strategy. *Advances in Strategic Management*, 26: 459–486.
10. Post, Preston, and Sachs 2002.
11. Post, Preston, and Sachs 2002.
12. Post, Preston, and Sachs 2002.
13. Doh, Lawton, and Rajwani 2012.
14. Aggarwal 2001: 92.
15. Aggarwal 2001: 92.
16. De Fouloy 2001.
17. Baron 1995a.

18. Bourgeois, L.J. and Brodwin, D.R. (1984). Strategic implementation: five approaches to an elusive phenomenon. *Strategic Management Journal*, 5(3): 241–264.

19. Lawton, T., Rajwani, T., and O'Kane, C. (2011). Strategic reorientation and business turnaround: the case of global legacy airlines. *Journal of Strategy and Management*, 4(3): 215–237.

20. Mitchell, Agle, and Wood 1997.

21. Jeffery 2009: 17.

22. Hunter, M.L., Le Menestrel, M., and De Bettignies, H.C. (2008). Beyond control: crisis strategies and stakeholder media in the Danone boycott of 2001. *Corporate Reputation Review*, 11(4): 335–350.

23. European Industrial Relations Observatory (2001). *Danone reignites controversy over redundancies in profitable firms.* <http://www.eurofound.europa.eu/eiro/2001/02/feature/fr0102133f.htm> (accessed December 1, 2012).

24. Hunter et al. 2008.

25. Hunter et al. 2008: 338.

26. Hunter et al. 2008.

27. Hunter et al. 2008.

28. Post, Preston, and Sachs 2002.

29. Jeffery 2009: 20.

30. Post, Preston, and Sachs 2002.

31. Jeffery 2009: 20.

32. Aggarwal 2001: 89–108; Aggarwal, V.K. (ed.) (2003). *Winning in Asia, American style: market and nonmarket strategies for success.* New York: Palgrave Macmillan.

33. Grayson, D. and Hodges, A. (2004). *Corporate social opportunity, 7 steps to make corporate social responsibility work for your business.* London: Greenleaf Publishing.

34. Jeffery 2009.

35. Post, Preston, and Sachs 2002.

36. Srivastava, A.K, Negi, G., Mishra, V., and Pandey, S. (2012), Corporate social responsibility: a case study of Tata Group. *IOSR Journal of Business and Management*, 3(5): 17–27.

37. Srivastava et al. 2012.

38. Adler, N.J., Brahim, R., and Graham, J. (1992). Strategy implementation: a comparison of face-to-face negotiations in the Peoples Republic of China and the United States. *Strategic Management Journal*, 13(6): 449–466; Bourgeois and Brodwin 1984.

39. Lexmark Corporate Social Responsibility Report (2011). <http://www1.lexmark.com/en_US/about-us/CSR-Report-2011.pdf> (accessed December 29, 2012).

40. Lexmark Corporate Social Responsibility Report 2011: 19.

41. H.J. Heinz Company Corporate Social Responsibility Report (2007). <http://www.heinz.com/CSR_2007/index.html> (accessed December 30, 2012): 1.

42. H.J. Heinz Company Corporate Social Responsibility Report 2007.

43. H.J. Heinz Company Corporate Social Responsibility Report 2007.

44. H.J. Heinz Company Corporate Social Responsibility Report 2007.

45. H.J. Heinz Company Corporate Social Responsibility Report 2007.

46. DeNicola, P., Freed, B.F., Passantino, S.C., and Sandstrom, K.J. (2010). *Handbook on corporate political activity: emerging corporate governance issues*. The Conference Board Research Report R-1472-10-RR <http://www.politicalaccountability. net/index.php?ht=a/GetDocumentAction/id/4084> (accessed December 1, 2012). In this chapter we draw heavily on the findings of this report produced by The Conference Board, a long established U.S. non-profit business membership and research group.

47. Royer, P.S. (2000). Risk management: the undiscovered dimension of project management. *Project Management Journal*, 31: 6–13.

48. Aggarwal 2001.

49. Aggarwal 2001; DeNicola et al. 2010: 21.

50. See <http://www.merck.com> (accessed June 12, 2013) and <http://www. dell.com> (accessed June 12, 2013) for more details.

51. DeNicola et al. 2010: 29. Merck was only one of many companies that contributed directly or indirectly—through PACs—to Richardson's campaign. Others included Ford Motor Company, Mississippi Restaurant Association, Liberty Mutual, and Pfizer.

52. Waller, D. (2006). Secrets of corporate giving. *Time*, May 15. <http://content.time. com/time/magazine/article/0,9171,1194037,00.html> (accessed January 2, 2013) and cited in DeNicola et al. 2010: 29. Also, for more information, visit the "Corporate Political Contributions" page on the Merck website: <http:// www.merck.com/about/public_policy/political_contributions/home.html> (accessed January 2, 2013).

53. DeNicola et al. 2010: 29.

54. DeNicola et al. 2010: 29.

55. Drinkard, J. (2006). Freddie Mac to pay $3.8 Million to Settle FEC allegations. *USA Today*. April 18. <http://usatoday30.usatoday.com/money/ companies/regulation/2006-04-18-freddie-mac_x.htm> (accessed January 2, 2013).

56. Federal Election Commission (2006). Federal Home Loan Mortgage Corporation ("Freddie Mac") pays largest fine in FEC history. <http://www.fec.gov/ press/press2006/20060418mur.html> (accessed December 30, 2012).

57. DeNicola et al. 2010; Keasey, K., Thompson, S., and Wright, M. (1997). *Corporate governance: economic and financial issues*. 1st ed. Oxford: Oxford University Press.

58. Keasey et al. 1997.

59. DeNicola et al. 2010.

60. Keasey et al. 1997.

61. Aggarwal 2001: 106.

11

Embracing New Frontiers

The winds and waves are always on the side of the ablest navigators.[1]

Edward Gibbon

In early 2010, Google, creator of the world's most widely used search engine and an increasingly diversified technology company, reported that it had been the target of a cyber attack emanating from China. The goal appeared to be to penetrate the email accounts of Chinese human-rights activists. In response, the company said it would no longer censor its results in China, effectively closing down its active operations in the country. Ultimately, Google moved its Greater China operation to Hong Kong, in effect bypassing the Chinese government and settling for partial access to the market on its own terms.

In 2006 and 2007, Coca-Cola was accused of using water that contained pesticides in its bottling plants in Kerala, India. An environmental group, the Center for Science and Environment (CSE), found that fifty-seven bottles of Coke and Pepsi products from twelve Indian states contained unsafe levels of pesticides. Kerala's minister of health, Karnataka R. Ashok, imposed a ban on the manufacture and sale of Coca-Cola products in the region. Coca-Cola then arranged to have its drinks tested in a British laboratory, which found that the amount of pesticides found in Pepsi and Coca-Cola drinks was harmless to the body. Coca-Cola subsequently ran numerous advertisements to regain consumers' confidence, but the scientific proof that Coca-Cola products did not contain pesticides was not convincing to state governments that had a history of antagonism toward large multinational investors, nor to a citizenry skeptical of the independence of regulatory agencies. Criticism of Coca-Cola's overall water usage soon prompted the company to make a broader commitment to global water conservation as part of a collaboration with the World Wide Fund for Nature (WWF),[2] one of the leading global conservation organizations.

Another example, from Chile, highlights how MNEs can fill voids created through institutional deficiencies—that is, a lack of, or weak enforcement of, laws and legislation. Deforestation is a widely accepted threat to biodiversity and climate stability in Latin America. Commercial forestry in the Amazon is one of the principal threats to biodiversity in this region. While there are many contributors to deforestation, demand for wood to produce furniture is a major culprit. Masisa—a Chilean wood-based board producer and forestry company—has advocated for improved environmental protection and higher standards. With total revenues of U.S. $1.3 billion in 2012, Masisa has more than ten industrial sites in Chile, Argentina, Brazil, Mexico, and Venezuela, and employs over 7,000 people. According to CEO Roberto Salas Guzmán, "We started talking about eco-efficiency in the 1990s. . . . Next, with respect to regulations, is to promote the use of biomass as energy in a sustainable way."[3] Beyond the legislative context, the company works closely with the WWF to protect forests. These governance standards have been very attractive for investors and their profits, because of their commitment to transparency and attempts to fill institutional voids.

From the examples above, we can see how institutional environments for nonmarket strategy differ widely around the world.[4] In this chapter, we examine different institutional systems in developed, developing, emerging, and transitional economies and draw implications for the design and structure of nonmarket strategies.

We begin with a brief review of the literature on institutional theory and how it has informed the strategies of firms that must adapt and adjust to such institutional environments. We draw from the international management literature that has explored new institutionalism,[5] the comparative capitalism literature, and the institutional economics perspectives of Douglas North and his disciples.[6] We describe how institutional voids (also termed deficits or discrepancies) between home and host countries pose challenges for firms seeking to understand the nonmarket environment in those systems.[7] We note that developed economies tend to function under a system of public ordering in which laws and regulations are used to protect private property and enforce contracts. In some environments these institutions are missing or deficient, most notably in developing and emerging economies. In these contexts, private ordering prevails. Under private ordering, governance relationships are derived from relationships and membership support rather than from formal legal contracts and obligations. Private ordering is particularly common in emerging markets, in which groups of local companies, business groups, and networks predominate to compensate for deficits in public ordering. In these contexts, strong government may exercise coercive force that also tends to favor state-owned enterprises—as is the case in China or Russia.[8]

These differences have direct implications for the organization and the implementation of nonmarket strategy. For example, under private ordering, enlisting allies who are within the government or who have government favor may be even more important than under public-ordered systems—direct, proactive lobbying may be frowned upon in favor of more subtle relationship building. This chapter will survey these contexts and derive practical implications for the design and structure of nonmarket strategy.

Factoring Institutions into Nonmarket Strategy

North defines the institutional environment as the formal and informal institutions that define the rules of the game in a society.[9] When this is applied to the business context, it can be argued that the institutional environment in which an organization operates exerts a strong influence on its behavior.[10] We understand the "behavior" of a commercial organization to be manifested in its corporate strategy. We disagree with neo-institutional theorists,[11] who argue that institutions generate strong pressure for conformity and thereby display substantial inertia. While this can indeed occur, it is not a given. Institutions—particularly governments—can display competences. Witness for example the actions of the European Commission in advancing market deregulation in Europe, often in the face of industry opposition.[12] Similarly, before the 2008 banking and property crisis, the Irish government pursued a proactive approach to industrial policy over a twenty-year period, encouraging and facilitating both the market entry and emergence of foreign and domestic companies in high-technology industries such as software and pharmaceuticals.

Given this book's emphasis on political as well as social arenas, it is important to identify two positions concerning the level of government intervention in market activity. Noninterventionist and interventionist political-economic types each align with orientations toward free-market economies and regulated industries through government policy. A third position is the deliberate use of more specific strategies, within industries, that nurture the relationships between organizations that foster network growth. While this third position concerns government intervention that focuses on the normative infrastructure between organizations, its specification in the literature is largely embryonic. The key question is: What role does institutional nurturing play in developing the relationship between firm structure and performance outcomes? We argue that public policy can make a difference in business performance and market competitiveness, and that not all government-based industrial intervention is necessarily market-distorting or "bad for business."

For instance, governments provide the legal and regulatory frameworks and enforcement mechanisms that determine the context of choice and action for managers and organizations.[13] Some scholars[14] have queried why there is a relative paucity of theoretical and empirical work exploring the effects of government on organizations and organizational behavior. Two research impediments have been advanced to at least partly explain this situation. First, it is difficult to isolate governmental effects from other influences. Secondly, there is a shortage of theory to isolate the causal mechanisms by which governments may affect other organizations and behaviors. While the first obstacle is challenging, it is not impossible to overcome through improved empirical modeling. The second obstacle may be overcome by looking beyond the narrow confines of "pure" management literature. In particular, political science, international relations/international political economy, and international business contain a wealth of literature that can assist in identifying the underlying instruments by which government can have an impact on firm structure and strategy.[15] Moreover, a significant body of related literature exists that examines the interaction of state policies and corporate strategies in shaping international business outcomes.[16]

A variety of perspectives and findings emerge from this literature on the role of government and of the state more broadly relative to companies in shaping economic competitiveness. Whether it is home or host government, the state can both help and hinder business in the formulation and implementation of strategy. A commonly used overarching term for this approach and influence is *industrial policy*.

Industrial Policy: Friend or Foe?

Industrial policy has many contrasting aspects: it can be either general or selective in nature; active, passive, or proactive in emphasis; vertical or horizontal in practice; and positive or negative in impact.[17] A general industrial policy promotes or protects the wider economy, while a selective version supports specific sectoral winners and losers in market competition. A vertical policy targets particular companies or industries for assistance, while its horizontal counterpart encourages widespread functional development in areas such as research and employee training.[18] At the risk of using normative language, *positive* or *competitive-focused* industrial policy facilitates structural adjustment and fair market competition, whereas *negative*, often *protectionist*, industrial policy obstructs structural adjustment and hinders open and equal competition. Ultimately, it can be argued that the success of industry is in part dependent on government's pursuit of the "right" measures, whether active or passive.[19]

Our starting point is the identification of two extreme positions regarding the extent to which governments intervene in business. At one extreme, non-intervention reflects a lack of purposeful manipulation by government of the competitive forces that shape industry growth and decline within a national economy. We term low levels of intervention as *passive* systems in terms of

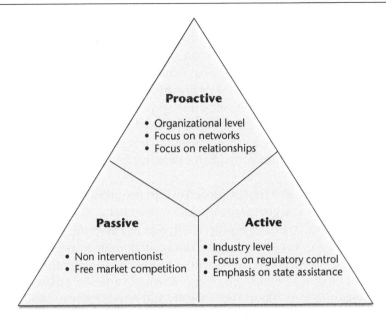

Figure 11.1 The three dimensions of government intervention

government policy and activity in manipulating the conditions within which organizations compete in any given society.

At the other extreme, high levels of intervention are conventionally marked by industrial policy that sets the conditions for industry competition and regulation. This high level of intervention reflects what we refer to as *active* systems in terms of government policy and activity toward manipulation and control of key industry conditions. Arguably, nation-states never exist at either extreme, and the comparison is best considered as a continuum between two fundamentally different political and economic orientations. In the newly emerging multipolar world order, variance has increased between the national points on this continuum because of the differences in forms of capitalism and the role of the state in Brazil, Russia, India, China, and South Africa (BRICS) and in other emerging economies. It is also important to highlight that active systems focus broadly on industry-level controls, with little active government intervention strategies at an organizational level. This is where we point out a third position.

Proactive systems are extensions of active systems. The key difference is that proactive systems focus on manipulation within the industry and, therefore, draw upon strategies that have an impact at the organizational level. A three-dimensional model therefore includes not only passive and active dimensions, but also proactive dimensions of institutional involvement in economic activity. The key characteristics are set out in Figure 11.1.

The empirical basis of Figure 11.1 is not clearly located in the literature, but we reiterate that there has been little systematic evidence that either passive or active government intervention, as conventionally defined, leads to more successful outcomes. Though our contribution of proactive types forms an even less clearly chartered area of institutional nurturing, the notion differs from the active model in one clear way: it represents a government's systematic and purposeful use of organizational-level strategies to grow and develop a successful network of organizational relationships, which in turn provide the relational infrastructure for industry and global competitiveness and success.

As we noted in Figure 11.1, the proactive type features a number of key characteristics, including a government's use of purposeful strategies, an organizational focus, an emphasis on the relationships between key organization actors, and a focus on providing the infrastructure for subsequent network development. However, the exploration of proactive intervention characteristics is still only in an embryonic form. When governments develop regulation, an organization is bound both legally and normatively to adopt certain policies or practices. Alternatively, dominant firms may demand that client firms adopt standardized practices, which results in coercive isomorphism. Together, mimetic, normative, and coercive isomorphism—treated in more detail below—represents three institutional forces that lead to the adoption of relatively limited sets of policies and practices.

The Politics, Markets, and Business Triangle

The South China Sea has been a source of tension between neighboring countries for centuries. Strains surfaced again during 2011 and 2012, sparking concern that the area could become a source of regional, if not global, conflict. The dispute centers on control of territory, particularly the Paracel and Spratly Islands chains.[20] China, Vietnam, and the Philippines are the main parties involved, but there are also rival sovereignty claims in the region advanced by Malaysia and Brunei. Why are so many countries at loggerheads over a sparsely populated stretch of ocean? As is so often the case, political and economic interests are closely aligned. Although there has been little detailed exploration of the area, it is believed to have vast reserves of natural resources. For instance, estimates of oil reserves vary from 28 to 213 billion barrels—the latter figure ten times the proven reserves of the United States.[21] The U.S. Energy Information Agency estimates that natural gas reserves in the area are even greater, and potentially as large as those of Qatar. The dispute continues, with no side appearing to back down.

As this example illustrates, inter-state relations and resource competition are frequently intertwined. World politics is, and always has been, influenced, if not determined, by a realist paradigm whereby state interests are paramount and conflict on an ongoing basis. This is turn affects firms and manifests in the nature and patterns of inter-firm cooperation and competition.[22] The overriding objective is to ensure balance of power and preserve order, despite periods of hegemony such as the U.S. experienced in the two decades following the end of the Cold War. In this view of the world, competition between great powers is the norm. This can occur directly, but in the interests of security and stability it often occurs indirectly via surrogates or allies. This was the way of the world throughout the Cold War, as the U.S. and Soviet Union vied for political influence and economic access across the globe. Ultimately, relations between the great powers shape the nature of the international system and the outcomes of regional conflicts. This is why the South China Sea territorial dispute, though it currently involves five regional players (six, if one includes Taiwan), may eventually morph into a contest between China and the U.S. The only real questions are whether this contest will occur directly or through surrogates and whether any subsequent conflict remains cold or turns hot in nature.

Similarly for inter-firm competition, the salient feature of business is that managers and entrepreneurs have to deal with a future they know little about because that is where risk and reward lie. Paradoxically, the only things we know about the future reside in the past. The past is recorded in accounts, in culture, in enduring structures and institutions, and in cultures and belief systems. How we read the past is, therefore, a clue to how we analyze the future. The interim conclusion is that the future can be segmented into two parts: the future that managers can shape by their own actions and the future they can anticipate but not affect in any meaningful way. As we discussed in Chapters 3 and 4, both futures involve complexity, but the latter, particularly its nonmarket elements, involves significantly greater uncertainty.

Institutional Environments and Strategic Alignment

As the world globalized, the strategy and organization literature increasingly embraced the complex interactions between organizations and their environments. Specifically, scholars of institutionalism have examined how firms that cross borders respond to different institutional environments. Obviously, government policy plays a critical role in firm performance, both at home and abroad. This is especially true for MNEs entering new markets, though, because of the vast amounts of uncertainty and resource control present in these new territories.[23] Hillman and Hitt's suggestion that "the success of business in the public policy arena is no less important than business success in the marketplace"[24] is especially the case in developing and emerging economies because of the variability and subjective nature of public-policy decisions in those environments. In many countries in which private or state ordering prevails, governmental policies are applied unevenly and based on personal preference or familial or other connections and subject to corruption, cronyism, and other illicit influence. Firms must, therefore, have the opportunity to use government policy to their advantage when entering new nations, specifically by producing public policy favorable to the position they are seeking in the marketplace.[25] They also, however, face new risks, and these risks can involve the presence (or absence) of institutional features that are quite distinct from those in their home markets.

Given different political agendas and actors in both home and host countries, research over the past four decades has typically focused on MNE responses to new environments to which they gain entry and in which they operate.[26] Two responses are typically explored under this scenario: the MNE accepts the political environment as a given and shapes itself to increase its legitimacy, or the MNE becomes an active player in bargaining with the host government.[27]

The first response is embedded in institutional theory, which suggests that in an effort to seek resources and legitimacy, the firm will simply take on the characteristics of the host environment.[28] As with other institutions, MNEs in this case are "socially constructed, routine-reproduced, program or rule systems."[29] Similarly, MNE responses may be characterized by passive reaction to government, that is, they are "reactive, with no direct participation in the public policy process."[30] Institutional theorists have proposed that MNEs must adapt and adjust to their local environments; in doing so they become isomorphic—that is, they become deeply embedded in the local environment in a consistent and similar way, such that their market and nonmarket strategies come to resemble one another, which results in convergence.[31]

However, others suggest that view to be widening, which can be the result of the second MNE response to host government pressures: actively working to change the current political state.[32] In fact, changes over the past few decades have shown that "relations between multinational corporations and host governments in developing countries have changed from being predominantly adversarial and confrontational to being non-adversarial and cooperative."[33]

North argues that businesses are a product of their institutional environments, which vary across the globe and can be categorized as either formal or informal.[34] Because of these differences, North contends that it is the interaction of institutions and organizations that shape business opportunities and practices in different countries over a period of time.[35] Even though research has shown that those organizations most successful in actively shaping public policy in different governmental settings are typically large powers, smaller firms have the same opportunities if they employ the right strategy.[36]

Hillman and Hitt refer to this type of strategy as "public policy shaping," by which they mean that it requires a proactive, behavior-based strategy aimed toward a specific policy objective.[37] Therefore, an MNE seeking to shape its environment can accomplish this task via one of two main approaches: discourse strategies or resource exchange strategies.[38] Discourse strategies emphasize the MNE's ability to affect the ideas, values, and norms of either a population or specific groups within a population.[39] Resource exchange strategies, conversely, focus on control over dependent resources within the host environment.[40]

Institutionalism, Comparative Capitalism, and Institutional Economics

Given that MNEs have a choice in how to respond to host government institutions—a point often ignored by mainstream theory—a research program has been conducted to explore how MNEs adapt to and, in some instances, seek to shape their environments.[41] In fact, scholars of what has been termed the "new institutionalism" highlight that institutional decisions affect MNE options and actions.[42] In other words, it is finally being recognized that accepting the status quo, in addition to being extremely difficult, might not be in the firm's best interest.

As MNEs enter many different countries around the world, they experience different types and intensities of institutional pressures. In such cases, it is difficult for them to accurately assess and comprehend the needs of these differing entities.[43] Therefore, there is a desire for MNEs to achieve supranational resolution by pushing for paralleled agendas across regions and countries.[44] However, when seeking to achieve this resolution, MNEs continue to experience isomorphic pressures to conform to their environments. According to Meyer and Rowan, these forces take three forms: coercive, mimetic, and normative pressures.[45]

Coercive isomorphic pressures result from other organizations on which the focal firm is dependent and can be exerted through government mandates, contract law, or financial reporting.[46] Under these circumstances, policymakers in support of the status quo[46] at times show strong resistance to isomorphic pressures, which creates a need for firm strategy to focus on those policymakers or government institutions likely to oppose the change. This type of policy transfer, termed *imposition*, represents the case in which external actors, such as the IMF, impose a type of cross-national policy convergence.[47] By directly appealing to these individual motivations, corporations will be more likely to see success in their transfer process.

Mimetic pressures, on the other hand, are simply the imitation of what is already in place and result from situations or environments plagued by uncertainty.[48] A home country will often make a conscious effort to agree to international standards, potentially to partake in the benefits of adoption or to avoid the costs of not adapting.[49] This voluntary adoption of standards, termed harmonization by researchers, represents the need of the home organization to stress the benefits of adoption to the focal country. In addition, given its negotiated nature, mimetic pressures are sometimes the result of direct negotiations between states and relevant actors, most often the policymakers of both the source and destination countries.[50] Under these circumstances, firm strategy will be most effective when it targets key policymakers and their constituents in both jurisdictions on an individual and a collective basis.

Normative isomorphic pressures represent themselves in networks or the licensing and crediting of educational achievement brought about by the state[51] and are most often accomplished using a diffusion strategy. Diffusion occurs when public decision-makers use policy knowledge and processes from other countries to create domestic regulations.[52] In these cases, policymakers must be persuaded to establish new regulations, which can be a seemingly easy task when many countries have adopted similar standards, which implies a need to conform. Because of the desire to stay abreast or ahead of the curve, competition will often be a driving force for normative diffusion strategies. To be most successful when developing these strategies, firms should cater to the most impressionable public officials.[53]

Institutional Differences, Discrepancies, and Voids

Khanna and Palepu have been most prominent in exploring and explicating the previously mentioned *institutional voids*—the absence of hard and soft infrastructure across product, labor, capital, and political/social markets that impedes entry and operation by foreign companies accustomed to more well-developed and sophisticated infrastructure.[54] They contend that qualitative analysis of the relative degree of advancement and the specific elements of institutional development in emerging markets can yield a more finely variegated and targeted approach to responding to, and at times filling, those voids. Indeed, they suggest that at its broadest level, firms' understanding of institutional variations between countries can guide strategies such that in some situations, the approaches to these institutional conditions may provide opportunities for "shaping," or influencing the policy context, in a manner that can benefit both the country environment and the firm. Examples would include encouraging a government to adopt or upgrade a regulation or standard—say for telecommunications, accounting, law, or environmental emissions—that a subject firm or firms may have already adopted and internalized to such a degree that they would have an advantage over local and global rivals when the standard is adopted.

Other situations, however, may prompt an "adapt" strategy. In these instances, the institutional conditions have already reached—or are on their way to reaching—a more mature state, and the firm or firms must adjust and adapt to those conditions accordingly. Google initially tried this approach in China but ultimately found the costs too high. The final option, which Khanna and Palepu describe as "withdraw" (or stay away), is appropriate for circumstances in which some aspect of the institutional categories they describe is so problematic that there is no viable recourse or logic for entering or remaining in a market. The quasi-nationalization of petrochemical assets in Venezuela has forced some foreign investors—notably those from the United States—to exit the country and accept the associated losses. Similarly, the more subtle "creeping expropriation" of oil and gas assets in Russia, as highlighted by Shell's forced withdrawal from its joint venture on Sakhalin Island and BP's saga with its joint venture partners and antagonists TNK and Rosneft, similarly underscore the reality that in some environments, the only viable and rational option is to get out.

Ordering Systems and Implications for Nonmarket Strategy

Boddewyn and Doh define collective goods as "those commodities, functions, and services that provide positive externalities such as health, education, communication, transportation, water, and electricity to local collectivities, and whose supply can be assured by public agencies and/or private for-profit and not-for-profit organizations."[55]

Collective goods represent resources necessary for survival, but their supply in emerging economies is often lacking, which results in institutional voids.[56] MNEs that wish to establish a presence in economies plagued by such voids will face challenges not only in how they enter, but in how they react to these problems, and either shape themselves or the environment to supply these collective goods.

Boddewyn and Doh borrow from institutional theory and transaction-cost economics to examine the governance relationships that arise from deficits in collective goods provision in emerging markets. They focus especially on how the specificity of the assets in question affects governance choices that emerge regarding whether MNEs and/or governments and NGOs can and should provide these goods. They describe three potential governance modes, each of which emanates from a transaction-cost analysis: (1) MNEs *contract* with the government and NGOs subsequently buy the goods from them; (2) MNEs, NGOs, and government agencies *ally* by collaborating and forming partnerships to supply these goods; or (3) MNEs *internalize* the responsibility.[57] In addition, Boddewyn and Doh have added a fourth possibility previously ignored in policy formation research, in which the MNE *assists* government agencies and/or NGOs by offering support or one-way donations for the purpose of developing a form of market economy where it previously had not existed.[58]

These types of exchanges are standard in public-ordering systems, which are characteristic of most developed economies. However, emerging economies are typically supplemented with *private-ordering systems* plagued by contractual hazards.[59] In the face of unsteady pricing and property rights,[60] this type of system develops legitimacy from personal relationships and networking; in the case of China, such a system may coexist with a strong, coercive government.[61] Table 11.1 provides a description of how variation in institutional settings and transaction costs affects preferred governance modes.

Ring et al. describe these relationship-based environments, in which the government does not have the same control as in public-ordering systems, as "nonfacilitative."[62] Strategy formulation in this environment depends on personal connections both inside and outside the organization, and these are often not based on trust.[63] While relationships are the key to success and many firms accordingly try to form different lines of rapport, all of them seem to be based on "suspicion, guardedness, and distrust," and create a sense of coldness.[64] Hence, in a public-ordering system, the provision of collective goods occurs through one of the three modes described by transaction-cost economics, while the fourth type provided by Boddewyn and Doh takes precedence in private- and state-ordering systems in which lines are blurred and relationships take precedence over well-defined rules and regulations.[65]

The goal of an enterprise entering an emerging economy or ones plagued by institutional voids and private-ordering systems is to find a way to provide collective goods to gain a competitive advantage.[66] These strategies are characterized as nonmarket because they require the firm to obtain the relevant permissions from the authorities, collaborating with NGOs and handling relations with local leaders, or from those who pursue objectives other than economic ones.[67] Therefore, to gain a competitive advantage in the environment in the supplying of these collective goods, the MNE is forced to find a way to obtain them at some type of cost advantage and to work in

Table 11.1. The combined impacts of institutional and organizational factors on the choice of governance mode for the provision of collective goods in emerging markets

Economic forum		Organizational factors	
		High asset specificity	Low asset specificity
Institutional factors	Public ordering prevails	1. Market contracting example: British Petroleum (BP) has hired Defense Systems Limited—a private security contractor—to train local forces to protect its pipelines in Colombia.	2. Alliance example: The German holding company, Textile Partners, and its Lithuanian subsidiary Utena are working with the German government-owned agency for international cooperation, GTZ, and the Lithuanian government on a Brazilian worker-training program.
	Private and/or state ordering prevails	3. Internalization example: In the diamond-mining industry, De Beers has taken on many traditional state functions within the mining regions of South Africa, while major oil companies in Nigeria have assumed responsibility for the supply of essential local collective goods.	4. Assistance example: The official China Youth Development Foundation's flagship Project Hope has raised hundreds of millions of dollars to build rural schools and provide scholarships for students from poor areas. Motorola, Coca-Cola and overseas foundations have contributed money to this project, while lobbying for the expansion of the market system in China.

Source: Boddewyn, J. and Doh, J.P. (2011). Global strategy and the collaboration of MNEs, NGOs, and governments for the provisioning of collective goods in emerging markets. *Global Strategy Journal*, 1: 345–361.

conjunction with those actors who have influencing power over nonmarket actors.[68] However, the unique nature of nonmarket environments poses various challenges to MNEs and strategy formulation in these areas.

Cross-border Nonmarket Strategy in Differing Institutional Environments

One goal of nonmarket strategy in these conditions can be to help transition the host community from a private-ordering state characterized by institutional voids to a more market-based economy capable of providing societal needs and more open business environments.[69] To shepherd this process, MNEs often partake in one of four strategies (bridging, buffering, supplement, and stimulate) to effectively manage relationships with external actors. Two of these are described by Pfeffer and Salancik and Hillman and Hitt as *bridging* and *buffering* strategies, given that it is essential that the MNE link with resource providers in the host country while at the same time acting to shelter the provision of collective goods against regulation.[70] Bridging constitutes more cooperative, affirmative strategies in which governmental and nongovernmental stakeholders are engaged as potential partners and collaborators. Buffering reflects a more defensive, protective stance in which companies seek to keep potentially threatening stakeholders at bay.

Nonmarket systems are often made up of different sets of business groups, described as "sets of legally separate firms bound together in persistent formal and/or informal ways."[71] Ring et al. describe this type of government system as "fragmented," meaning that the environment is made up of many actors with no centralized authority to resolve or dispute opposing goals and views.[72] Because of this, governments uphold conflicting regulations with a lack of uniformity in law creation.[73]

Therefore, the provision of collective goods will tie MNEs to these groups in some fashion, which means that nonmarket strategy becomes crucial in terms of integrating and identifying common interests with the right strategic partners.[74] Influencing these institutions can be challenging and complex; yet, the potential to exploit underdeveloped markets as an opportunity to gain competitive advantage can be powerful.[75] However, overt manipulation may be viewed skeptically and challenged, which means that the MNEs will be successful only if there are obvious shared benefits.[76]

In addition, the incoming subsidiary may also be placed in direct competition with other firms trying to provide collective goods.[77] In such a case, a strategy to raise rivals' costs typically prevails—the firm attempts to become the first mover and take advantage of the benefits that go along with that status while displacing rivals, which are then subject to higher costs.[78] An example is Southwestern Bell, which entered the Mexican telecommunications market early in the liberalization process by partnering with the incumbent carrier, which secured the firm a dominant insider position vis-à-vis international rivals that came later to the market.

Another strategy, termed the *supplement strategy*, strives to give back to the community to gain legitimacy and honor, which is intended to offset negative effects that might arise upon entering a new market.[79] CEMEX, the global building materials giant, has a long track record of pursuing supplement strategy. For instance, CEMEX established Patrimonio Hoy, a housing microfinance program, to expand lending to low-income families in several Latin American countries. In addition to the social benefits of such an initiative and the implications for bottom-of-the-pyramid growth[80] in the company's core businesses, the program increased CEMEX's social legitimacy and helped to defuse potential political and social opposition to its market expansion and business activities. In the same sense, a *stimulate strategy* may also work. This aims at assisting the local community with a longer-term project—for example, improving infrastructure[81]—that leads community members to shift their previously held norms and beliefs toward a public-ordering system.[82] The U.S. multinational AES, an electricity generation and distribution company, was eager to build a $550 million dam in Uganda, but was met with objections from environmentalists and local opponents who said the project was ecologically damaging, financially flawed, and disrespectful to the Nile's ancestral spirits. Yet, in spite of the problems, AES was able to secure financing and begin construction after it conducted environmental assessments showing that the dam would have a relatively small impact. The company also helped to modernize local schools, built a local cultural center, and compensated and resettled affected residents. "In all respects, the project's resettlement efforts are outstanding in the global context," a report noted.[83]

No matter which strategy is implemented, MNEs face challenges when trying to implement change in a nonmarket environment. The vast differences between private- and public-ordering systems impose wide-ranging differences on government and nongovernment actors in these locations. In addition, MNEs are faced with the burden of a double failure: not only do they risk failing in traditional markets characterized by well-developed ordering systems, but also failing in regard to institutional voids plaguing emerging economies.[84]

Conclusions and Managerial Implications

In this chapter we have explored how differing institutional conditions pose both challenges and opportunities for firms. On the one hand, companies that are unprepared for significant variation in institutional conditions—especially when confronting institutional voids—can be severely constrained in their ability to enter and operate effectively under those conditions. Both Google and Coca-Cola were stopped in their tracks in efforts to advance their products and services in China and India respectively. Each adjusted and adapted their approaches to those institutional requirements. In Google's case, a withdraw strategy appeared to be the most appropriate and viable response. In Coca-Cola's case, the company adapted to the pressures and constraints and used the experience to address a broader set of concerns regarding its water practices globally.

This chapter suggests several broad implications for the development of alignment between market and nonmarket strategies:

- Institutional environments differ considerably around the world, and what works in one context is unlikely to succeed elsewhere.

- These international institutional differences have important implications for market and nonmarket strategies and the relationships between the two.

- Some environments limit or curtail certain practices or strategies and, therefore, reduce the range of strategic options available to the firm.

- Companies have a range of potential strategic initiatives that are tailored to the specifics of the institutional environment and make the most of company resources and capabilities.

In Chapter 12 we will look at the process and practice of leading alignment: Who leads strategic alignment and how is it factored into the design and delivery of corporate strategy? We explore how different forms of network capital, particularly social, are leveraged to ensure corporate success in nonmarket arenas. The chapter draws together arguments and insights from previous chapters and makes the overall case for strategy alignment as a business principle and management practice.

Notes

1. Gibbon, E. (1826). *The history of the decline and fall of the Roman Empire.* New York: Harper: vol. 6: 315.
2. The WWF was formerly the World Wildlife Fund, a name that it retains in Canada and the U.S.
3. Boston Consulting Group and World Economic Forum 2011.
4. Khanna et al. 2005.
5. Scott, W.R. (1995). *Institutions and organizations.* Thousand Oaks, CA: Sage.
6. North, D.C. (1986). The new institutional economics. *Journal of Institutional and Theoretical Economics,* 142: 230–237; North 1990; North, D.C. (1991). Institutions. *Journal of Economic Perspectives,* 5: 97–112.
7. Khanna et al. 2005.
8. Boddewyn, J. and Doh, J.P. (2011). Global strategy and the collaboration of MNEs, NGOs, and governments for the provisioning of collective goods in emerging markets. *Global Strategy Journal,* 1: 345–361.
9. North 1991.
10. Henisz, W.J. and Zelner, B.A. (2001). The institutional environment for telecommunications investment. *Journal of Economics & Management Strategy,* 10(1): 123–148.
11. Particularly Scott W.R. (2001). *Institutions and organizations.* 2nd ed. London/Thousand Oaks, CA: Sage; Scott W.R. (2003). *Organizations: rational, natural and open systems.* 5th ed. Upper Saddle River, NJ: Prentice-Hall; Scott W.R and Meyer J.W. (1994). *Institutional environments and organizations: structural complexity and individualism.* London/ Thousand Oaks, CA: Sage.

12. Lawton, T.C. (1999a). Governing the skies: conditions for the Europeanization of airline policy. *Journal of Public Policy*, 19(1): 91–112; Lawton, T.C. (2002). *Cleared for take-off: structure and strategy in the low fare airlines business*. Ashgate studies in aviation economics and management. Aldershot, U.K./Burlington, VT: Ashgate Publishing Limited; Hatzopoulos, V. (2012). *Regulating services in the European Union*. Oxford: Oxford University Press.

13. Pearce, J.L. (2001b). *Organization and management in the embrace of government*. Mahwah, NJ: LEA Publishers.

14. Pearce 2001b.

15. Boddewyn 1988; Ring et al. 1990; Rugman, A.M. and Verbeke, A. (1990*). Global corporate strategy and trade policy*. London and New York: Routledge; Rugman, A.M. and Verbeke, A. (1992). Multinational enterprise and national economic policy. In P.J. Buckley and M. Casson (eds.). *Multinational enterprises in the world economy: essays in honour of John Dunning*. Aldershot, U.K.: Edward Elgar: 194–211; Lenway and Rehbein 1991; Brewer 1992a; Boddewyn 1993; Boddewyn and Brewer 1994; Baron 1995a.

16. Vernon, R. (1971). *Sovereignty at bay*. New York: Basic Books; Boarman, P. and Schollhamer, H. (eds.) (1975). *Multinational corporations and governments*. New York: Praeger; Doz, Y. and Prahalad, C.K. (1980). How MNCs cope with host government intervention. *Harvard Business Review*, 58(3): 149–157; Fagre, N. and Wells, L.T. (1982). Bargaining power of multinationals and host governments. *Journal of International Business Studies*, 13(2): 9–23; Kim, W.C. (1988). The effects of competition and corporate political responsiveness on multinational bargaining power. *Strategic Management Journal*, 9(3): 289–295; Behrman, J.N. and Grosse, R. (1990). *International business and governments: issues and institutions*. Columbia, SC: University of South Carolina Press; Stopford and Strange 1991; Murtha and Lenway 1994; Rugman and Verbeke 1998; Hillman et al. 1999; Ramamurti 2001; Schuler et al. 2002.

17. Lawton, T.C. (1999b). Introduction: concepts defined and scenes set. In T.C. Lawton (ed.). *European industrial policy and competitiveness: concepts and instruments*. Basingstoke: Macmillan and New York: St. Martin's Press: 1–22.

18. Lawton, T.C. (1999c). Evaluating European competitiveness: measurements and models for a successful business environment. *European Business Journal*, 11(4): 195–205.

19. Barberis, P. and May, T. (1993). *Government, industry and political economy*. Buckingham: Open University Press.

20. Different names exist for these islands, depending on country and language perspective.

21. BBC (2012). *Q&A: South China Sea dispute*. 27 June. <http://www.bbc.co.uk/news /world-asia-pacific-13748349> (accessed 17 December 2012).

22. Porter 1980; Porter, M.E. (1990). *The competitive advantage of nations*. New York: MacMillan; Morgenthau, H. (1967). *Politics among nations*. 4th ed. New York: Knopf; Waltz, K. (1979). *Theory of international politics*. New York: McGraw-Hill.

23. Hillman and Hitt 1999; Shaffer 1995; Boddewyn 1988; Jacobson, C., Lenway, S., and Ring, P. (1993). The political embeddedness of private economic transactions. *Journal of Management Studies*, 30: 453–478.

24. Hillman and Hitt 1999: 826.

25. Hillman and Hitt 1999: 826.

26. Dahan et al. 2006.

27. Dahan et al. 2006.

28. Dahan et al. 2006; DiMaggio and Powell 1983; Oliver 1991; Zucker, L.G. (1987). Institutional theories of organization. *Annual Review of Sociology*, 13: 443–464.

29. Jepperson 1991: 149. See also Dahan et al. 2006.

30. Hillman and Hitt 1999: 827; Weidenbaum 1980.

31. Dahan et al. 2006; DiMaggio and Powell 1983; Drezner, D.W. (2001). Globalization and policy convergence. *International Studies Review*, 3(1): 53–78.

32. Dahan et al. 2006.

33. Ramamurti 2001: 23, citing Dunning, H. (1998). An overview of relations with national governments. *New Political Economy*, 3(2): 280–284 (280). See also Vernon, R. (1998). *In the hurricane's eye*. Cambridge, MA: Harvard University Press; Weigel, D.R., Gregory, N.F., and Dileep, M.W. (1997). *Foreign direct investment*. Washington, DC: International Finance Corporation; United Nations (1999). *World investment report 1999: foreign direct investment and the challenge of development: overview*. New York and Geneva: UNCTAD.

34. Keim and Hillman 2008; North, D. (2001). Lobbying, euro-style. *National Journal*, 33(36): 2742–2746.

35. Keim and Hillman 2008: 48.

36. Keim and Hillman 2008: 51.

37. Hillman and Hitt 1999: 827; Weidenbaum 1980.

38. Dahan et al. 2006; Birnbaum, P. (1985). Political strategies of regulated organizations as functions of context and fear. *Strategic Management Journal*, 6: 135–150.

39. Dahan et al. 2006; Benford, R.D. and Snow, D.A. (2000). Framing processes and social movements: an overview and assessment. *Annual Review of Sociology*, 26: 611–639; Dejean, F., Gond, J-P., and Leca, B. (2004). Measuring the unmeasured: an institutional entrepreneurship strategy in an emerging industry. *Human Relations*, 57: 741–764; DiMaggio 1988; DiMaggio, P.J. (1991). Introduction. In W.W. Powell and P.J. DiMaggio (eds.). *The new institutionalism in organizational analysis*. Chicago, IL: University of Chicago Press: 1–38; Suchman 1995.

40. Dahan et al. 2006; Pfeffer, J. and Salancik, G.R. (1978). *The external control of organizations: a resource dependence perspective*. New York, NY: Harper & Row.

41. Dahan et al. 2006; Tsebelis 1991; Oliver 1991; Djelic and Quack 2003.

42. Dahan et al. 2006; Bulmer 1994; Levy and Egan 2003; Pollack 1996.

43. Dahan et al. 2006; Hillman and Wan 2005; Kostova and Roth 2002.

44. Dahan et al. 2006; Egan 2002.

45. Dahan et al. 2006; DiMaggio and Powell 1983; Meyer, J.W. and Rowan, B. (1977). Institutional organizations: formal structures as myths and ceremony. *American Journal of Sociology*, 80: 340–363.

46. Dahan et al. 2006.

47. Dahan et al. 2006; Collier, D. and Messick, R.E. (1975). Prerequisites versus diffusion: testing alternative explanations of social security adoption. *American Political Science Review*, 69(4): 1299–1315; Drezner 2001; Dolowitz, D. and Marsh, D. (2000). Learning from abroad: the role of policy transfer in contemporary

policy-making. *Governance: an international journal of policy, administration, and institutions*, 13(1): 5–23.

48. Dahan et al. 2006.
49. Dahan et al. 2006.
50. Dahan et al. 2006.
51. Dahan et al. 2006.
52. Dahan et al. 2006; Dolowitz and Marsh 2000.
53. Dahan et al. 2006.
54. Khanna et al. 2005.
55. Boddewyn and Doh 2011: 347.
56. Boddewyn and Doh 2011: 349.
57. Boddewyn and Doh 2011: 350.
58. Boddewyn and Doh 2011: 350; Seifert, B., Morris, S.A., and Bartkus, B.R. (2004). Having, giving, and getting: slack resources, corporate philanthropy, and firm financial performance. *Business & Society*, 43(2): 135–161.
59. Boddewyn and Doh 2011: 351.
60. Boddewyn and Doh 2011: 351.
61. Boddewyn and Doh 2011: 352; Peng, M.W. (2003). Institutional transitions and strategic choices. *Academy of Management Review*, 28(2): 275–296.
62. Ring, P.S., Bigley, G.A., D'Aunno, T., and Khanna, T. (2005). Perspectives on how governments matter. *Academy of Management Review*, 30(2): 308–320.
63. Ring et al. 2005: 312.
64. Ring et al. 2005: 312.
65. Boddewyn and Doh 2011; Brehm, J. and Rahn, W. (1997). Individual-level evidence for the causes and consequences of social capital. *American Journal of Political Science*, 41(3): 999–1023.
66. Boddewyn and Doh 2011: 356; Porter 1991; Madhok, A. (2002). Reassessing the fundamentals and beyond: Ronald Coase, the transaction cost and resource-based theories of the firm and the institutional structure of production. *Strategic Management Journal*, 23(6): 535–550.
67. Boddewyn and Doh 2011: 353.
68. Boddewyn and Doh 2011: 353.
69. Boddewyn and Doh 2011: 354.
70. Boddewyn and Doh 2011: 354; Pfeffer and Salancik 1978; Hillman and Hitt 1999; Scott, W.R. (1992). *Organizations: rational, natural, and open systems*. Englewood Cliffs, NJ: Prentice-Hall.
71. Boddewyn and Doh 2011: 355; Granovetter, M. (1985). Economic action and social structure: the problem of embeddedness. *American Journal of Sociology*, 91(3): 481–510.
72. Ring et al. 2005: 313.
73. Ring et al. 2005: 313.
74. Boddewyn and Doh 2011: 355.
75. Boddewyn and Doh 2011: 355.
76. Boddewyn and Doh 2011; Ahuja, G. and Yayavaram, S. (2011). Explaining influence rents: the case for an institutions-based view of strategy. *Organization Science*, 22: 1631–1652.

77. Boddewyn and Doh 2011: 356.

78. Boddewyn and Doh 2011: 356; McWilliams et al. 2002; Aulakh, P.S. and Kotabe, M. (1997). Antecedents and performance implications of channel integration in foreign markets. *Journal of International Business Studies*, 28(1): 145–175.

79. Boddewyn and Doh 2011.

80. Prahalad, C.K. and Hart, S.L. (2002). The fortune at the bottom of the pyramid. *Strategy+Business*, 26: 54–67; Prahalad, C.K. (2004). *The fortune at the bottom of the pyramid*. Upper Saddle River, NJ: Pearson Prentice Hall; Hart, S.L. (2005). *Capitalism at the crossroads*. Upper Saddle River, NJ: Pearson Prentice Hall; London, T. and Hart, S. L. (2004). Reinventing strategies for emerging markets: beyond the transnational model. *Journal of International Business Studies*, 35(5): 350–370.

81. Boddewyn and Doh 2011: 359–360.

82. Boddewyn and Doh 2011: 360; Peng, M.W. and Luo, Y. (2000). Managerial ties and firm performance in a transition economy: The nature of a micro-macro link. *Academy of Management Journal*, 43(3): 486–501.

83. Turner, M. (2001). Uganda's dam-builders search for consensus. *Financial Times*, 1 October: 15.

84. Boddewyn and Doh 2011: 360; Buckley, P.J. and Casson, M. (1976). *The future of the multinational enterprise*. London and New York: Macmillan; Khanna and Palepu 1997.

12

Leading for Advantage

While we are postponing, life speeds by.[1]

Seneca

Business leaders generally accept that building and maintaining relationships is critical to developing successful and aligned competitive strategies
for the political and social arenas. The role of the top management team and
company board in forging and sustaining these nonmarket relationships may
vary. Sometimes it is symbolic—a company's CEO meets with a country's
president—and intended merely to affirm in the public sphere what is already
going on in more discreet surroundings. On other occasions, it is facilitative—
a chairperson calls in favors from his or her professional network (deploying
social capital) to gain political access for members of the executive team. Often
it is instrumental—the COO went to college with the head of Greenpeace USA
and arranges to meet her for lunch to catch up about old times and to find
out about emergent campaigns and potential alliances. In most cases, it is
opportunistic, as executives engage whenever and wherever to create business
opportunities and defend company interests. Farther down the corporate hierarchy, it is routine, as directors of external affairs and sustainability managers
carefully establish and continually cultivate connections with civil servants,
regulatory officials, NGO managers, and other stakeholders.

In this final chapter we discuss how effective strategic leadership recognizes
the strengths and limitations of existing internal and external relationships.
We consider how leaders can find the means to energize and progressively
improve their connections with relevant political and social actors and agents,
including connections within relational networks such as those linked to
board governance (nonexecutive directors, shareholders, and so on), external customer and supplier groups, media, NGOs, and grassroots organizations. We argue that effectual aligned strategy must recognize, reinforce, and

exploit existing networks and then build upon them to develop new network connections where appropriate. Networking assumptions are formed and expressed through a self-reinforcing system of connectivity that tends to lead toward social capital accumulation.[2]

Leveraging Networks and Social Capital

Building on Gulati's notion of expanding network resources beyond those that generate social capital, we recognize that different types of networks can be acquired, exchanged, and converted into value forms within the political and social environments.[3] As the structure and distribution of networks presents the inherent structure of the social world, an understanding of network formation can help elucidate the structure and functioning of relationships. We argue that companies must look at different forms of networks and their structural distribution and develop those that are most suitable to particular social and political challenges, especially lobbying or interest representation to shape policy.

Relating the idea to business success, one can note that in any field of human endeavor there is stratification, and in any industry there is a hierarchy. Political and social strategy in the top stratum is dominated by companies that set industry policy parameters. In the bottom stratum, subversive political and social strategies emerge from industry upstarts or mavericks. Successful strategic leaders—regardless of their industry stratum—can access and leverage network resource types.[4] Such social capital can be converted into power within their organization and market, and into authority and legitimacy within their industry, which allows these companies to deliver substantial value for stakeholders and to win their strategic games.[5]

Elaborating on ideas developed earlier in the book, this final chapter advances a fresh way of thinking about the practice and principles of strategic leadership within the political and social arenas. The potential for fast-track business growth can only be realized when an organization has a dynamic and capable leader or leadership team. Value-creating political and social activities cannot occur without an active and focused leadership. A number of distinct and complementary characteristics are needed to be an effective strategic leader, particularly in a nonmarket context. We discuss these and clarify how leading and implementing nonmarket strategy is similar to and different from leading and delivering market strategy. We end with some thoughts on how best to proactively align strategy in both the market and nonmarket domains to release both corporate and societal value in the process. We also argue that in successfully aligned companies, political capabilities sit alongside social capabilities—and market capabilities such as positioning, pricing, and marketing—in a strategic toolkit that includes tactics such as lobbying, PR campaigns, and other nonmarket practices.

Before advancing to these issues and ideas, we need to revisit two questions touched on in earlier chapters but not fully answered: Where in a company does the design and development of nonmarket strategy occur, and who is best placed to lead the delivery of nonmarket initiatives and ensure alignment between market and nonmarket strategy? In practice, there are no agreed answers to either question. For many companies, the design and development are outsourced to consultancies. For most, the delivery and alignment are led by the top management team, with the board chairperson occasionally playing a role. In addition, the two main pillars of nonmarket activity—political and regulatory engagement and social and environmental initiatives—are largely separate within corporate structures.

At computer technology giant Dell, for example, nonmarket matters are largely dealt with in-house at a senior level, but managers conducting CPA and those responsible for CSR are functionally separate, which thus reduces Dell's ability to create strategy alignment. Dell's vice president (VP) of corporate responsibility (a position created in 2008) presides over a Department for Corporate Responsibility. She has three direct reports—the executive director for sustainability, the executive director for global giving and community engagement, and the principal environmental strategist—signifying the three areas of emphasis.[6] This VP reports to the chief marketing officer (CMO), who in turn reports to founder and CEO Michael Dell.

CPA is undertaken separately. There is a vice president for government affairs, who reports to the chief legal counsel, who in turn reports to Michael Dell. The chief legal or general counsel (who is also a senior vice president and secretary of the company) oversees the global legal department as well as government affairs, compliance, and ethics.[7] All are located at corporate headquarters in Austin, Texas. In addition, Dell has a vice president for corporate communications, who reports to the CMO and to Michael Dell. It is clear that Dell has elevated but not aligned or integrated nonmarket strategy. Vice presidents directly tasked with analyzing and responding to the nonmarket are only two levels of report away from the company's founder and CEO, but the reporting structures are different: corporate responsibility, sustainability, and PR and communications report through the CMO to the CEO, while legal, government, and regulatory affairs report to the general counsel, who reports to the CEO. Dell's relatively flat hierarchy ensures that all of these executives do communicate, but their activities, initiatives, and objectives are, for the most part, siloed. In multidivisional global companies that have grown in part through acquisition, this functional separation is often more pronounced. For instance, in the case of Ben & Jerry's and Unilever, CSR (including sustainability) is managed and implemented by Ben & Jerry's from its head office in Burlington, Vermont. CPA, encapsulating government and regulatory affairs, is undertaken by senior Unilever executives based in London and Rotterdam.[8]

We argue that nonmarket strategy is too important to be formulated outside the company by those who may not understand the firm's values and culture. We further contend that strategy alignment is vital to ensure competitive advantage and too valuable to be undertaken on an ad hoc basis by business leaders with other priorities. Accordingly, we advance the notion of a new, top-team-level position responsible for nonmarket strategy design, development, and delivery. This function would ideally sit alongside the CEO, Chief Operating Officer COO, Chief Financial Officer CFO, and other executive board members. Relevant titles might include Chief External Officer (CEO), Chief Policy Officer (CPO), and Chief External Engagement Officer (CEEO). In circumstances where it may be difficult to create a new board-level position, this role could be part of the CEO's office or affiliated—or even merged—with the role of Chief Strategy Officer (if such a position exists). As the following example, already mentioned in Chapter 6, illustrates, when companies elevate nonmarket strategy to a senior executive level, it can strengthen market position and feed into competitive advantage.

Why you Need a CEEO[9]

In the mid-1990s Thomas Kropp managed Lufthansa's government and regulatory affairs office in Brussels, with a total team of nine people.[10] The airline's "corporate embassy" to the EU was one of the first of its kind among European airlines and the most substantial in terms of resource commitment. Its mandate was to monitor and influence the EU policymaking process as it affected air transport and specifically Lufthansa Group.

Like other major airlines at the time, Lufthansa was under growing pressure to increase fuel efficiency, reduce emissions, and adopt an overall social responsibility and sustainability strategy. Much of this pressure was being exerted at a European level, as policy authority for air transport shifted from national capitals to EU institutions in Brussels. As a result, airlines' external affairs emphasis also shifted away from bilateral international traffic rights, airport slot allocations, and engagement with national legislators toward a more integrated, pan-European approach that transcended narrow, short-term political and social objectives. Lufthansa recognized this necessity well in advance of its industry peers. Further, as the demands placed on the company increasingly emanated from multiple jurisdictions ranging from the EU to consumer pressure groups, the company shifted its attention to broader issues of customer rights, infrastructure, and competition.

Structure followed strategy as new teams were created under the overall external affairs function around political affairs, social responsibility, environmental sustainability, and international relations. Recognizing the increasingly transnational nature of the social and political pressures facing the group, Lufthansa invested further in external affairs offices in Brussels and Washington, DC, engaging with legislators and administrators, international organizations, NGOs, and trade associations. Lufthansa's chief executive routinely served as chairman of the influential Association of European Airlines. The air carrier gained first-mover advantage by building a corporate strategy that closely aligned its business objectives and market positions with its political obligations and social responsibilities. Kropp and his team further recognized that the narrow process of lobbying for influence was being superseded by the more transparent interest representation approach to policy shaping. At an EU level, a preference had emerged for a broader and more inclusive approach to policy consultation. When forging new policy and regulations, it was common for EU politicians and civil servants to create representative committees, drawing on all relevant stakeholder groups, including environmental NGOs, consumer groups, and others. When the issues related to air transportation, one company became the default industry representative: Lufthansa, represented either by its chief executive officer or by its senior government affairs executives.

Thomas Kropp has since moved from Brussels back to Lufthansa's headquarters in Frankfurt. As senior vice president and head of Group International Relations and Government Affairs, he is a key member of Lufthansa's corporate strategy leadership team. In essence, Kropp is Lufthansa's CEEO, having overseen the corporation's emergence as Europe's most politically astute, socially aware, and environmentally responsive air transport group. It is no coincidence that during his tenure Lufthansa also emerged from near collapse in 1991 to being one of the largest and most successful air transport groups in Europe and globally. As public opinion and the regulatory landscape shifted, Lufthansa's de facto CEEO was adept at moving proactively and seizing opportunities to propel Lufthansa into the pilot's seat of European public policy's new journey. In contrast, other national flag carriers, such as Alitalia and Iberia, failed to recognize or respond rapidly to changing external contexts and new environmental realities. Their lobbying and communications efforts remained nationally focused, their external affairs structures remained fragmented and under-resourced, and their approaches were tactical rather than strategic. Today these external relations laggards have been subsumed by stronger rivals or are heavily indebted and on the brink of bankruptcy. In contrast, Lufthansa's market success, supported by its ability to anticipate political and social trends and respond preemptively to external constituencies, provides a compelling case for companies to have a board-level CEEO.

The Challenges of Implementing Alignment[11]

An important challenge for the CEEO or equivalent is executing strategy alignment—understanding the differences between a company's market and nonmarket environment, and advancing a coherent and integrated strategic approach.[12] The key is to transform perceived nonbusiness issues into strategic opportunities to build a sustainable competitive advantage. Bach and Allen advance four factors that drive investment in nonmarket strategy: multiple audiences that companies navigate simultaneously in distinct nonmarket environments, the globalization of nongovernmental organizations, new regulatory hurdles with fresh nonmarket challenges, and the constant search for a competitive edge.[13]

However, a firm can face both internal and external challenges in implementing alignment.[14] Internal limitations usually arise as a result of lack of commitment, particularly from the top management team. External challenges can arise from the political or regulatory environment or from interactions with activists or interest groups that change the nature of the competitive game.[15] More generally, market and nonmarket activities are not always complementary, which forces firms to face trade-offs and limit nonmarket activities to focus on the development of market activities. We argue that in the modern world economy, making trade-offs that deprioritize nonmarket strategy initiatives and activities is ultimately self-defeating. In the past, firm performance was determined, at least in part, by how effectively and efficiently a firm's market strategy was implemented.[16] This point still holds but needs to be augmented to reflect the increased importance of nonmarket strategy implementation to firm performance, particularly in a multipolar world.[17] The challenge, therefore, is to be able to build frameworks to allow predictions and consequently adapt to all the changes occurring in the market and nonmarket to ensure that the firm has a sustainable strategy.[18] Zajac et al. emphasize the importance of having a "distinctive analytical approach that simultaneously considers how multiple organizational and environmental factors should affect strategic fit over time, as well as subsequent firm performance."[19] Identifying specific environmental and organization factors is fundamental for a firm to achieve a strategic fit that will allow it to have a successful and sustainable strategy.

A core element in ensuring the successful implementation of an aligned strategy is the management of stakeholder needs and expectations.[20] Identifying key stakeholders is particularly important. For instance, the

French food products group Danone identified medical institutions as being key stakeholders and redefined its strategy to "bring health through food to as many people as possible."[21] In the same way, the French multinational Saint-Gobain identified its customers and the government as its key stakeholders. This led the company to build its strategy around innovative high-quality products that help clients in their business while providing environmentally friendly solutions that comply with, and even go beyond, government regulations.[22] A company's nonmarket initiatives have to match its core competences to be coherent and successful; therefore, it makes both business and societal sense for Saint-Gobain to produce energy-saving products, just as it does for Danone to provide healthy products. As a result, as Hillman and Keim argue, when a company's societal efforts are directly tied to its primary stakeholder, investments may not only benefit stakeholders but also result in increased shareholder wealth.[23]

The Practice of Leading Alignment

The emergence of China, India, Brazil, Indonesia, Turkey, Nigeria, Colombia, Vietnam, and other economies around the world has brought with it considerable business opportunity. As the Chinese concept of yin and yang demonstrates, opposite forces are interconnected and interdependent—with opportunity comes challenge. Questions of how to enter and make money in an overseas market are rendered infinitely more problematic by the three Cs of *context*, *culture*, and *complexity*. Many challenges in a multipolar world are cultural, and others are frequently political (complexity) or social (context). This book sends a clear message to business leaders: a strategic approach to crafting and managing external nonmarket relations is integral to market success. This is particularly pertinent in international business. We argue that proactive companies can create a new, unified senior executive role to manage the political–regulatory and social–cultural environments, and that this role and resultant actions can defend or advance the competitive advantage of the business.

As companies increasingly face concurrent and coordinated pressures from governmental and civil society stakeholders, the traditional separation between legislative/regulatory affairs functions and corporate activities focused on a broader set of stakeholders that include NGOs, community groups, and other nongovernmental actors may no longer be viable. Issues like climate change, financial regulation and disclosure, cybercrime and terrorism, and the labor and human rights of workers in developing countries all require proactive strategies directed toward both political and social actors.

Yet most companies maintain distinct and separate offices for these functions, which can lead to uncoordinated and at times competing—even conflicting—objectives and outcomes. In this book we have shown that strategic alignment and functional integration can lead to more effective corporate actions and policies, ultimately serving to protect or promote the competitive advantage of the corporation.

A Framework for Responding to External Issues

Throughout the last eleven chapters, we considered a range of organizations, engaging directly through senior-level interviews and indirectly through archival data spanning twenty years. We analyzed and evaluated various approaches to nonmarket strategy (or lack thereof) to derive insights that can help guide company policies and practices. For instance, in the case of Germany's Lufthansa Group and India's Tata Group, two distinct conglomerates with unique organizational structures and market positions, both elected to move toward a coordinated approach to political and social issues and each elevated this function such that it had an impact on decision-making at the highest levels of the businesses. For most companies the challenges posed by social and political actors command attention, responsiveness, and action at the top-team level. Closer alignment of the political and social affairs functions with each other and with the business strategy is a first step in ensuring that these issues are disseminated and acted upon from the C-suite down. We argue that most companies would be well served to recognize the interdependencies between the political and social arenas and the actors engaged within each and to organizationally unify related business and management functions. This suggests a new profile for those overseeing both functions in the form of the CEEO. Such integration can assist top management teams when dealing with the major social and political issues of today. The main challenges to realizing such a development are how to configure this integrated nonmarket function and how to manage an assimilated external environment.

In Table 12.1 we introduce five structural options for managing the external environment. In practice, examples exist for all approaches apart from the first, where nonmarket engagement is driven by the agenda and actions of the CEO and/or top management team (TMT). The influence of political and legal/regulatory affairs (the functional manifestation of what we previously referred to as CPA) can be significant in highly regulated industries. The strategic authority of corporate responsibility or sustainability executives can be visible in organizations that have built their competitive differentiation and advantage on social awareness and engagement.

Table 12.1. Five structures for managing the external environment

Focus	Purpose	Decision making	Key benefits
CEO/TMT- driven	Key external relations decisions taken by the CEO/ TMT	Top-down, clear chain of command	Rapid and decisive action
Political and Legal Affairs (PLA)-driven	Political and Legal Affairs executive has primary responsibility	Political and regulatory issues are to the fore when taking corporate decisions	Long-term political and policy network benefits can accrue, which can lead to inclusivity in the legislative consultation process
CSR/Sustainability-driven	CSR (or equivalent) executive has primary responsibility	CSR issues of higher importance than PLA issues when taking decisions	Long-term NGO and civil society networks can accrue, which can result in joint branding and the enhancement of corporate reputation
CSR/PLA split (equal importance)	CSR and PLA executives both have input and authority	CSR and PLA issues arise in the executive agenda	Development of technical ability and competences in both CSR and PLA issues
Chief External Engagement Officer	CEEO is responsible for both CSR and PLA issues and activities	The CEEO has a key role in the corporate executive suite	Elevation of CSR and PLA issues to the C-suite and alignment of business units with central CSR/ PLA purpose and direction

Examples of the fifth option, creating a CEEO (or equivalent) role, are more limited in practice. Companies such as Coca-Cola and IKEA have developed distinctive and high-level executive roles that engage both political and social contexts in an integrated approach. These executives are empowered to make strategic decisions on various social and political issues, working closely with the chief executive and TMT to strengthen long-term competitive advantage. The CEO and TMT can identify those who are best qualified to take on the role of the CEEO (a blended skill set is required) and decide how to make the most of this new top-level executive.

Throughout this book we have discussed the distinct but interconnected nature of CSR and CPA as the two key pillars of nonmarket strategy. We have illustrated how, in large companies, these are distinct activities with dedicated personnel and resources. The practical overlap and communication exchange are often absent, which results in a bifurcated nonmarket strategy. We argue that the alignment of market and nonmarket strategy is more likely to occur and to contribute to competitive advantage if a company first integrates—or at least internally aligns—its political and social affairs functions. In Table 12.2, we advance a four-stage process that firms can use to functionally integrate their political/regulatory and social/sustainability personnel and activities.

Table 12.2. Four stages in creating a Chief External Engagement Officer support team

Stage	Purpose	Managers involved	Outcome
1. Advocate	Create the conditions and urgency for the integration	TMT and CSR/PLA teams	A time plan and route map to create a unified office
2. Resource	Provide the necessary resources (human and financial primarily)	TMT	A budget and resource plan for the new office
3. Establish	Create the new office and link to other departments	TMT and internal communications team	A series of communications about the new office and its purpose and intent
4. Initiate	Agree and disseminate strategic priorities of the new office	The new, integrated office and CEEO	A set of key initiatives and objectives for the new office that are clearly communicated

Making a Case for Value Chain Alignment

Business leaders must consider one last network resource when attempting to align for advantage. In principle, if not always in practice, the relationship between a company and its supply-chain partners has shifted from a purely transactional to a more strategic level. Cost pressures and the internationalization of markets have resulted in the increased preponderance of outsourcing and offshoring. This means that a firm is increasingly dependent on other firms—often in distant locations—to deliver the efficiency and effectiveness that underpin its business strategy. Consequently, most senior executives recognize that achieving and retaining competitive advantage in market arenas has become a shared endeavor. But, by and large, this realization has not extended to the nonmarket arena. Business leaders often overlook the importance of supply-chain partners in building and delivering a nonmarket strategy. More acutely, trouble may be beckoning if the leadership of a company neglects to align its nonmarket strategy with the words and deeds of those companies that are to produce, deliver, or service its products. When this occurs, market value and competitiveness can rapidly be eroded or lost. Two high-profile examples of the problems that can occur when there is a lack of nonmarket alignment between a firm and its supply-chain partners involve Apple and BP.

An explosion in May 2011 at a factory in Chengdhu, China, killed two workers and injured twelve. The factory was owned by Foxconn, one of China's largest electronics manufacturers. In the West, we often hear nothing of the industrial accidents that occur regularly across China. What was different on this occasion? The workers in the area where the explosion occurred were polishing the covers of new iPads, one of the world's most in-demand consumer electronic devices. The iPad is a flagship product of Apple Inc., one of the world's most valuable companies and one that prides itself on being a highly responsible business (its website states that "Apple is committed to the highest standards of social responsibility across out worldwide supply chain"). Foxconn, one of Apple's most important manufacturing partners, is no stranger to controversy and is frequently criticized for its factory workers' welfare. Though Foxconn and Apple are separate companies in different parts of the world, certain elements in the media and some advocacy groups directed their criticisms over the incident at Apple, arguing that Apple calls the shots in the supply chain and, therefore, must take at least some responsibility for the actions of its suppliers. The California-based company responded with press releases and a more muscular approach to enforcing its supplier code of conduct.

The 2010 Deepwater Horizon oil spill is another example of how the actions (or inactions) of a supplier can damage the reputation, brand, and even financial stability of a corporation. Eleven men died and seventeen were injured when an explosion occurred at an oil drilling unit in the Gulf of Mexico. The resulting oil discharge was the largest accidental marine spill in the history of the industry. Deepwater Horizon was owned by Transocean, leased to BP, and operated by Halliburton. Who was to blame: the supplier, the lessee, or the operator of the equipment? Investigations indicate that all were at fault, as the accident was the result of a loss of control over pressure in the well (the responsibility of both BP and Halliburton) together with the failure of the valve's blowout preventer (Transocean's responsibility). After the initial explosions, the blowout preventer's emergency functions failed to seal the well, which allowed the spill to happen.[24] This suggests that while the loss of life was due to human or equipment error at BP/Halliburton, the environmental disaster that followed was the fault of Transocean. The media and the public largely overlooked this fact, as BP bore the brunt of criticism and initial censure and took the most significant share price hit of all the companies involved in the venture. This was a huge PR blow to a corporation that only ten years before had rebranded itself, through a high-profile advertising campaign, as one of the most environmentally friendly companies in the industry.

So, why have both Apple and BP seen their reputations tarnished, and in BP's case suffered financial cost and share price decline, as a result in whole or in part of the actions of supply-chain partners? The answer is, in part, social media and the Internet, which allow awareness of these events and activities to spread faster and more widely. It is also due to the increased reliance of companies on outsourcing and offshoring of business activities, usually to reduce cost. This phenomenon has resulted in increasingly closer and more aligned operations between contractor and contracted, regardless of geographical location. But at a strategic level, less alignment typically occurs, especially in the area of social responsibility. The principle of strategic alignment has two dimensions: a balanced and mutually reinforcing approach to business strategy, political activity, and social responsibility both inside a corporation *and* outside with supply-chain partners. Aligned strategies reconcile a company's internal objectives and external demands and turn this reconciliation into a source of competitive advantage. For instance, as we mentioned previously, Coca-Cola works with its supply-chain partners to encourage water conservation and efficiency practices in China—an initiative that has environmental sustainability overtones but is equally valuable to the company's market-growth strategy in China, which is dependent on a consistent and sanitary water supply.

As the Apple and BP examples illustrate, companies need to devote more time and resources to aligning strategically with supply-chain partners. This means working toward a mutual understanding of corporate vision, values, objectives, and market positions, and requires sharing and adhering to a similar approach to social responsibility and to the environment in which the entire supply chain operates. Therefore, the concept of alignment has two primary elements: the internal alignment of a company's market and nonmarket strategy values and objectives, and the external alignment of both with the strategies of strategic supply-chain partners. Combined with an internal alignment with corporate policy and culture to ensure effective implementation, this is the approach through which a company can optimize nonmarket strategy competitive advantage.

Conclusions and Managerial Implications

In *Aligning for Advantage*, we have proposed an approach for aligning a company's business objectives and market positions with its political requirements and social obligations. While academic research to date acknowledges that companies should be viewed not as separate from, but embedded within, the political and social environments in which they operate,[25] it has rarely offered concrete ideas about how this can be accomplished. While most scholars and practitioners agree that political and social strategies must be aligned with overall corporate strategy to have impact and be successful,[26] the process of achieving this orientation is rarely discussed.

The practical outcomes of our research can assist senior managers in two ways: to develop a more nuanced, practical, and realistic approach to alignment, and to acquire unique insights into how this process is addressed by executives across various sectors and countries. In summary, we have shown that:

- A realistic and realizable stance for most companies is a balanced and mutually reinforcing approach to corporate strategy, political activity, and social responsibility.

- In some instances, alignment may mean deep partnerships with governments or other stakeholders that are embedded in a core business strategy.

- In other situations, alignment may take the form of looser collaborations with outside organizations and individuals, with some coordination of commercial activities that includes ongoing and meaningful communication.

- In either case, the relationship between the nonmarket and market strategies should be conscious and deliberate, not accidental or artificially constructed.

Typically, alignment will reflect features of both of these examples, rather than an all-or-nothing, integrated, "built in" position, in which companies establish a competitive differentiation predicated on responsibility, sustainability, or deep partnership with government; or a "bolt on" approach, in which companies allocate resources to social and political initiatives only to offset specific stakeholder criticisms, embellish their citizenship credentials, or gain influence for specific purposes. Aligned strategies seek to reconcile the sometimes conflicting external demands that a company encounters, modulate those demands in a way that is appropriate for the firm's geographic and market positions, and leverage the overall nonmarket strategy such that it contributes to organizational success. In a multipolar world, the winning companies of the future must ensure that they engage proactively with the nonmarket and are structurally and strategically aligned for advantage.

Notes

1. Seneca, L.A. (1969). *Letters from a stoic: epistulae morales ad Lucilium.*Translated by R.A. Campbell. London: Penguin.
2. Nohria, N. and Eccles, R. (eds.) (1992). *Networks and organizations: structure, form, and action.* Boston, MA: Harvard Business School Press.
3. Gulati, R. (1999). Network location and learning: the influence of network resources and firm capabilities on alliance formation. *Strategic Management Journal*, 20(5): 397–420.
4. Nahapiet and Ghoshal 1998.
5. Morten T., Hansen, J., Podolny, M., and Pfeffer, J. (2001). So many ties, so little time: a task contingency perspective on corporate social capital in organizations. In S.M. Gabbay and R.T.A.J. Leenders (eds.). *Social capital of organizations.* New York: JAI Press: 21–57.
6. Telephone interview conducted by Thomas Lawton with Michele Glaze, Giving Manager (North America), Dell. Ms Glaze was at corporate headquarters in Austin, Texas and the interview took place on March 22, 2012.

7. Telephone interview conducted by Thomas Lawton with Michele Glaze 2012. See also <http://content.dell.com/us/en/corp/d/bios/leadership-lawrence-tu> (accessed March 23, 2012).
8. Interview conducted by Thomas Lawton with Jostein Solheim 2012.
9. Our thanks to Sotirios Paroutis of Warwick Business School for his input into this section.
10. One of the authors, Thomas Lawton, visited Lufthansa's "corporate embassy" in 1995 and met with Mr. Kropp for research purposes.
11. This section draws on the work of Juliette Scheidecker and Marie-Alicia Tardy and their 2012 EMLYON Business School Masters thesis supervised by Thomas Lawton.
12. Husted, B.W. and Allen, D.B. (2011). *Corporate social strategy: stakeholder engagement and competitive advantage*. Cambridge, U.K.: Cambridge University Press.
13. Husted and Allen 2011.
14. Bonardi, J.P. (2008). The internal limits to firms nonmarket activities. *European Management Review*, 5(3): 165–174.
15. Bonardi, J.P. and Keim, G.D. (2005). Corporate political strategies for widely salient issues. *Academy of Management Review*, 30(5): 555–576.
16. Galbraith, J.R. and Kazanjian, R.K. (1986). Organizing to implement strategies of diversity and globalization: the role of matrix designs. *Human Resource Management*, 25(1): 37–54.
17. Doh, Lawton, and Rajwani 2012.
18. Zajac et al. 2000.
19. Zajac et al. 2000: 432.
20. Freeman 1984; Freeman, R.E. (1994). The politics of stakeholder theory. *Business Ethics Quarterly*, 4(4): 409–421; Freeman, R.E. (2004). The stakeholder approach revisited. *Zeitschrift für Wirtschafts- und Unternehmensethik*, 5(3): 228–241; Donaldson and Preston 1995.
21. This is Danone's Food, Nutrition and Health Charter mission statement and can be found at <http://research.danone.com/index.php?option=com_danoneconte nt&cid=37> (accessed April 10, 2013).
22. For further details, see Saint-Gobain (2011) *Building our environment together.* Sustainable Development Report. <http://www.saint-gobain.com/files/Saint-Gobain-RADD-GB.pdf> (accessed April 10, 2013).
23. Hillman, A.J. and Keim, G.D. (2001). Shareholder value, stakeholder management, and social issues: what's the bottom line? *Strategic Management Journal*, 22(2): 125–139.
24. For further details, see the report into the spill published in 2011 by a U.S. federal government special commission: <http://www.oilspillcommission.gov/final-report> (accessed April 10, 2013).
25. Hillman and Hitt 1999.
26. Baron 1995a.

Index

Abidjan 162
Abrams, Frank W. 151, 153
abuse of power 60
  see also bribes; corruption; scandals
accountability 29, 32, 178, 180–1
Acme Motors 82
adaptive strategies 66
AEA (Association of European Airlines) 121, 213
AES Corporation 203
Afghanistan 47, 57
Africa x, 14, 22
  sub-Saharan 107
  see also Algeria; Egypt; Ethiopia; Gambia;
    Ghana; Ivory Coast; Kenya; Libya;
    Morocco; Nigeria; South Africa; Tanzania;
    Tunisia; Uganda
Afrique Secours et Assistance 162
Agle, B. R. 20 n.(46), 154, 155, 166 n.(4), 167
  nn.(23-7), 178, 187 n.(20)
Agmark 151
AHC (US Alliance for Healthcare
  Competitiveness) 75–6
Air France 140, 144
  see also KLM
Airbus 44
airlines 8, 13, 45, 102, 129, 131 n.(28), 144,
  205 n.(12)
  budget 105
  global 94, 187 n.(19)
  legacy 90 n.(0), 187 n.(19)
  long-haul 35, 126
  major 94, 212
  national 121
Algeria 107
alignment 42, 89, 158, 185, 217, 221
  challenges of implementing 214–15
  creating 146, 152, 157
  early example of the art of 26–7
  enhanced 179
  ensuring 66
  establishing 3–21, 180
  external/internal 220
  functional 102
  implications for development of 203
  intellectual and moral underpinnings 26

organizations must slowly develop
  culture of 180
practice of leading 215–16
specific approach to 108, 116
stakeholder, nonmarket, strategic
  importance of 165
trust 159
value chain 218–20
see also strategic alignment
Alitalia 213
Allen, D. B. vii, x n.(5), 5, 17 n.(9), 69 n.(4), 214
Alliance for a Green Revolution in Africa 151
American Bankers Association 115
American Libraries Association 135
American Textile Manufacturers Institute 79
antidumping 79
Appalachian Energy 82
Apple Inc. 13, 218–19, 220
Arab Spring (2011) 57, 66
Arctic National Wildlife Refuge 173
Argentina 58, 190
Aristotle 33
Arkansas 81
Ashok, Karnataka R. 189
Asia 65–6
  Southeast 107
  see also Afghanistan; Bangladesh; Brunei;
    Cambodia; China; India; Indonesia;
    Malaysia; Philippines; Thailand; Vietnam;
    also under Middle East
Asia-Pacific x, 14, 27, 205 n.(21)
Association of the British Pharmaceutical
  Industry 79
Athabasca 165
Attac (French antiglobalization association) 178
Austin 211
Australia 47, 121
  Department of Immigration and Citizenship
    163, 169 nn.(91-2), 170 nn.(93-7)
  Maritime Crew Visa 163
Aveeno 3

Bach, D. vii, x n.(5), 5, 17 n.(9), 69 n.(4), 214
Bangladesh 32
Bank of America Merrill Lynch xi, 13

Index

Galang, R. M. N. 163, 164, 169 nn.(82/88-9), 170 nn.(99-100/102-4/107-8)
Galbraith, J. R. 94, 109 nn.(6-8), 110 n.(30), 222 n.(16)
Gambia 107
Gargiulo, M. 149 n.(63)
Gates, Bill 24, 25, 33, 35
GATT (General Agreement on Tariffs and Trade) 79
Gedajlovic, E. 104, 111 n.(58)
General Electric 140
General Mills 32
General Motors 95
Genoa 23
Germany vii, 24, 121, 159, 164
  Bündnis 90/Die Grünen 168 n.(57)
  decision to close down nuclear power plants 57
  GTZ agency 151, 201
  see also Deutsche Telekom; Lufthansa
Ghana 27, 32
Gibbon, Edward 189, 204 n.(1)
Giddens, A. 10, 19 n.(37)
Gilpin, R. 7, 17 nn.(17-18)
Gingrich, Newt 135
GlaxoSmithKline 93
Glaze, Michele 221 n.(6), 222 n.(7)
globalization 10, 20 n.(53), 28, 106, 206 n.(31), 214, 222 n.(16)
Goldman Sachs 32, 115
Google 13, 75, 189, 199, 203
Gordon, S. 86, 92 n.(53)
government ownership 84–5, 201
GrandMet 27
Grattan, Henry 26
Gray, V. 81, 91 n.(28-9)
Great Depression (1930s) 24, 25
Great Recession (2008-12) 24, 25
Green Party (France) 178
Greenfield, Jerry 26, 173
Greenhouse Gas Protocol 181
Greenpeace 164, 209
Grier, K. 80–1, 91 n.(26), 131 n.(21)
Groseclose, T. 126, 133 n.(76)
Grossman, G. M 117, 131 nn.(13-15)
Grunig, J. E. 94, 95, 109 nn.(10/12)
Grupo Balbo 13, 159
Guay, T. 20 n.(56-7), 21 n.(58-9)
Guinness, Arthur 23, 26–7, 36
Gulati, R. 149 n.(63), 210, 221 n.(3)
Gulf of Mexico 32, 57, 134 n.(83), 219
Gulf states (Middle East) 10

Häagen-Dazs 173
Hafer, C. 86, 92 n.(53)
Halliburton 219
Hamada, K. 121, 132 n.(38)

Hansen, W. 18 n.(28), 86, 92 n.(52), 131 n.(11)
HARITA (Horn of Africa Risk Transfer for Adaptation) 151
Harvey, C., 40 n.(35), 49 n.(3)
Heathrow airport 35
Heinz 13, 181, 187 nn.(41-5)
Helpman, E. 117, 131 nn.(13-15)
Hillman, A. J. 9, 16 n.(5), 18 nn.(21/24), 21 n.(58), 50 n.(19), 73 n.(78), 79, 80, 82, 83, 87, 90 n.(4), 91 nn.(20-3/34/41-2), 94, 109 nn.(5-6), 110 n.(21), 131 n.(22), 141–2, 148 n.(50), 149 n.(59), 150 n.(81), 196, 197, 201, 205 nn.(16/24), 206 nn.(25/30/34-7/43), 207 n.(70), 215, 222 nn.(23/25)
Hitt, M. A. 9, 20 n.(19), 79, 83, 87, 91 nn.(20-1/34/41-2), 131 n.(22), 196, 197, 201, 205 n.(24), 206 nn.(25/30/37), 207 n.(70), 222 n.(25)
Hong Kong 25, 189
Howton, S. D. & S. W. 109 n.(0)
Hudson's Bay Company 23
Human Resources Without Borders 162
Hunter, M. L. 178, 187 n.(22/24-7)
Hussein, M. E. A. 141, 148 n.(49)
Hutchison Whampoa 25

IATA (International Air Transport Association) 121, 126
Iberia (airline) 213
ICICI Bank 13, 174–5, 186 n.(7)
IFMA (International Financial Management Association) 115
IMF (International Monetary Fund) 120, 198
imitative behavior, *see* mimetic behavior
implicit knowledge 138
inclusiveness 117, 118, 158, 213
  developing 162–3
India 28, 41, 44, 116, 121, 143, 203
  capitalism and role of the state 193
  emergent economy 215
  Mauryan Empire 23
  see also Bhopal; Kerala; Tata
Indonesia 27, 107, 215
industrial policy 43, 131 n.(27), 192–4
  proactive approach to 191
Industrial Revolution 36
industry structure 153, 163
information and communications 13, 46, 87
information value 15, 135–50
integrity 158, 161–2, 181, 185
  performance with 183
Intel 182
intellectual property rights 120, 146 n.(3), 177, 186
  promoting stricter international regulations on 79
  see also PIPA; SOPA